# The Lighter Side of Chocolate

RICH HOT COCOA
• PAGE 21 •

CHOCOLATE—PEANUT BUTTER SPREAD
• PAGE 30 •

MORNING MOCHA
• PAGE 22 •

CHOCOLATE-ALMOND
GRANOLA
• PAGE 33 •

SPANISH HOT CHOCOLATE
WITH ORANGE, ESPRESSO, AND SPICE • PAGE 25 •

DOUBLE GINGER CHOCOLATE-CHIP SCONES
• PAGE 36 •

MULTIGRAIN
POWER PANCAKES
WITH CHOCOLATE &
WALNUTS
• PAGE 48 •

EXOTIC SPICE
TRUFFLES
• PAGE 99 •

CHOCOLATE
CINNAMON ROLLS
• PAGE 58 •

BUTTERSCOTCH-CHOCOLATE CHUNK BARS
• PAGE 107 •

VERY BEST BROWNIES
• PAGE 114 •

CHOCOLATE-CHOCOLATE CHUNKERS
• PAGE 74 •

BAKEHOUSE
CHOCOLATE CHIPPERS
• PAGE 78 •

BROWNIE BLISS CAKE
• PAGE 128 •

ALMOND JOYFUL
TUNNEL CAKE
• PAGE 137 •

BANANA–CHOCOLATE CHIP MINI BUNDTS
• PAGE 165 •

EXOTIC
CHOCOLATE-DATE CAKE
• PAGE 148 •

RICH, OLD-FASHIONED
CHOCOLATE PUDDING • PAGE 169 •

CHOCOLATE PANNA COTTA
• PAGE 176 •

VERY CHOCOLATE CHEESECAKE
• PAGE 153 •

CHOCOLATE FRAMBOISE
MILK SHAKE
• PAGE 181 •

FAVORITE DOUBLE-CHOCOLATE CUPCAKES
• PAGE 162 •

MILK CHOCOLATE CRÈME BRÛLÉE
• PAGE 183 •

EXOTIC, SPICED
PUMPKIN SOUP
• PAGE 217 •

CHOCOLATE SOUFFLÉS WITH RASPBERRY SAUCE
• PAGE 184 •

COCOA-RUBBED CHICKEN
WITH BARBECUE TABLE MOP • PAGE 223 •

CHOCOLATE FUDGE ICE CREAM
• PAGE 188 •

GRILLED PORK KEBABS
WITH CUBAN COCOA-RUM GLAZE • PAGE 225 •

LIME TORTILLA SOUP WITH SHRIMP &
CHIPOTLE CHILES • PAGE 214 •

BEEF AND BEER CHILI
WITH LIME CREMA
• PAGE 236 •

# ENLIGHTENED Chocolate

## Also by Camilla V. Saulsbury

*Cookie Dough Delights*

*Brownie Mix Bliss*

*Cake Mix Cookies*

*No-Bake Cookies*

*Puff Pastry Perfection*

*Panna Cotta*

# ENLIGHTENED
## *Chocolate*

*More Than 200 Decadently Light, Easy-to-Make, and Inspired Recipes*
*Using Dark Chocolate and Unsweetened Cocoa Powder*

## CAMILLA V. SAULSBURY

CUMBERLAND HOUSE
NASHVILLE, TENNESSEE

Enlightened Chocolate
Published by Cumberland House Publishing, Inc.
431 Harding Industrial Drive
Nashville, TN 37211

Cover design: JulesRulesDesign
Text design: Lisa Taylor

**Library of Congress Cataloging-in-Publication Data**
Saulsbury, Camilla V.
  Enlightened chocolate : more than 200 decadently light, easy-to-make, and inspired recipes using dark chocolate and unsweetened cocoa powder / Camilla V. Saulsbury.
    p. cm.
  Includes bibliographical references and index.
  ISBN-13: 978-1-58182-607-4 (hardcover)
  ISBN-10: 1-58182-607-9 (hardcover)
1.  Cookery (Chocolate)  I. Title.
  TX767.C5S28 2007
  641.6'374—dc22

2007028469

Printed in Canada
1 2 3 4 5 6 7 — 12 11 10 09 08 07

*To Kevin*

# CONTENTS

# ACKNOWLEDGMENTS

Heartfelt thanks to my family, friends, and all of the wonderful people at Cumberland House Publishing, all of whom make writing and cooking for a living all it's cracked up to be.

Special thanks to Lindsey Vineyard, Kirsten Escobar, and Mercy Cannon—three extraordinary women and exceptional friends who, although they may not know it, made the final writing of this book possible.

And finally, to Carl Keen, Ph.D., for planting the seed of inspiration for this book in my brain. Thank you for your wisdom and encouragement.

# ENLIGHTENED Chocolate

# INTRODUCTION

EAT MORE CHOCOLATE—it's good for you.

It sounds like a mandate straight from the mouth of Willy Wonka.

The good news for chocoholics everywhere is that it's not fiction. Clinical research over the past decade increasingly indicates that consumption of antioxidant-rich chocolate and cocoa is associated with health benefits from improved cardiovascular function to reduced bad cholesterol levels to increased alertness. Hurrah!

Alas, don't hold your breath for prescriptions of chocolate ganache cake or daily swims in Mr. Wonka's river of chocolate anytime soon. That's because of one bittersweet barrier in the case for the health benefits of chocolate: it is high in fat and calories. Consider the average chocolate bar: one 1.5-ounce bar alone has about 240 calories and 13 to 14 grams of fat (about half of which are the saturated, heart-clogging kind). This holds true for many favorite chocolate treats, too: one cup of premium chocolate ice cream, for example, has 540 calories and 36 grams of fat, 22 of which are saturated.

But a solution to the chocolate fat and calorie quandary exists. Within the following pages you'll find more than 200 recipes that let you have your chocolate in an "enlightened" manner, namely with less fat, fewer calories, and maximum chocolate flavor. Chocolate cake, chocolate cookies, chocolate snacks, even chocolate for breakfast and dinner—the recipes are all here, and they're all scrumptious.

Before saying anything further, though, it's important for me to emphasize what this book is, as well as what it isn't.

It is, first and foremost, a cookbook, one I've filled with luscious, inviting chocolate recipes. All are straightforward and rely on easy-to-find ingredients. Nothing will daunt, not even the Chocolate Soufflé with Raspberry Sauce or Chocolate Crème Brûlée. It's an ideal collection for any chocolate fanatic who loves to cook with and eat chocolate without overloading on fat and calories.

*Enlightened Chocolate* isn't a diet or health-food book. The new way of looking at chocolate and cocoa as beneficial ingredients inspired me to look for new ways to use and appreciate them in cooking and baking. The recipes are lighter in fat and calories, have lots of fresh ingredients, and include the chocolate products with the highest antioxidant levels, namely dark chocolate and natural cocoa powder. I developed these recipes to inspire you to use more chocolate and cocoa, and thus enjoy more of their many healthful benefits. But in the end, my driving force was always flavor—the very best chocolate flavor.

We're used to seeing chocolate as a dessert or sweet treat, and this collection is no exception. With one chapter each devoted to chocolate cake, chocolate cookies, and other chocolate desserts, the possibilities for satisfying a chocolate sweet tooth are vast. From Double Chocolate Chunk Cookies to Peanut Butter–Swirled Brownies to Chocolate-Grand Marnier Soufflé Cake, there's no shortage of decadent chocolate options. Just as enticing, the desserts incorporate fresh, light, and healthful ingredients whenever possible and follow fundamental, widely recognized guidelines for healthy eating: no more than 10 grams of fat per serving with an emphasis on keeping saturated fat particularly low.

But why stop at chocolate as a confection? That very question led to my development of the two remaining chapters in the book: Chocolate, Morning to Noon, and Savory Chocolate.

As for chocolate for breakfast or a midmorning pick-me-up—could there be a better reason to rise and shine? For busy weekdays, think chocolate yogurt with fresh berries, a ginger-chocolate scone on the go, or perhaps a favorite morning mocha, smoothie, or spicy hot chocolate. For midmorning snacks, Cashew-Chocolate Kashi Bars, Chocolate Fruit Chews, and Salty-Sweet Chocolate Popcorn will tide you over until lunchtime, deliciously. On the weekend, the Chocolate Ricotta Muffins and Bittersweet Chocolate Waffles can't be missed—they're perfect pajama-lounging, paper-reading fare.

The final chapter on savory chocolate may sound unusual, but think again. The complex flavors of both dark chocolate and unsweetened cocoa powder lend themselves exquisitely to savory recipes, bringing new dimensions to main dishes, sides, and snacks. Rather than imparting an identifiable "chocolate" flavor, dark chocolate and cocoa powder enhance, deepen, and bind the flavors of many savory foods, much in the same manner as other multiuse seasonings, such as soy sauce, Worcestershire sauce, and balsamic vinegar.

Chocolate and cocoa are particularly well-suited to hot and spicy foods—a classic example is Mexican mole, a dark, intense sauce made with chiles, spices, and chocolate. Savory chocolate and cocoa can also play a subtle, complementary role to chicken and lamb, even fish, especially when paired with bright, fresh ingredients or lightly sweet flavors, such as honey or tart cherries.

So which recipe to try first? Oh, that's a hard one. Among my favorites...Spanish Hot Chocolate with Orange, Espresso & Spice...Strawberries & Cream Chocolate Layer Cake . . . Mudslide Cookies . . . Chocolate, Caramel & Rum Flan . . . Beef & Beer Chili with Lime Crema...and, of course, Very Best Brownies. I suggest you make them all. Each and every option is proof positive that you can have your chocolate and eat it, too.

To chocolate!

## A Brief Early History of Chocolate as "Medicine"

*Chocolate when carefully prepared, is a wholesome and agreeable form of food is very suitable for persons of great mental exertion, preachers, lawyers and above all travellers . . . it agrees with the feebles stomaches, has proved beneficial in cases of chronic illness and remains the last resource in the diseases of the pylorus.*
—Brillat-Savarin 1755–1826

The ancient Maya certainly knew their stuff: in addition to monumental discoveries in astronomy, math, agriculture and construction, they deduced connections between chocolate and health thousands of years before Western science.

The Maya were the first to create what we now know as chocolate by cultivating the theobroma cacao tree, fermenting, drying and roasting the beans, and then grinding the kernels to produce cocoa mass (chocolate liquor). They used these products both as stimulants and soothing balms. Mayan warriors, for example, slugged one of the world's first sports drinks—an unsweetened concoction made from ground cocoa beans—to boost their energy prior to battle.

The Aztecs, too, adopted cacao as a food and medicine when they arrived in the central valley of Mexico. The Florentine Codex, a massive compilation of Aztec culture written in 1590, offers some of the most extensive documentation of the ways in which they used cacao as a medicinal cure-all. They used every part of the cacao: the beans were used to treat intestinal complaints, cure infections, remedy coughs, and alleviate fever, shortness of breath, and faintness of heart; the cacao fruit pulp was concentrated and then drunk by pregnant women to ease delivery; cacao leaves were applied to wounds as antiseptics; cacao oil was used to relieve cracked lips; and cacao flowers were used to treat fatigue.

Christopher Columbus is thought to be the first European to carry cocoa beans back to Europe, around 1502. But his presentation of the dark brown beans, which looked like little more than shriveled almonds, received an underwhelming response from Spain's Queen Isabella and King Ferdinand. It was Hernando Cortés, the great Spanish explorer, who grasped the commercial possibilities of cacao, penning an enthusiastic letter about the frothy cacao beverages of the New World to the emperor of Spain in 1520. But it wasn't until 1544, when Dominican friars took a delegation of Maya to Spain, with beaten chocolate gifts in tow, that chocolate captured the palate—and imagination—of the Western world.

Despite myriad developments in the culinary possibilities of chocolate, medicinal uses of chocolate throughout Europe persisted. Sixteenth to early twentieth-century manuscripts in Europe and New Spain discuss the use of cacao in emaciated patients for everything from fostering weight gain, stimulating the nervous systems of exhausted patients, improving digestion and elimination, and stimulating the kidneys, as well as improving a host of maladies from anemia, poor appetite, mental fatigue, poor breast milk production, tuberculosis, fever, gout, kidney stones, reduced longevity, and low virility.

Events went full circle when English colonists carried chocolate with them to England's colonies in North America. Chocolate consumption in Colonial North America was rare, largely due to its high cost, but apothecary shop advertisements of the time nevertheless reveal its use as a healing product, used to treat asthma, cholera, dysentery, smallpox, typhus, and yellow fever.

Even as health uses of chocolate ceded to culinary ones in both Europe and America, nineteenth-century pharmaceutical companies kept the connection alive by using chocolate as a vehicle for administering bitter-tasting medicines. This chocolate-coated practice gave rise to the modern candy industry in both the United States and Europe.

## CHOCOLATE & HEALTH TODAY

Put into historical perspective, the research renaissance of chocolate and health seems downright logical, perhaps even overdue. Chocoholics may even wonder, what took so darn long?!!!

Scientific interest in chocolate was revived just over a decade ago as something of a whim. A couple of nutritionists were conducting research on the health benefits of red wine and, for kicks or curiosity (or both), decided to test some chocolate from a nearby vending machine. To their surprise and delight, they discovered chocolate had huge quantities of antioxidants, the same good-for-you chemicals as found in red wine, berries, vegetables, and tea. Thank heavens for inquiring minds.

## CHOCOLATE: ANTIOXIDANT SUPERSTAR

In the decade since, a flurry of research across the globe has uncovered more good news of the potential health-giving attributes of chocolate. It turns out that chocolate is rich in certain essential vitamins and minerals, namely magnesium, copper, and iron, and lesser amounts of calcium, zinc, Vitamin A, niacin, and phosphorus. But it is chocolate's high level of antioxidants that remains central to scientific inquiries.

So what are antioxidants? In short, they are phytochemicals, vitamins, and other nutrients that protect the body's cells from damage caused by free radicals. Free radicals cause all manner of cellular damage and are formed as part of the body's natural metabolism as well as by environmental factors, including smoking, pesticides, pollution, and radiation. Antioxidants have the property to neutralize free radicals and are essential to how the body detoxifies itself.

Antioxidants are also present in a wide range of foods, including red wine, leafy greens, tea, and blueberries. But chocolate is a particularly potent source; for example, an ounce of dark chocolate has five times as many antioxidants as an ounce of blueberries. Dark chocolate (i.e., bittersweet and unsweetened) and unsweetened cocoa powder have the greatest health-giving properties because they are packed with a particular type of antioxidants called flavonoids (also commonly referred to as bio-flavonoids). Scientists are further discovering that it is likely the large amounts of a subclass of flavonoids found in chocolate and cocoa products—flavonols—boast the strongest antioxidant activity and may contain other health-promoting attributes.

The data are extensive and compelling, especially given that multiple independent labs are coming to the same or similar conclusions about the benefits of chocolate flavonols. What follows is a quick overview of some of the significant findings to date. A brief caveat, though—keep in mind that these are emerging, not conclusive, findings. Despite all the remarkable things chocolate may do for health, scientists are still trying to figure out exactly how and why flavonols work as they do.

## CHOCOLATE MAY BE ESPECIALLY BENEFICIAL TO HEALTH BY:

- Improving blood flow and elasticity in blood vessels (by easing inflammation, opening blood vessels, preventing platelets from adhering to the lining of blood vessels, inhibiting blood clotting, and helping to prevent plaque formation in the arteries).
- Lowering blood pressure.
- Improving overall heart health and reducing the risk of death from cardiovascular disease.

- Decreasing LDL (bad) cholesterol as well as the body's inflammatory immune responses.
- Improving insulin resistance and sensitivity.
- Increasing alertness, lessening pain, and promoting a general feeling of well-being.
- Promoting healthy brain function, including boosting short-term memory and problem-solving abilities.
- Serving as a good energy source because it releases slowly into the bloodstream and does not elevate insulin levels. This is because dark chocolate has a low glycemic index rating (around 22), making it a good option for endurance activities and even weight training routines.
- Potentially reducing the risk of cancer.
- Remedying coughs (due to the theobromine in chocolate).

## CHOCOLATE AND STRESS REDUCTION: IT'S NOT ALL IN YOUR HEAD

No, you weren't imagining that sense of calm that enveloped you the last time you savored a few pieces of dark chocolate. Granted the sensory pleasures—taste, smell, mouth feel—associated with eating chocolate had something to do with the soothing effects, but there's more to it than that.

One explanation has to do with magnesium. Chocolate has a high level of magnesium, about 56 mg in a 2-ounce bar of dark chocolate. Stress causes the body to deplete its supplies of magnesium, ultimately leading to biochemical imbalances. It is hypothesized that the magnesium in chocolate helps restore the body's magnesium balance, resulting in a mild sedative effect.

Chocolate also contains a compound called anandamide, a neurotransmitter that targets the same brain structures as THC, the active ingredient in cannabis. Now don't get too excited—to make a substantial impact on the brain's own natural anandamide levels, experts estimate you would need to eat several pounds of chocolate. It's more likely that chocolate works indirectly to produce a "high." As well as anandamide, chocolate also contains two hard-to-pronounce, and even harder-to-spell, chemicals (N-oleo-lethanolamine and N-linoleoylethanolamine) known to slow the breakdown of anandamide. It's thought that chocolate might therefore work by prolonging the action of this natural stimulant in the brain.

Finally, chocolate triggers the release of endorphins in our brains. Endorphins are those feel-good molecules, a class of neurotransmitters produced by the body and used internally as a pain killer. Enhanced endorphin-release lowers blood pressure and reduces the chocolate-eater's sensitivity to pain. Endorphins, in combination with the pure enjoyment of eating chocolate, likely contribute to the bliss induced by a few nibbles of a dark chocolate truffle.

### SELECTING CHOCOLATE: GO FOR PREMIUM

There may come a time in the not-too-distant future when, in addition to taste, flavonol-level will be an option for selecting chocolates. Until then, choose the best quality brand you can afford, both from a chocolate-for-health and chocolate-for-taste perspective.

Premium brands are more likely to use premium beans, yielding, well, premium chocolate with the greatest, most complex flavor. Variations in processing can lower the amount of healthy flavonols even in a higher percentage of cacao. Choosing a premium chocolate does not guarantee the highest amount of flavonols, but premium brands of chocolate are more likely to be made with care, blended and roasted in small batches with close attention to each step in the chocolate making.

The following general rules will also help in choosing chocolate for maximum health benefit (and, coincidentally, for incredible chocolate flavor):

- The darker the better.
- The higher the cocoa content the better.
- The less fat the better.
- The less sugar the better.

### WHAT DO THE PERCENTAGES (E.G., 56%, 62%, 70%, 82%) MEAN?

The percentages indicate by weight the amount of ingredients derived from the cacao bean that is in the chocolate. The remaining percentage is sugar and a small amount of vanilla and soy lecithin. For example, a 70 percent bittersweet chocolate is 70 percent cocoa solids (cocoa mass and cocoa butter), 30 percent sugar, vegetable lecithin, and vanilla. Note that all of the recipes in this book that call for bittersweet chocolate were tested with 70 percent bittersweet chocolate.

### SELECTING COCOA POWDER: GO "NATURAL"

Unsweetened cocoa powder stands in for chocolate in a good many of the recipes in this collection. It has 60 percent less fat than unsweetened chocolate, but tremendous chocolate flavor, making it an ideal solution for "enlightened" chocolate recipes. And besides being low in fat and calories, a USDA study found that among all chocolate products, standard cocoa powders have the greatest concentrations of antioxidants and flavonols.

Cocoa powder is made when chocolate liquor is pressed to remove three quarters of its cocoa butter. The remaining cocoa solids are processed to make fine unsweetened cocoa powder. Thus, cocoa powder is the purest concentration of the part of chocolate that has all the good stuff, health-wise.

Two types of unsweetened cocoa powder are available: Dutch process (alkalized) and natural (nonalkalized).

Dutch process unsweetened cocoa powder is made by treating cocoa, which is naturally quite acidic, with an alkali, such as potassium carbonate, to reduce the harshness of the cocoa, deepen its color, and neutralize its acids. Because it is neutral and does not react with baking soda, Dutch process cocoa powder must be used in recipes calling for baking powder, unless there are other acidic ingredients in sufficient quantities used.

Natural unsweetened cocoa powder is simply untreated cocoa powder; it is rarely labeled with the word *natural* on the package, but will simply say unsweetened cocoa powder or unsweetened cocoa. When natural cocoa (an acid) is used in recipes calling for baking soda (an alkali), it creates a leavening action that causes the batter to rise when placed in the oven.

If using cocoa powder to derive some of its health benefits, opt for natural over Dutch process—the alkali in the latter destroys most of the beneficial flavonols. Good-quality natural cocoa powders deliver tremendous chocolate depth, allowing the inherent fruitiness and natural full flavor of the cacao bean to shine through. Note that natural cocoa powder was used for the testing of all the recipes in this collection.

Good old-fashioned Hershey's Brand Cocoa Powder is probably the most familiar natural cocoa powder and is readily available at grocery stores. But for deeper chocolate flavor (I'm talking knock-your-socks-off delicious), do try a premium brand. My favorites? Scharffen Berger, Green & Black's, and Dagoba (the latter two are organic). Good chocolates and cocoas are like fine wines—each has distinctive nuances of flavor. So shop around and enjoy sampling and experimenting with multiple varieties until you find the ones that best suit your taste. See the appendix for on-line sources.

### SUBSTITUTING NATURAL COCOA POWDER FOR DUTCH PROCESS

Natural cocoa powder can be substituted, measure for measure, for Dutch process cocoa powder in nearly every case with one major exception: baking recipes with leaveners (i.e., baking powder or baking soda). Because natural cocoa powder is more acidic than Dutch process cocoa powder, the leavening typically needs adjustment.

To make the switch from Dutch process to natural, adjust the 1½ teaspoons baking powder in recipe to ½ teaspoon baking powder plus ¼ teaspoon baking soda. This is not a 100 percent guarantee, but it will work in many cases.

## THE ENLIGHTENED CHOCOLATE PANTRY

### Chocolate & Cocoa Powder

**Bittersweet Chocolate:** Bittersweet chocolate is available in varying percentages (as described previously). Although I tested with 70 percent bittersweet chocolate, and higher percentages contain more flavonols, feel free to experiment and choose the percentage that best suits your taste.

Dark chocolate has a very stable shelf life, but that's not to say it will last indefinitely. For best results, store chocolate in a cool, dry place, with limited contact to heat and moisture. Refrigeration is not necessary unless you live in a particularly humid climate.

If your chocolate develops a white or gray sheen, it does not mean that it has spoiled. This is referred to as "bloom" and can occur because the chocolate got warm enough for the cocoa butter's crystalline bonds to break and re-form in irregular patterns ("fat bloom"); or water has condensed on the chocolate's surface ("sugar bloom"). Bloom does not damage the chocolate for cooking purposes, but may make the chocolate grainy and less palatable for eating plain.

Freezing chocolate is not recommended; when you freeze it and then thaw it out, it will have a greater tendency to bloom.

**Unsweetened Baking Chocolate:** Typically sold in packages of 1-ounce or 2-ounce blocks, unsweetened baking chocolate is dark chocolate without any sugar added. Although commonly available in supermarkets, it is also being offered from a number of premiere chocolate companies (e.g., Scharffen Berger). It's worth the splurge if your wallet allows.

**Miniature Semisweet Chocolate Chips:** Used in less than five recipes in the collection, miniature semisweet chocolate chips are a good way to add a lot of chocolate flavor without adding too much fat and calories. As an alternative, an equal amount of finely chopped bittersweet chocolate may be used.

**Cocoa Powder:** Natural cocoa powder (not Dutch process) is used in all of the recipes in this collection. Although cocoa powder packaging should state whether it is Dutch process or not, you can also determine cocoa powder type by sight: if it is dark to almost black, it is Dutch process; if it is natural, it is much lighter and more typically brownish-reddish in color.

Measure cocoa powder by lightly spooning it into the appropriate size dry measuring cup and leveling it off with the straight edge of a knife or spatula. Tapping the measuring cup will result in an inaccurate measure.

It's best to store cocoa away from herbs and spices and other aromatic substances, as it picks up other flavors relatively easily. Store it in an airtight container in a cool, dark place for up to one year.

## Flours

**All-Purpose Flour:** Made from a blend of high-gluten hard wheat and low-gluten soft wheat, all-purpose flour is a fine-textured flour milled from the inner part of the wheat kernel and contains neither the germ nor the bran. All-purpose flour comes either bleached or unbleached; they can be used interchangeably.

**Regular Whole Wheat Flour:** Fuller-flavored than all-purpose flour, whole wheat flour contains the wheat germ, which means that it also has a higher fiber, nutritional, and fat content. Because of the fat, it should be stored in the refrigerator to prevent rancidity.

**Whole Wheat Pastry Flour:** A fine-textured, soft wheat flour that includes the wheat germ. It can be used interchangeably with all-purpose flour in most recipes. In most of the recipes in this book I've used it in combination with all-purpose flour, but feel free to increase the proportion of the whole wheat pastry flour to replace more or all of the all-purpose.

It is extremely important not to substitute regular whole wheat flour for the whole wheat pastry flour; the results will be coarse, leaden, and possibly inedible.

You can find whole wheat pastry flour at well-stocked supermarkets as well as natural food stores. Store it in a ziplock plastic bag in the refrigerator (for the same reasons as regular whole wheat flour).

**Cake Flour:** Finely ground, soft white flour. It is low in protein, which means it will develop less gluten during mixing and yield particularly tender baked goods. For a quick substitute, replace 2 tablespoons of flour with cornstarch for each cup of all-purpose flour.

## Sweeteners

**Granulated White Sugar:** Granulated white sugar is the most common sweetener used throughout this collection. It is refined cane or beet sugar. If a recipe in the book calls for sugar without specifying which one, use granulated white sugar. Once opened, store granulated sugar in an airtight container in a cool, dry place.

**Brown Sugar:** Brown sugar is granulated sugar that has some molasses added to it. The molasses gives the brown sugar a soft texture. Light brown sugar has less molasses and a more delicate flavor than dark brown sugar. If a recipe in the book calls for brown sugar without specifying which one, use light brown sugar. Once opened, store brown sugar in an airtight container or ziplock plastic bag to prevent clumping.

**Powdered Sugar:** Powdered sugar (also called confectioners' sugar) is granulated sugar that has been ground to a fine powder. Cornstarch is added to prevent the sugar from clumping together. It is used in recipes where regular sugar would be too grainy.

**Turbinado Sugar:** Turbinado sugar is raw sugar that has been steam-cleaned. The coarse crystals are blond in color and have a delicate molasses flavor. It is typically used for decoration and texture atop baked goods.

**Corn Syrup:** Corn syrup is a thick, sweet syrup made by processing cornstarch with acids or enzymes. Light corn syrup is further treated to remove any color. Light corn syrup is very sweet, but does not have much flavor. Dark corn syrup has coloring and flavoring added to make it caramel-like. Unopened containers of corn syrup may be stored at room temperature. After opening, store corn syrup in the refrigerator to protect against mold. Corn syrup will keep indefinitely when stored properly.

**Honey:** Honey is the nectar of plants that has been gathered and concentrated by honey bees. Any variety of honey may be used in the recipes throughout this collection. Unopened containers of honey may be stored at room temperature. After opening, store honey in the refrigerator to protect against mold. Honey will keep indefinitely when stored properly.

**Maple Syrup:** Maple syrup is a thick liquid sweetener made by boiling the sap from maple trees. Maple syrup has a strong, pure maple flavor. Maple-flavored pancake syrup is not recommended as a substitute for pure maple syrup as it is corn syrup with coloring and artificial maple flavoring added. Unopened containers of maple syrup may be stored at room temperature. After opening, store maple syrup in the refrigerator to protect against mold. Maple syrup will keep indefinitely when stored properly.

**Molasses:** Molasses is made from the juice of sugar cane or sugar beets that is boiled until a syrupy mixture remains. Light molasses is lighter in flavor and color and results from the first boiling of the syrup. Dark molasses, dark in both flavor and color, is not as sweet as light molasses. It comes from the second boiling of the syrup. Light and dark molasses may be used interchangeably in the recipes in this collection. Blackstrap molasses is thick, very dark, and has a bitter flavor; it is not recommended for the recipes in this collection. Unopened containers of molasses may be stored at room temperature. After opening, store molasses in the refrigerator to protect against mold. Molasses will keep indefinitely when stored properly.

## Fats & Oils

**Butter:** When it comes to flavor, nothing compares to real butter. But because it is high in saturated fat, it is used in small quantities throughout this collection. All of the recipes in this collection were tested with unsalted butter unless otherwise stated.

Fresh butter should have a delicate cream flavor and pale yellow color. Butter quickly picks up off-flavors during storage and when exposed to oxygen; once the carton is opened, place it in a ziplock plastic food bag or airtight container. Store it away from foods with strong odors, especially items such as onions or garlic.

To melt butter, cut the specified amount of butter into small pieces, place in a small saucepan, and allow to melt over the lowest heat setting of the burner. Once the butter has melted, remove the pan from the heat and cool. To speed the cooling, pour the melted butter into a small bowl or liquid measuring cup.

To soften butter, let the needed amount of butter stand 30–45 minutes at room temperature. Cutting the butter into small chunks will reduce the softening time to about 15 minutes. If time is really limited, try grating the cold butter on the large holes of a cheese grater. The small bits of butter will be soft in just a few minutes. Avoid softening butter in the microwave. It will typically melt at least part of the butter, even if you are watching it closely.

**Canola Oil:** Pressed from rapeseed, canola oil is a neutral-flavored vegetable oil that is extremely low in saturated fat and quite high in monounsaturated fat. It is used extensively throughout this collection.

**Nonstick Cooking Spray:** Nonstick cooking spray is canned oil that has been packed under pressure and dispersed by a propellant. It is flavorless, coats pans evenly, and allows for easier removal of the cooled and chilled bars throughout this collection.

**Nonstick Baking Spray with Flour:** Nonstick baking spray with flour is the same as nonstick cooking spray, only with the addition of flour in the spray. It eliminates the step of greasing and flouring cake pans, saving time as well as significant fat and calories. It is especially useful for Bundt-style baking pans. The two most common brands are Bakers Joy® and PAM® For Baking. If you have ever had half of a cake fall out of the pan, you will never want to be without this product—it is a minor miracle.

*Dairy & Eggs*

**Milk:** Both low-fat and nonfat milk are used in a wide range of recipes in this collection. Be sure to note when low-fat milk is used—the extra fat is needed in that recipe, so non-fat milk should not be substituted. Similarly, do not substitute fresh low-fat or nonfat milk for canned evaporated fat-free milk; the latter has a richness similar to cream that fresh milk does not.

**Eggs:** All of the fat in an egg is contained in the yolk. To reduce the fat in many of the recipes, I cut back on the whole eggs and substituted egg whites.

Select clean, fresh eggs that have been handled properly and refrigerated. Do not use dirty, cracked, or leaking eggs that may have a bad odor or unnatural color when cracked open. They may have become contaminated with harmful bacteria such as salmonella. Cold eggs are easiest to separate; eggs at room temperature can be beaten to high volume for use in such recipes as meringues and angel food cake. Note that all of the recipes in this book were developed using large eggs.

**Refrigerated Egg Substitute:** Egg substitute is made from real eggs, but only the whites, so it has a fraction of the fat and calories of whole eggs. Vitamins and other nutrients that would otherwise be lost when the yolk is removed are typically added. The product can be frozen if unopened. Once the product has been opened, it must be used within a week.

**Low-Fat Buttermilk:** Commercially prepared buttermilk is made by culturing skim or low-fat milk with bacteria. It has a distinctive tang that, when added to baked goods like cakes, yields a tender, moist result and a slightly buttery flavor.

**Nonfat and Low-Fat Yogurt:** Yogurt is acidic, like buttermilk, and tenderizes baked goods. It also makes an excellent substitution for sour cream in a wide range of recipes.

**Reduced-Fat & Fat-Free Cream Cheese:** All of the recipes in this book use "brick"-style cream cheese; the fat-free and reduced fat (also called Neufchatel) are typically sold in 8-ounce rectangular packages.

To soften cream cheese, unwrap it and cut it into chunks with a sharp knife. Let it stand at room temperature 30–45 minutes until softened. For speed softening, place the chunks of cream cheese on a microwavable plate or in a microwavable bowl and microwave on high for 15 seconds. If necessary, microwave 5 or 10 seconds longer.

**Fat-Free Ricotta Cheese:** Ricotta is a rich, fresh cheese with a texture that is slightly grainy, but still far smoother than cottage cheese. It's white, moist and has a slightly sweet flavor. The fat-free variety is readily available and adds considerable richness to baked goods and cheesecakes.

**Canned Evaporated Fat-Free Milk:** Produced by evaporating nearly half the water from fresh fat-free milk, this thick and slightly sweet product is an excellent option for replacing heavy cream in a wide range of recipes from desserts to sauces. It is best used in recipes that are cooked or that have other strong flavors to conceal the slightly cooked flavor of the milk.

**Canned Sweetened Condensed Fat-Free Milk:** Sweetened condensed milk has been a baking staple for decades, but the fat-free variety is relatively new to the kitchen. This is one of those rare products that does not suffer much—if at all—from losing its fat. It is readily available in supermarkets (the fat-free version typically has a green label).

**Reduced-Fat & Fat-Free Cottage Cheese:** Makes a great addition to cheesecakes and dips when puréed in a food processor and combined with other flavorful ingredients.

*Flavor Enhancers*

Fat has great flavor, so when you cut it back, you need to add some flavor back. The following are some of my favorite big, bold flavor enhancers, used throughout this collection.

**Instant Espresso Powder:** Stronger than regular coffee powder, a small amount of this potent powder dramatically enhances the flavor of chocolate and cocoa. It is now available in most supermarkets.

**Spices:** All of the recipes in this book use ground, as opposed to whole, spices. Freshness is everything with ground spices. The best way to determine if a ground spice is fresh is to open the container and smell it. If it still has a strong fragrance, it is still acceptable for use. If not, toss it and make a new purchase.

**Vanilla Extract:** Vanilla extract adds a sweet, fragrant flavor to reduced-fat baked goods and is particularly good for enhancing the flavor of chocolate. It is produced by extracting the flavor of dried vanilla beans with an alcohol and water mixture. It is then aged for several months. The three most common types of beans used to make vanilla extract are Bourbon-Madagascar, Mexican, and Tahitian.

Store vanilla extract in a cool, dark place, with the bottle tightly closed, to prevent it from evaporating and losing flavor. It will stay fresh for about two years unopened and for one year after being opened.

Imitation vanilla flavoring can be substituted for vanilla extract, but it may have a slight or prominent artificial taste depending on the brand. It is about half the cost of real vanilla extract; however it's worth the extra expense of splurging on the real thing.

**Zest:** The name for the colored outside layer of citrus peel. The oils in the zest are intense in flavor. Use a microplane grater or the small holes of a box grater to grate the zest. Avoid grating the white layer (pith) just below the zest; it is very bitter.

**Liqueurs & Spirits:** Alcohol adds significant flavor and dimension to reduced-fat recipes. You needn't buy an entire bottle for a recipe; look for the miniature-size bottles (like the kind on airplanes) at liquor stores; they typically contain 2 fluid ounces (¼ cup) and are a frugal option.

## Measuring Ingredients

**Measuring Dry Ingredients:** When measuring a dry ingredient such as cocoa powder, sugar, spices, or salt, spoon it into the appropriate-size dry measuring cup or measuring spoon, heaping it up over the top. Next, slide a straight-edged utensil, such as a knife, across the top to level off the extra. Be careful not to shake or tap the cup or spoon to settle the ingredient or you will have more than you need.

**Measuring Liquid Ingredients:** Use a clear plastic or glass measuring cup or container with lines up the sides to measure liquid ingredients. Set the container on the counter and pour the liquid to the appropriate mark. Lower your head to read the measurement at eye level.

**Measuring Chocolate:** Chocolate packaged specifically for baking is typically sold in 1-ounce or 2-ounce increments, making it easy to measure the amount of chocolate needed in a recipe by the ounce. Premium chocolate bars are also sold in ounce increments (e.g., 1.5-, 4-, 5-, or 6-ounce); cut or break off the amount needed and then proceed with the recipe directions for chopping, melting, etc. A small kitchen scale is also a useful investment for measuring chocolate by the ounce.

**Measuring Syrups, Honey, and Molasses:** Measure syrups, honey, and molasses as you would other liquid ingredients, but lightly spray the measuring cup or container with nonstick cooking spray before filling. The syrup, honey, or molasses will slide out of the cup without sticking, allowing for both accurate measuring and easy clean-up.

**Measuring Moist Ingredients:** Some moist ingredients, such as brown sugar, coconut, and dried fruits, must be firmly packed into the measuring cup to be measured accurately Use a dry measuring cup for these ingredients. Fill the measuring cup to slightly overflowing, then pack down the ingredient firmly with the back of a spoon. Add more of the ingredient and pack down again until the cup is full and even with the top of the measure.

**Measuring Butter:** Butter is typically packaged in stick form with markings on the wrapper indicating tablespoon and cup measurements. Use a sharp knife to cut off the amount needed for a recipe.

¼ cup = ½ stick = 4 tablespoons = 2 ounces
½ cup = 1 stick = ¼ pound = 4 ounces
1 cup = 2 sticks = ½ pound = 8 ounces
2 cups = 4 sticks = 1 pound = 16 ounces

**Measuring Cream Cheese:** Like sticks of butter, bricks of cream cheese are typically packaged with markings on the wrapper indicating tablespoon and cup measurements. Use a sharp knife to cut off the amount needed for a recipe.

**Measuring Spices, Salt, Baking Powder, & Baking Soda:** Use the standard measuring spoon size specified in the recipe and be sure the spoon is dry when measuring. Fill a standard measuring spoon to the top and level with a spatula or knife. When a recipe calls for a dash of a spice or salt, use about $\frac{1}{16}$ of a teaspoon. A pinch is considered to be the amount of salt that can be held between the tips of the thumb and forefinger, and is also approximately $\frac{1}{16}$ of a teaspoon.

**Measuring Nuts:** Spoon nuts into a dry measuring cup to the top. Four ounces of nuts is the equivalent of 1 cup chopped nuts.

**Measuring Extracts & Flavorings:** Fill the standard measuring spoon size specified in the recipe to the top being careful not to let any spill over. It's a good idea to avoid measuring extracts or flavorings over the mixing bowl because the spillover will go into the bowl and you will not know the amount of extract or flavoring you have added.

# 1. *Chocolate*, MORNING TO NOON

RICH HOT COCOA, MORNING MOCHA, DAIRY-FREE HOT CHOCOLATE, SPANISH HOT CHOCOLATE WITH ORANGE, ESPRESSO, & SPICE, CHOCOLATE RASPBERRY MORNING MILKSHAKE, CHOCOLATE POWER PROTEIN SMOOTHIE, CHOCOLATE-PEANUT BUTTER SMOOTHIE, CHOCOLATE YOGURT WITH FRESH BERRIES, CHOCOLATE-PEANUT BUTTER SPREAD, CHOCOLATE SCHMEAR, CHOCOLATE OATMEAL, CHOCOLATE -ALMOND GRANOLA, THREE-GRAIN CHOCOLATE BREAKFAST CEREAL WITH WALNUTS & TROPICAL FRUITS, CHOCOLATE, CHERRY, & APRICOT MUESLI, DOUBLE GINGER- CHOCOLATE CHIP SCONES, MOCHA-PECAN SCONES, CHOCOLATE RICOTTA MUFFINS, COCOA -APPLE MUFFINS WITH PECAN STREUSEL, CHOCOLATE-FLECKED MULTIGRAIN MUFFINS, COCOA CRUNCH STREUSEL COFFEE CAKE, MOLASSES WHOLE WHEAT BRAN BREAD, CHOCOLATE-CINNAMON TOASTING BREAD, MULTIGRAIN POWER PANCAKES WITH CHOCOLATE & WALNUTS, CHOCOLATE FRENCH TOAST, BITTERSWEET CHOCOLATE WAFFLES WITH BERRY COMPOTE, SILVER DOLLAR CHOCOLATE PANÇAKES WITH RASPBERRY SAUCE, CHOCOLATE-CARDAMOM FRENCH TOAST CASSEROLE, OVEN-PUFFED PANCAKE WITH CHOCOLATE & FRUIT, ORANGE CREPES WITH DARK CHOCOLATE DRIZZLE, CHOCOLATE CINNAMON ROLLS, NO-BAKE ENERGY BARS WITH TOASTED OATMEAL, ALMONDS & CHOCOLATE, CHOCOLATE ENERGY FRUIT CHEWS, DOUBLE CHOCOLATE HEALTH-NUT BARS, AND MORE...

# *Hot Cocoa*

*With cocoa this good, it would be a shame to confine it to mornings alone. An ample dose of vanilla extract and good-quality unsweetened cocoa powder are the key ingredients to a sinfully rich chocolate drink with a lighter fat and calorie profile.*

| | |
|---|---|
| 4 CUPS 1% LOW-FAT MILK | ¼ CUP SUGAR |
| ½ CUP UNSWEETENED COCOA POWDER (NOT DUTCH PROCESS), SIFTED | 2 TEASPOONS VANILLA EXTRACT |

Place the evaporated and low-fat milk in a medium, heavy-bottomed saucepan. Heat until very hot, but not boiling.

In a small bowl whisk the cocoa powder and sugar until well blended. Add ¼ cup of the hot milk and stir until the mixture forms a paste.

Pour the cocoa paste and the vanilla into the hot milk and stir until the mixture is completely smooth. Divide the hot cocoa between 4 mugs and serve immediately. **Makes 4 servings.**

## Variations

**Mayan Hot Cocoa:** Prepare as directed, adding 1 teaspoon cinnamon, ¼ teaspoon almond extract, and a pinch of cayenne pepper to the cocoa-sugar mixture.

**Peppermint Hot Cocoa:** Prepare as directed, replacing the vanilla with 1 teaspoon pure peppermint extract.

**Gingered Hot Cocoa:** Prepare as directed, adding 2 teaspoons ground ginger to the cocoa-sugar mixture.

**Exotic Spice Hot Cocoa:** Prepare as directed, replacing the sugar with an equal amount of firmly packed light brown sugar and adding ¾ teaspoon ground cardamom, ½ teaspoon ground cinnamon, ⅛ teaspoon ground cloves, and a pinch of cayenne pepper to the cocoa-sugar mixture.

NUTRITION PER SERVING (1 MUG):
CALORIES 173; FAT 3.7G (POLY .13G, MONO 1.13G, SAT 2.35G); PROTEIN 10G;
CHOLESTEROL 12.2MG; CARBOHYDRATE 30G.

# Mocha

*Forget the local coffeehouse and have your coffee drink in the comfort of home. For a frothy mocha, prepare the mixture in a blender, in batches, until it's frothy.*

---

½ CUP UNSWEETENED COCOA POWDER (NOT DUTCH PROCESS)

½ CUP PACKED LIGHT BROWN SUGAR

2½ TABLESPOONS INSTANT ESPRESSO OR COFFEE POWDER

1½ TEASPOONS VANILLA

PINCH OF SALT

1 CUP COLD WATER

4 CUPS 1% LOW-FAT MILK

---

In a large, heavy-bottomed saucepan combine the cocoa powder, brown sugar, espresso powder, the vanilla, a pinch of salt, and water and heat the mixture over low heat, whisking, until the cocoa powder is dissolved and the mixture is a smooth paste.

Gradually add the milk. Heat the mixture over moderately low heat, whisking, until it is hot, but do not let it boil. Divide between 4 mugs and serve immediately. **Makes 4 servings.**

NUTRITION PER SERVING (1 MUG):
CALORIES 233; FAT 3.7G (POLY .13G, MONO 1.13G, SAT 2.35G);
PROTEIN 10.2G; CHOLESTEROL 12.2MG; CARBOHYDRATE 46G.

# Hot Chocolate

*You don't have to be vegan or lactose-intolerant to love this hot chocolate. It's a great way to incorporate soy into your diet in the most delicious way possible. The cornstarch is undetectable—it thickens the hot chocolate slightly, creating an extra-rich-tasting cocoa, without adding fat. Use the very best possible cocoa powder—it makes all the difference. For additional variations, see the options for Rich Hot Cocoa (page 21)—they can all be applied to this recipe, too.*

| | |
|---|---|
| ¼ CUP WATER | 2 TABLESPOONS SUGAR |
| 1 TABLESPOON CORNSTARCH | 2 TEASPOONS VANILLA EXTRACT |
| 2 CUPS PLAIN, UNSWEETENED SOY MILK (OR UNSWEETENED RICE MILK) | ⅛ TEASPOON CINNAMON |
| 3 TABLESPOONS UNSWEETENED COCOA POWDER | |

Whisk the water and cornstarch in a small bowl until blended; set aside.

Place the soy milk in a medium, heavy-bottomed saucepan. Heat until very hot, but not boiling.

In a small bowl whisk the cocoa powder and sugar. Toss to blend well. Add about 3 tablespoons of the hot soy milk and stir until the mixture forms a paste.

Add the cocoa paste, vanilla, cinnamon, and cornstarch mixture to the hot soy milk and stir until the mixture is completely smooth. Cook 1–2 minutes longer until mixture thickens slightly. Divide between 2 mugs and serve immediately. **Makes 2 servings.**

**Variation**

**Dairy-Free Mocha:** Prepare as directed, adding 2 teaspoons instant espresso powder to the cocoa-sugar mixture.

NUTRITION PER SERVING (1 MUG):
CALORIES 185; FAT 5.2G (POLY 1.9G, MONO 1.1G, SAT .9G); PROTEIN 12G;
CHOLESTEROL 0MG; CARBOHYDRATE 27G.

# SPICY CHOCOLATE

## Chai Tea

*This Indian-inspired version of chai combines black tea, spices, milk, and cocoa powder to create an aromatic, complex cuppa. It is the perfect cozy drink for a chilly winter day.*

| | |
|---|---|
| 1 2-INCH PIECE FRESH GINGER, CUT INTO THIN ROUNDS | 6 BAGS OF BLACK TEA (PREFERABLY DARJEELING) |
| 2 CINNAMON STICKS | 2 CUPS 2% LOW-FAT MILK |
| 2 TEASPOONS BLACK PEPPERCORNS | ½ CUP PACKED LIGHT BROWN SUGAR |
| 10 WHOLE CLOVES | ⅓ CUP UNSWEETENED COCOA POWDER (NOT DUTCH PROCESS) |
| 6 CARDAMOM PODS | |
| 6 CUPS COLD WATER | |

Combine the ginger, cinnamon sticks, peppercorns, cloves, and cardamom pods in medium saucepan. Using a mallet or back of large spoon, lightly crush or bruise spices. Add 6 cups water; bring to boil over high heat. Reduce heat to medium-low, partially cover pan, and simmer gently 10 minutes. Remove from heat.

Add tea bags and steep 5 minutes. Discard tea bags. Whisk in the milk, brown sugar, and cocoa powder. Bring tea just to simmer over high heat, whisking until sugar dissolves. Strain chai into teapot. Divide between 6 mugs and serve immediately. **Makes 6 servings.**

NUTRITION PER SERVING (1 MUG):
CALORIES 123; FAT 2.2G (POLY .07G, MONO .88G, SAT. 1.1G);
PROTEIN 3.5G; CHOLESTEROL 6.5MG; CARBOHYDRATE 25G.

# Spanish Hot Chocolate

## WITH ORANGE, ESPRESSO, & SPICE

*I nearly swooned when I had a cup of hot chocolate in Seville several years back. The warming elixir—distinguished by the addition of spice—had a richness closer to pure melted chocolate than hot cocoa. Its rich, frothy texture is achieved by heating and beating it several times. A standard metal whisk does the trick.*

| | |
|---|---|
| 1⅓ CUPS 1% LOW-FAT MILK | 3   2X1-INCH STRIPS ORANGE ZEST |
| ⅔   CUP CANNED FAT-FREE EVAPORATED MILK | ½   TEASPOON INSTANT ESPRESSO OR COFFEE |
| ¼   CUP UNSWEETENED COCOA POWDER (NOT |     POWDER |
|     DUTCH PROCESS) | ⅛   TEASPOON GROUND NUTMEG |
| 3   TABLESPOONS HONEY | ⅛   TEASPOON GROUND CLOVES |
| ½   OUNCE BITTERSWEET CHOCOLATE, | |
|     CHOPPED | |

Combine all ingredients in a medium, heavy-bottomed saucepan. Stir over low heat until chocolate melts. Increase heat and bring just to boil, stirring often. Remove from heat and whisk until frothy.

Return pan to heat and bring just to a boil again. Repeat heating and whisking once again. Discard orange zest. Pour hot chocolate into 2 mugs. **Makes 2 servings.**

**Cook's Note:** The hot chocolate may be prepared up to a day in advance. Cool and refrigerate in a covered container. Just before serving, bring just to boil, remove from heat, and whisk until frothy.

NUTRITION PER SERVING (1 MUG):
CALORIES 205; FAT 6.4G (POLY .23G, MONO 2.0G, SAT 4.1G); PROTEIN 14G;
CHOLESTEROL 20MG; CARBOHYDRATE 24G.

# CHOCOLATE-RASPBERRY

# *Morning Milkshake*

*Chocolate and raspberries were made for each other. This milkshake is great at any time of day, but what a way to start the morning.*

---

2 CUPS FROZEN UNSWEETENED RASPBER-
RIES (DO NOT THAW)

1 CUP PLAIN FAT-FREE YOGURT

1 CUP LIGHT (REDUCED SUGAR) CRANBERRY
JUICE

3 TABLESPOONS HONEY

3 TABLESPOONS UNSWEETENED COCOA
POWDER (NOT DUTCH PROCESS)

1 LARGE RIPE BANANA, PEELED AND SLICED

Combine all ingredients in a blender; process until smooth. Strain mixture through a sieve; discard seeds. **Makes 4 servings.**

NUTRITION PER SERVING (1 CUP):
CALORIES 160; FAT 1.1G (POLY .25G, MONO .24G, SAT .42G); PROTEIN 5G;
CHOLESTEROL 1.2MG; CARBOHYDRATE 37G.

CHOCOLATE

# Power Protein Smoothie

*Power indeed! With a double dose of soy protein, this simple-to-assemble smoothie will keep you in high gear for hours. But it's the great flavor that will have you making it morning after morning.*

1   MEDIUM SLICED RIPE BANANA, FROZEN

½   CUP LITE SILKEN TOFU

½   CUP LITE PLAIN SOYMILK

2   TABLESPOONS UNSWEETENED COCOA
    POWDER (NOT DUTCH PROCESS)

1   TABLESPOON HONEY

1   TEASPOON VANILLA EXTRACT

Place all ingredients in a blender and process until smooth. Pour into a tall glass and serve immediately. **Makes 1 serving.**

NUTRITION PER SERVING (1 GLASS):
CALORIES 299; FAT 4.1G (POLY 1.4G, MONO .97G, SAT 1.2G); PROTEIN 16G;
CHOLESTEROL 0MG; CARBOHYDRATE 59G.

# CHOCOLATE–PEANUT BUTTER

## *Smoothie*

*Who can resist the combination of chocolate and peanut butter? Not me. In smoothie form, it makes a perfect reason to rise and shine. Be sure to freeze the banana—it's essential for creating a thick, milkshake-like texture.*

½ CUP FAT-FREE MILK

2 TABLESPOONS UNSWEETENED COCOA POWDER (NOT DUTCH PROCESS)

2 TABLESPOONS REDUCED-FAT CREAMY PEANUT BUTTER

1 LARGE SLICED RIPE BANANA, FROZEN

1 8-OUNCE CARTON VANILLA FAT-FREE YOGURT

Place all ingredients in a blender and process until smooth. Pour into 2 tall glasses and serve immediately. **Makes 2 servings.**

NUTRITION PER SERVING (1 GLASS):
CALORIES 260; FAT 7.1G (POLY 1.9G, MONO 3.2G, SAT 1.9G);
PROTEIN 13G; CHOLESTEROL 1.2MG; CARBOHYDRATE 41G.

# Chocolate Yogurt

## WITH FRESH BERRIES

*I am crazy for yogurt—I can hardly imagine a day without it. And while I'll eat it plain, sweetened, or flavored most any way, I think this chocolate yogurt trumps all, especially when sweetened with honey and topped with berries.*

| | |
|---|---|
| 2 CUPS FAT-FREE PLAIN YOGURT | 1 TEASPOON VANILLA EXTRACT |
| 3 TABLESPOONS UNSWEETENED COCOA POWDER (NOT DUTCH PROCESS) | ½ CUP ASSORTED FRESH OR FROZEN, THAWED BERRIES (E.G., RASPBERRIES, |
| ¼ CUP HONEY | BLUEBERRIES, OR SLICED STRAWBERRIES) |

In a medium bowl whisk the yogurt, cocoa powder, honey, and vanilla until well blended and smooth. Divide yogurt between 2 bowls and top each with ¼ cup berries. **Makes 2 servings.**

»ⓒ» **Cook's Note:** The yogurt may be prepared ahead of time and stored in the refrigerator, in a covered container, for up to 1 week. Stir before serving and top with berries.

NUTRITION PER SERVING (1 CUP YOGURT AND ¼ CUP BERRIES):
CALORIES 298; FAT 1.7G (POLY .15G, MONO .48G, SAT .90G);
PROTEIN 16G; CHOLESTEROL 4.9MG; CARBOHYDRATE 61G.

# Chocolate-Peanut Butter Spread

*So good, and so easy to throw together, you'll wonder why you didn't think of this spread your-self. Spread it on bread, English muffins—anything toast-able—for a very good morning, or spread on whole grain bread with raspberry jam for a PB & J extraordinaire.*

| | |
|---|---|
| 1 CUP REDUCED-FAT CREAMY PEANUT BUTTER | ¼ CUP UNSWEETENED COCOA POWDER (NOT |
| 2 TABLESPOONS HONEY | DUTCH PROCESS) |
| 2 TABLESPOONS HOT WATER | 1½ TEASPOONS VANILLA EXTRACT |

Combine all of the ingredients in a medium bowl until blended and smooth. Transfer to a covered container and refrigerate. Makes about 1¼ cups. **Makes 16 servings.**

◈ **Cook's Note:** The spread will keep in a covered container in the refrigerator for up to 1 month.

NUTRITION PER SERVING (1½ TABLESPOONS):
CALORIES 104; FAT 6.3G (POLY 1.9G, MONO 3.0G, SAT 1.4G);
PROTEIN 5G; CHOLESTEROL 0MG; CARBOHYDRATE 9G.

# Chocolate Schmear

*Your morning bagel will never be the same. Spread the schmear on solo, or pair it with your favorite jam. You can adjust the sweetness according to your preference.*

3½ TABLESPOONS PACKED LIGHT BROWN
    SUGAR

2   TABLESPOONS UNSWEETENED COCOA
    POWDER (NOT DUTCH PROCESS)

1   8-OUNCE PACKAGE REDUCED-FAT CREAM
    CHEESE, SOFTENED

2   TABLESPOONS FAT-FREE MILK

1   TEASPOON VANILLA EXTRACT

Sift the brown sugar and cocoa powder into a small bowl; set aside. Beat the cream cheese, milk, and vanilla with an electric mixer set on medium speed until blended and fluffy. Beat in the cocoa mixture until well blended. **Makes 16 servings.**

**Cook's Note:** The schmear will keep in a covered container in the refrigerator for up to 1 week.

NUTRITION PER SERVING (1½ TABLESPOONS):
CALORIES 45; FAT 2.6G (POLY .09G, MONO .75G, SAT 1.7G); PROTEIN 2G;
CHOLESTEROL 8MG; CARBOHYDRATE 4G.

# Chocolate Oatmeal

*For quick comfort in a bowl, look no further—this makes the grayest morning bright. Although a drizzle of milk with fresh berries is my favorite topping, a dollop of vanilla yogurt with sliced bananas is an equally irresistible way to start the day.*

2 CUPS FAT-FREE MILK

1 CUP OLD-FASHIONED OATS

3 TABLESPOONS PACKED DARK BROWN SUGAR

2 TABLESPOONS UNSWEETENED COCOA POWDER (NOT DUTCH PROCESS)

⅛ TEASPOON SALT

Place the milk in a medium saucepan. Bring milk to a simmer over medium-low heat.

Stir in the remaining ingredients. Reduce heat to low and cook 5 minutes, stirring occasionally. Serve immediately. **Makes 4 servings.**

NUTRITION PER SERVING (ABOUT 1 CUP):
CALORIES 165; FAT 2.1G (POLY .45G, MONO .57G, SAT .54G);
PROTEIN 7.6G; CHOLESTEROL 2.3MG; CARBOHYDRATE 32G.

# CHOCOLATE-ALMOND

## *Granola*

*I have fond memories of my mother's homemade granola, rich with nuts, honey and toasted-oat goodness. My version ups the ante with chocolate two ways—cocoa powder and bittersweet chocolate—while keeping the fat and calories to a minimum. Spoon it up with milk, sprinkle it on yogurt, or pack a handful in a small plastic bag for a midmorning boost.*

4   CUPS OLD-FASHIONED OATS

1   CUP SLIVERED ALMONDS

3   TABLESPOONS PEPITAS (RAW GREEN
     PUMPKINSEEDS)

1½ TEASPOONS GROUND CINNAMON

¼   TEASPOON SALT

½   CUP WATER

⅔   CUP HONEY

3   TABLESPOONS UNSWEETENED COCOA
     POWDER (NOT DUTCH PROCESS)

2   TABLESPOONS PACKED LIGHT BROWN SUGAR

2   TABLESPOONS CANOLA OIL

½   TEASPOON ALMOND EXTRACT

1   OUNCE BITTERSWEET CHOCOLATE, FINELY
     CHOPPED

Preheat oven to 325°F. Spray a 15x10x1-inch jelly roll pan with nonstick cooking spray.

In a large bowl combine the oats, almonds, optional pepitas, cinnamon, and salt.

In a small saucepan combine the water, honey, cocoa powder, brown sugar, and oil; bring to a boil. Remove from heat and stir in almond extract. Pour over oat mixture; toss to coat. Spread oat mixture evenly onto prepared pan.

Bake 35 minutes, stirring every 10 minutes. Place in a large bowl; stir in chocolate. Cool completely. **Makes 20 servings.**

»⊙» **Cook's Note:** Granola may be stored in an airtight container for up to 1 week.

NUTRITION PER SERVING (¼ CUP):
CALORIES 159; FAT 6.6G (POLY 1.6G, MONO 3.5G, SAT .88G);
PROTEIN 4G; CHOLESTEROL 0MG; CARBOHYDRATE 24G.

# Three-Grain Chocolate Breakfast Cereal

## WITH WALNUTS & TROPICAL FRUITS

*Whole grains, nuts, dried fruits, and chocolate—this homemade cereal has everything you need to start the day right. Spoon it into a bowl with milk or vanilla yogurt, and top with fresh fruit.*

| | |
|---|---|
| ½ CUP MAPLE SYRUP | ¼ CUP UNSWEETENED COCOA POWDER (NOT |
| ⅓ CUP HONEY | DUTCH PROCESS) |
| 3 TABLESPOONS CANOLA OIL | 1 TEASPOON GROUND CINNAMON |
| 1½ TABLESPOONS VANILLA EXTRACT | ¼ TEASPOON GROUND NUTMEG |
| 4½ CUPS OLD-FASHIONED OATS | 2 OUNCES BITTERSWEET CHOCOLATE, FINELY |
| 1 CUP UNCOOKED QUICK-COOKING BARLEY | CHOPPED OR GRATED |
| ¾ CUP CHOPPED WALNUTS | 1 CUP PREPACKAGED DRIED TROPICAL FRUIT |
| ½ CUP TOASTED WHEAT GERM | BITS |

Preheat oven to 325°F. Spray a 15 x 10 x 1-inch jelly roll pan with nonstick cooking spray.

In a small bowl whisk the maple syrup, honey, oil, and vanilla until blended.

In a large bowl combine the oats, barley, walnuts, wheat germ, cocoa powder, cinnamon, and nutmeg. Add syrup mixture; stir well to coat. Spread oat mixture evenly onto prepared pan.

Bake 30 minutes, stirring every 10 minutes. Stir in chocolate and dried fruit bits. Cool completely. Transfer cereal to an airtight container. **Makes 24 servings.**

»☉► **Cook's Note:** Cereal can be stored in an airtight container for up to 1 week.

NUTRITION PER SERVING (⅓ CUP):
CALORIES 190; FAT 6.5G (POLY 3.5G, MONO 1.2G, SAT 1.2G);
PROTEIN 4G; CHOLESTEROL 0MG; CARBOHYDRATE 31G.

# CHOCOLATE, CHERRY, & APRICOT

## *Muesli*

*Muesli, which means "mixture" in German, was conceived and developed as the perfect health food by Swiss nutritionist Dr. Bircher-Benner more than a century ago. It can include raw or toasted cereals (oats, wheat, millet, barley, etc.), dried fruits (such as raisins, apricots, and apples), nuts, bran, wheat germ, sugar, and dried-milk solids. Chocolate is an ideal addition.*

| | |
|---|---|
| 1⅓ CUPS OLD-FASHIONED OATS | ¼ CUP CHOPPED DRIED APRICOTS |
| 1 CUP PLAIN FAT-FREE YOGURT | ¼ CUP CHOPPED DRIED CHERRIES |
| 1 CUP FAT-FREE MILK | 1 OUNCE BITTERSWEET CHOCOLATE, FINELY |
| ⅓ CUP COARSELY CHOPPED PECANS, TOASTED | CHOPPED |
| ¼ CUP HONEY | |
| ¼ CUP TOASTED WHEAT GERM | |

Combine all of the ingredients in a medium bowl, stirring well. Chill 2 hours. Serve cold. **Makes 5 servings.**

NUTRITION PER SERVING (½ CUP):
CALORIES 308; FAT 9.4G (POLY 2.4G, MONO 4.1G, SAT 2.0G); PROTEIN 10G;
CHOLESTEROL 1.9MG; CARBOHYDRATE 51G.

# DOUBLE GINGER CHOCOLATE-CHIP

# *Scones*

*Scones and lazy Saturday mornings go hand in hand. A fragrant hit of ginger and a handful of chopped chocolate guarantee these scones as winners. But be sure to save and freeze any leftover scones for quick and delicious weekday breakfasts. Individually wrapped, they take a mere 15 minutes to thaw.*

| | |
|---|---|
| 1 CUP WHOLE WHEAT PASTRY FLOUR (OR ALL-PURPOSE FLOUR) | ½ CUP PLUS 2 TEASPOONS FAT-FREE MILK, DIVIDED USE |
| 1 CUP ALL-PURPOSE FLOUR | 1 TEASPOON VANILLA EXTRACT |
| ¼ CUP PACKED LIGHT BROWN SUGAR | 1 LARGE EGG WHITE |
| 2½ TEASPOONS GROUND GINGER | 2½ OUNCES BITTERSWEET CHOCOLATE, CHOPPED |
| 1½ TEASPOONS BAKING POWDER | 3 TABLESPOONS CHOPPED CRYSTALLIZED GINGER |
| ½ TEASPOON SALT | 2 TEASPOONS TURBINADO (RAW) SUGAR |
| 5 TABLESPOONS CHILLED UNSALTED BUTTER, CUT INTO SMALL PIECES | |

Preheat oven to 425°F. Line a cookie sheet with parchment paper.

In a large bowl whisk the flours, brown sugar, ground ginger, baking powder, and salt. Cut in butter with a pastry blender or 2 knives until mixture resembles coarse meal.

In a small bowl combine ½ cup milk, vanilla, and egg white. Add milk mixture to flour mixture, stirring just until moist (dough will be soft). Turn dough out onto a lightly floured surface. Sprinkle surface of dough with the chocolate and crystallized ginger. With floured hands, knead 4 times or just until the chocolate and ginger are incorporated.

Pat dough into an 8-inch circle on the prepared cookie sheet. Cut dough into 12 wedges, cutting into, but not through, it. Brush remaining 2 teaspoons milk over surface of dough and sprinkle with turbinado sugar.

Bake 16–18 minutes or until golden. Serve warm, or cool on a wire rack. **Makes 12 scones.**

NUTRITION PER SERVING (1 SCONE):
CALORIES 183; FAT 7.4G (POLY .37G, MONO 2.8G, SAT 3.9G);
PROTEIN 4G; CHOLESTEROL 13.7MG; CARBOHYDRATE 27G.

# Scones

*Although lower in fat, these have the tender crumb you'd expect of traditional—and higher calorie—scones. Cut through the circle of dough, but do not separate the wedges. This allows them to bake as one large scone, and they will be much moister than scones baked separately.*

⅔ CUP PLUS 2 TEASPOONS FAT-FREE MILK, DIVIDED USE

2½ TABLESPOONS INSTANT ESPRESSO OR COFFEE POWDER

1 TEASPOON VANILLA EXTRACT

1 LARGE EGG, LIGHTLY BEATEN

1 CUP ALL-PURPOSE FLOUR

1 CUP WHOLE WHEAT PASTRY FLOUR (OR ALL-PURPOSE FLOUR)

¼ CUP UNSWEETENED COCOA POWDER (NOT DUTCH PROCESS)

⅓ CUP SUGAR

1¼ TEASPOONS BAKING POWDER

¾ TEASPOON BAKING SODA

¾ TEASPOON SALT

¼ TEASPOON GROUND CINNAMON

¼ CUP (½ STICK) CHILLED UNSALTED BUTTER, CUT INTO SMALL PIECES

3 TABLESPOONS FINELY CHOPPED PECANS

2 TEASPOONS TURBINADO (RAW) SUGAR

Combine ⅔ cup milk and the espresso powder in a microwave-safe bowl. Microwave on HIGH 1 minute; stir until espresso dissolves. Cover and chill completely. Stir in vanilla and egg.

Preheat oven to 425°F.

Combine the flours, cocoa powder, sugar, baking powder, baking soda, salt, and cinnamon in a medium bowl; cut in butter with a pastry blender or 2 knives until the mixture resembles coarse meal. (The flour mixture and butter can also be combined in a food processor; pulse until mixture resembles coarse meal.) Stir in pecans. Add milk mixture, stirring just until moist (dough will be sticky).

Turn the dough out onto a lightly floured surface; knead lightly 4 times with floured hands. Pat dough into an 8-inch circle on a baking sheet coated with cooking spray. Cut dough into 10 wedges; do not separate. Brush the dough with the remaining 2 teaspoons milk and sprinkle with turbinado sugar.

Bake 18–20 minutes or until browned. Serve warm. **Makes 10 scones.**

NUTRITION PER SERVING (1 SCONE):
CALORIES 190; FAT 7.5G (POLY .83G, MONO 3.2G, SAT 3.0G); PROTEIN 5G;
CHOLESTEROL 34.4MG; CARBOHYDRATE 28G.

# CHOCOLATE RICOTTA

*Muffins*

*Fat-free ricotta cheese is the stealth ingredient here, making these double-chocolate muffins both tender and rich.*

---

1⅓ CUPS ALL-PURPOSE FLOUR

1 CUP WHOLE WHEAT PASTRY FLOUR (OR ALL-PURPOSE FLOUR)

½ TEASPOON SALT

1 TEASPOON BAKING POWDER

1 TEASPOON BAKING SODA

6 TABLESPOONS UNSWEETENED COCOA POWDER (NOT DUTCH PROCESS)

⅔ CUP SUGAR

2 OUNCES BITTERSWEET CHOCOLATE, FINELY CHOPPED

1 CUP FAT-FREE RICOTTA CHEESE

¼ CUP (½ STICK) UNSALTED BUTTER, MELTED

1 LARGE EGG

2 LARGE EGG WHITES

1⅓ CUPS FAT-FREE MILK

1 TEASPOON VANILLA EXTRACT

---

Preheat oven to 350°F. Spray 14 standard-size muffin cups with nonstick cooking spray.

In a large bowl whisk the flours, salt, baking powder, baking soda, cocoa powder, sugar, and chopped chocolate.

In another large bowl mix the ricotta cheese with the butter. Add the egg and egg whites, mixing well. Whisk in the milk and vanilla. Fold into dry ingredients until just combined (be careful not to overmix or the muffins will be tough). Scoop batter into the 14 prepared muffin cups.

Bake 20–25 minutes or until a toothpick inserted in the center comes out clean. Transfer pans to a wire rack and cool. Serve warm or at room temperature. **Makes 14 muffins.**

NUTRITION PER SERVING (1 MUFFIN):
CALORIES 194; FAT 6.0G (POLY .35G, MONO 2.2G, SAT 3.0G);
PROTEIN 7G; CHOLESTEROL 29MG; CARBOHYDRATE 31G.

# Cocoa-Apple Muffins

## WITH PECAN STREUSEL

*If you have read about the health benefits of flax seed (it lowers cholesterol and is good for the heart), and wondered how to incorporate it into your diet, baking is the answer. The oil in the flax seeds adds incredible moistness, eliminating the need for much extra oil or butter. And the taste is delicious: nutty and rich. Who knew healthy eating could be so easy and delicious?*

| | |
|---|---|
| 1 CUP ALL-PURPOSE FLOUR | 1 CUP LOW-FAT BUTTERMILK |
| ½ CUP WHOLE WHEAT FLOUR | 1 TABLESPOON CANOLA OIL |
| ⅓ CUP PLUS 2 TEASPOONS UNSWEETENED COCOA POWDER (NOT DUTCH PROCESS), DIVIDED USE | 1 TEASPOON VANILLA EXTRACT |
| | 2 LARGE EGGS, LIGHTLY BEATEN |
| | 2 CUPS FINELY CHOPPED GRANNY SMITH APPLE (ABOUT 1 LARGE) |
| ¾ CUP FLAXSEED MEAL | ½ CUP GOLDEN RAISINS |
| ¾ CUP PLUS 2 TABLESPOONS PACKED DARK BROWN SUGAR, DIVIDED USE | ¼ CUP FINELY CHOPPED PECANS |
| 1 TEASPOON BAKING POWDER | 1 TABLESPOON BUTTER, CHILLED, CUT INTO BITS |
| 1 TEASPOON BAKING SODA | |
| ¼ TEASPOON SALT | |

Preheat oven to 350F°. Spray 18 standard-size muffin cups with nonstick cooking spray.

In a medium bowl whisk the flours, ⅓ cup cocoa powder, flaxseed, ¾ cup brown sugar, baking powder, baking soda, and salt. Make a well in the center of the mixture.

In a small bowl whisk the buttermilk, oil, vanilla, and eggs; add to flour mixture, stirring just until moist. Fold in apple and raisins. Spoon batter into 18 muffin cups coated with cooking spray.

To prepare streusel, combine the pecans, butter, remaining 2 tablespoons brown sugar and remaining 2 teaspoons cocoa powder in a small bowl, stirring with a fork until crumbly. Sprinkle streusel evenly over muffin tops.

Bake 18–20 minutes or until muffins spring back when touched lightly in center. Remove from pans immediately; place on a wire rack. Serve warm or at room temperature. **Makes 1½ dozen muffins.**

NUTRITION PER SERVING (1 MUFFIN):

CALORIES 146; FAT 4.7G (POLY 2.2G, MONO 1.3G, SAT 1.1G); PROTEIN 4.5G;

CHOLESTEROL 25.1MG; CARBOHYDRATE 23G.

# Multigrain Muffins

*Whole grains are cool again, and they taste as delicious as can be in these chocolate-laden muffins. Be sure to let the batter stand for 15 minutes before baking; it allows the whole wheat flour and oats to absorb some liquid, yielding a tender muffin.*

| | |
|---|---|
| 1 CUP WHOLE WHEAT FLOUR | ½ TEASPOON SALT |
| ¼ CUP SUGAR | 1½ CUPS QUICK-COOKING OATS |
| ¼ CUP PACKED DARK BROWN SUGAR | ⅔ CUP CHOPPED PITTED DATES |
| 2 TABLESPOONS TOASTED WHEAT GERM | 1 CUP LOW-FAT BUTTERMILK |
| 2 TABLESPOONS FLAXSEED MEAL | ¼ CUP CANOLA OIL |
| 2 TABLESPOONS UNSWEETENED COCOA POWDER (NOT DUTCH PROCESS) | 1 TEASPOON VANILLA EXTRACT |
| | 1 LARGE EGG, LIGHTLY BEATEN |
| 1½ TEASPOONS BAKING SODA | ½ CUP BOILING WATER |
| 1 TEASPOON GROUND CINNAMON | 2 OUNCES BITTERSWEET CHOCOLATE, CHOPPED |

In a large bowl whisk the flour, sugar, brown sugar, wheat germ, flaxseed meal, cocoa powder, baking soda, cinnamon, and salt until blended. Stir in the oats and dates. Make a well in the center of the mixture.

In a small bowl whisk the buttermilk, oil, vanilla, and egg; add to flour mixture, stirring just until moist. Stir in boiling water. Let batter stand 15 minutes. Stir in chocolate.

Preheat oven to 375°F. Spray 12 standard-size muffin cups with nonstick cooking spray.

Spoon batter into prepared muffin cups. Bake 18–20 minutes or until muffins spring back when touched lightly in center. Remove muffins from pans immediately. Place on a wire rack and cool. **Makes 12 muffins.**

NUTRITION PER SERVING (1 MUFFIN):
CALORIES 219; FAT 8.9G (POLY 2.3G, MONO 3.9G, SAT 1.9G); PROTEIN 6G;
CHOLESTEROL 19.3MG; CARBOHYDRATE 33G.

# CHOCOLATE CHUNK
# Strawberry Muffins

*You don't have to be a kid to get a kick out of the strawberry jam surprise hidden in each of these muffins. And yes, they are every bit as good with other varieties of jam and preserves, including two of my favorites, ginger marmalade and orange marmalade.*

1¼ CUPS ALL-PURPOSE FLOUR

½ CUP WHOLE WHEAT PASTRY FLOUR (OR ALL-PURPOSE FLOUR)

½ CUP PLUS 1 TABLESPOON SUGAR, DIVIDED USE

1½ TEASPOONS BAKING POWDER

½ TEASPOON SALT

¾ CUP FAT-FREE MILK

3 TABLESPOONS UNSALTED BUTTER, MELTED

1 LARGE EGG, LIGHTLY BEATEN

½ CUP STRAWBERRY JAM

1½ OUNCES BITTERSWEET CHOCOLATE, FINELY CHOPPED

Preheat oven to 400°F. Spray 12 standard-size muffin cups with nonstick cooking spray.

In a medium bowl whisk the flours, ½ cup sugar, baking powder, and salt until blended. Make a well in the center of the mixture. In a small bowl whisk the milk, butter, and egg; stir well. Add to flour mixture, stirring just until moist.

Spoon about 1 tablespoon batter into each of the prepared muffin cups. Spoon 2 teaspoons jam into center of each muffin cup (do not spread over batter). Mix chocolate into the remaining batter; top jam with remaining batter. Sprinkle tops of muffins evenly with the remaining 1 tablespoon sugar.

Bake 20–22 minutes or until muffins spring back when touched lightly in center. Remove from pan. Cool completely on wire rack. **Makes 12 muffins.**

NUTRITION PER SERVING (1 MUFFIN):
CALORIES 196; FAT 4.9G (POLY .28G, MONO 1.9G, SAT 2.5G); PROTEIN 3G;
CHOLESTEROL 26MG; CARBOHYDRATE 35G.

# PETITE CHOCOLATE-ALMOND MARBLED

## Coffee Cakes

*Mini Bundt pans look very much like standard-size muffin pans, with the exception of their heavier weight and decorative designs. The molded designs make these petites especially charming, but in a pinch, a muffin tin will work just fine.*

| | |
|---|---|
| ¼ CUP PACKED LIGHT BROWN SUGAR | 1 LARGE EGG, LIGHTLY BEATEN |
| ¼ CUP SLICED ALMONDS, TOASTED | 2 LARGE EGG WHITES, LIGHTLY BEATEN |
| 1½ TABLESPOONS UNSWEETENED COCOA POWDER (NOT DUTCH PROCESS) | ½ TEASPOON ALMOND EXTRACT |
| 1 OUNCE BITTERSWEET CHOCOLATE, CHOPPED | ¾ CUP FAT-FREE PLAIN YOGURT |
| 1½ TEASPOONS CINNAMON, DIVIDED USE | 1¼ CUPS ALL-PURPOSE FLOUR |
| ¼ CUP (½ STICK) UNSALTED BUTTER, MELTED | 1 TEASPOON BAKING POWDER |
| | ½ TEASPOON BAKING SODA |
| 2 TABLESPOONS UNSWEETENED APPLESAUCE | ¼ TEASPOON SALT |
| ½ CUP SUGAR | 2 TABLESPOONS POWDERED SUGAR |

Preheat oven to 325°F. Spray the cups of a 12-cup mini Bundt pan (½ cup molds) with nonstick cooking spray.

In a small bowl combine the brown sugar, almonds, cocoa powder, chocolate, and 1 teaspoon cinnamon; set aside.

In a small bowl whisk the butter, applesauce, sugar, egg, egg whites, almond extract, and yogurt. In a large bowl mix the flour, baking powder, baking soda, salt, and remaining ½ teaspoon cinnamon. Add the yogurt-egg mixture, stirring until just blended.

Place about 1 tablespoon batter in the bottom of prepared Bundt molds. Divide chocolate filling evenly among molds. Fill molds evenly with remaining batter.

Bake 11–13 minutes until cakes are firm to the touch and edges are brown and pull away from sides of pan. Cool 5 minutes in pan. Turn out on a rack and cool with flat side down. Lightly dust with powdered sugar before serving. **Makes 12 cakes.**

NUTRITION PER SERVING (1 MINI CAKE):
CALORIES 185; FAT 6.7G (POLY .62G, MONO 2.8G, SAT 2.8G);
PROTEIN 5G; CHOLESTEROL 28.7MG; CARBOHYDRATE 28G.

## CHOCOLATE JUMBLE

# *Breakfast "Cookies"*

*Soft and cake-y, these jumbo cookies more closely resemble muffin tops, but there's something irresistible about eating milk and a "cookie" for breakfast. The sentiment is even stronger with the addition of chopped chocolate.*

| | |
|---|---|
| ¾ CUP PACKED LIGHT BROWN SUGAR | 1½ CUPS WHOLE WHEAT PASTRY FLOUR (OR |
| ¼ CUP (½ STICK) UNSALTED BUTTER, MELTED | ALL-PURPOSE FLOUR) |
| 1 LARGE EGG | ½ CUP UNPROCESSED BRAN |
| 2 LARGE EGG WHITES | ½ TEASPOON BAKING SODA |
| ⅓ CUP DRIED MIXED FRUIT BITS | ¼ TEASPOON GROUND CINNAMON |
| 1½ OUNCES BITTERSWEET CHOCOLATE, | ¼ TEASPOON GROUND GINGER |
| CHOPPED | 3 TABLESPOONS SLICED ALMONDS |
| 1 TEASPOON VANILLA EXTRACT | 2 TEASPOONS TURBINADO ("RAW") SUGAR |
| | (OR REGULAR SUGAR) |

Preheat oven to 350°F. Line 2 baking sheets with parchment paper.

In a large bowl whisk the brown sugar, butter, egg, and egg whites. Stir in the fruit bits, chopped chocolate, and vanilla.

In a separate bowl whisk the flour, bran, baking soda, cinnamon, and ginger. Add the flour mixture to egg mixture, stirring just until moist.

Drop by level ¼ cup measures on prepared sheets. Sprinkle evenly with the almonds and sugar.

Bake 11–13 minutes or until almost set. Cool 2 minutes on sheets. Remove from sheets and cool completely on wire racks. **Makes 10 cookies.**

NUTRITION PER SERVING (1 COOKIE):
CALORIES 212; FAT 7.6G (POLY .83G, MONO 2.7G, SAT 3.4G);
PROTEIN 5G; CHOLESTEROL 33.4MG; CARBOHYDRATE 34G.

## COCOA BANANA

# Mini Muffins

*Everyone needs a great recipe that can be thrown together anytime for a wide range of circumstances. These mini muffins are just such a recipe. Not too sweet, they are made with ingredients you likely always have on hand—bananas, oats, flour, cocoa powder—and everybody, including you, will love them. Freeze the extras in a large ziplock bag—they thaw in about 5 minutes.*

¾   CUP ALL-PURPOSE FLOUR

½   CUP WHOLE WHEAT PASTRY FLOUR (OR
    ALL-PURPOSE FLOUR)

1   CUP QUICK-COOKING OATS

½   CUP SUGAR

⅓   CUP UNSWEETENED COCOA POWDER (NOT
    DUTCH PROCESS)

1   TEASPOON BAKING POWDER

½   TEASPOON BAKING SODA

¼   TEASPOON SALT

⅔   CUP MASHED RIPE BANANAS (ABOUT 2
    SMALL BANANAS)

½   CUP FAT-FREE MILK

5   TABLESPOONS UNSALTED BUTTER, MELTED

2   LARGE EGG WHITES, LIGHTLY BEATEN

1   TEASPOON VANILLA EXTRACT

2   TABLESPOONS SIFTED POWDERED SUGAR

Preheat oven to 400°F. Line 36 miniature muffin cups with paper baking cups or spray bottoms only with nonstick cooking spray.

In a large bowl whisk the flours, oats, sugar, cocoa powder, baking powder, baking soda, and salt until blended. In a medium bowl mix the bananas, milk, butter, egg whites and vanilla until blended. Add banana mixture to dry ingredients all at once; stir just until dry ingredients are moistened. Divide batter evenly among muffin cups, filling almost full.

Bake 10–12 minutes or until a wooden pick inserted in the center comes out clean. Cool muffins in pan on wire rack 5 minutes. Remove from pan. Cool completely.

Sprinkle with powdered sugar. Store tightly covered. **Makes 3 dozen muffins.**

**Cook's Note:** To make standard-size muffins, line 12 medium muffin cups with paper baking cups. Proceed as recipe directs. Bake 20–25 minutes or until a wooden pick inserted in the center comes out clean.

NUTRITION PER SERVING (1 MINI MUFFIN):
CALORIES 67; FAT 2.1G (POLY .20G, MONO .55G, SAT 1.2G);
PROTEIN 2G; CHOLESTEROL 4.3MG; CARBOHYDRATE 11G.

# COCOA CRUNCH STREUSEL
# Coffee Cake

*Move over doughnuts—this buttery, cocoa streusel-filled, mocha-iced cake has ten times the flavor and a fraction of the fat.*

½ CUP PACKED DARK BROWN SUGAR

½ CUP NUTLIKE CEREAL NUGGETS (SUCH AS GRAPE-NUTS)

2½ TABLESPOONS UNSWEETENED COCOA POWDER (NOT DUTCH PROCESS), DIVIDED USE

2½ TEASPOONS INSTANT ESPRESSO OR COFFEE POWDER, DIVIDED USE

1 TEASPOON GROUND CINNAMON

1¾ CUPS ALL-PURPOSE FLOUR

1 CUP SUGAR

1 TEASPOON BAKING SODA

½ TEASPOON BAKING POWDER

½ TEASPOON SALT

1 CUP FAT-FREE PLAIN YOGURT

1 TEASPOON VANILLA EXTRACT

½ CUP (1 STICK) BUTTER, SOFTENED

½ CUP EGG SUBSTITUTE

1½ CUPS POWDERED SUGAR, SIFTED

2 TABLESPOONS HOT WATER

Preheat oven to 350°F. Spray an 8-inch square baking pan with nonstick cooking spray.

In a small bowl whisk the brown sugar, cereal, 2 tablespoons cocoa powder, 2 teaspoons espresso powder, and cinnamon until blended. Set aside.

Lightly spoon flour into dry measuring cups; level with a knife. In a large bowl combine the flour, sugar, baking soda, baking powder, and salt. Add yogurt, vanilla, butter, and egg substitute; beat with an electric mixer on low speed 1 minute or until combined. Spread half of batter into the prepared pan. Sprinkle with cereal mixture; top with remaining half of batter.

Bake for 43–47 minutes or until a wooden pick inserted in center comes out clean. Transfer to a wire rack and cool in pan.

In a small bowl combine powdered sugar, hot water, remaining ½ teaspoon espresso powder, and remaining ½ tablespoon cocoa; spread glaze evenly over top of cake. Cut into 16 pieces. **Makes 16 servings.**

NUTRITION PER SERVING (1 PIECE):
CALORIES 242; FAT 6.3G (POLY .41G, MONO 1.6G, SAT 3.8G);
PROTEIN 4G; CHOLESTEROL 15.7MG; CARBOHYDRATE 44G.

# MOLASSES WHOLE WHEAT

# *Bran Bread*

The cocoa powder in this dark, delicious bread will come as a surprise to those who taste it. All they'll taste is the hearty, molasses and whole grain flavor, akin to Boston brown bread. The cocoa enhances the semisweet flavors of the brown sugar, molasses, and bran. Toast it up in the morning for breakfast on the go, or nibble a thin slice with a cup of early afternoon tea.

| | |
|---|---|
| 2⅓ CUPS WHOLE WHEAT FLOUR | 1   TEASPOON SALT |
| 1½ CUPS UNPROCESSED WHEAT BRAN | ¼   CUP FIRMLY PACKED DARK BROWN SUGAR |
| ¼   CUP UNSWEETENED COCOA POWDER (NOT DUTCH PROCESS) | 2   CUPS LOW-FAT BUTTERMILK |
| | ½   CUP DARK MOLASSES (NOT BLACKSTRAP) |
| 1½ TEASPOONS BAKING SODA | OPTIONAL: ½ CUP RAISINS |

Preheat oven to 350°F. Spray an 8½-inch loaf pan with nonstick cooking spray. Position oven rack to middle position.

In a large bowl whisk the flour, bran, cocoa powder, baking soda, salt, and brown sugar. In another bowl stir together the buttermilk and the molasses, stir the mixture into the flour mixture until the batter is combined well, and stir in the raisins, if desired. Spoon the batter into the prepared pan.

Bake in the middle of oven for 1 hour to 1 hour and 10 minutes or until the bread sounds hollow when tapped. Transfer bread to wire rack and cool in the pan 15 minutes. Invert bread onto the rack and cool completely. **Makes 1 loaf, 16 slices.**

NUTRITION PER SERVING (1 SLICE):
CALORIES 133; FAT 1.2G (POLY .28G, MONO .28G, SAT .48G);
PROTEIN 5G; CHOLESTEROL 1.2MG; CARBOHYDRATE 30G.

# CHOCOLATE-CINNAMON

# *Toasting Bread*

*Toast is one of life's unsung pleasures. Elevate it further with this homey chocolate-cinnamon bread. When toasted, the flecks of chocolate get melt-y, eliminating the need for further butter or any other topping. But . . . truth be told, I find it hard to resist spreading a teaspoon of peanut butter or raspberry jam on top.*

| | |
|---|---|
| 1 LARGE EGG YOLK | 3 OUNCES BITTERSWEET CHOCOLATE, COARSELY CHOPPED |
| 1 CUP WATER | |
| 2 CUPS UNBLEACHED BREAD FLOUR | 1 TABLESPOON UNSALTED BUTTER |
| 1 CUP WHOLE WHEAT BREAD FLOUR | 1 TEASPOON SALT |
| ¼ CUP UNSWEETENED COCOA POWDER (NOT DUTCH PROCESS) | ⅓ CUP PACKED LIGHT BROWN SUGAR |
| | 2 TEASPOONS BREAD-MACHINE YEAST |
| 1½ TEASPOONS CINNAMON | |

Whisk the egg yolk and water in a small bowl; pour into bread pan of bread machine. In a medium bowl whisk the flours, cocoa powder, cinnamon and chocolate; sprinkle into pan, covering the water-egg mixture. Add the butter, salt, and brown sugar in opposite corners of the pan. Make a shallow indentation in the center of the pan; spoon yeast into the indentation.

Set the machine to the basic/normal setting for a small loaf. Press start. At the end of the baking cycle, turn out onto a wire rack. Cool completely. **Makes 1 loaf, 14 slices.**

NUTRITION PER SERVING (1 SLICE):
CALORIES 165; FAT 4.0G (POLY .38G, MONO 1.4G, SAT 2.0G);
PROTEIN 4.4G; CHOLESTEROL 16.5MG; CARBOHYDRATE 30G.

# Multigrain Power Pancakes

## WITH CHOCOLATE & WALNUTS

*If you think chocolate-chip pancakes are fussy fare for little girls' slumber parties, then you need to whip up a batch of these hearty flapjacks. Chock-full of good-for-you and good-tasting things, they'll sustain you through the most rigorous of activities—deliciously.*

1¼ CUPS WHOLE WHEAT PASTRY FLOUR (OR ALL-PURPOSE FLOUR)

⅓ CUP UNCOOKED FARINA (SUCH AS CREAM OF WHEAT)

⅓ CUP PACKED LIGHT BROWN SUGAR

1 TEASPOON BAKING SODA

1 TEASPOON BAKING POWDER

½ TEASPOON SALT

1½ CUPS FAT-FREE MILK

¼ CUP UNSWEETENED APPLESAUCE

1 TEASPOON VANILLA EXTRACT

1 LARGE EGG, LIGHTLY BEATEN

2 OUNCES BITTERSWEET CHOCOLATE, FINELY CHOPPED

¼ CUP COARSELY CHOPPED WALNUTS

OPTIONAL: MAPLE SYRUP

In a large bowl combine the flour, farina, brown sugar, baking soda, baking powder, and salt, stirring with a whisk. Combine milk, applesauce, vanilla, and egg in a medium bowl, stirring until well blended. Add milk mixture to flour mixture, stirring until well combined. Let batter stand 5 minutes.

Heat a nonstick griddle or skillet over medium heat; coat pan with nonstick cooking spray. Pour a scant 3 tablespoons batter per pancake onto pan; sprinkle each with chocolate and walnuts. Cook 1 minute or until tops are covered with bubbles and edges look cooked. Carefully turn pancakes over, and cook 1 minute or until bottoms are lightly browned.

Repeat procedure with remaining batter, chocolate, and walnuts. If desired, serve with maple syrup. **Makes 8 servings.**

NUTRITION PER SERVING (2 PANCAKES):
CALORIES 202; FAT 5.8G (POLY 2.0G, MONO 1.5G, SAT 2.0G);
PROTEIN 5.6G; CHOLESTEROL 27MG; CARBOHYDRATE 34G.

# Chocolate French Toast

*Here French toast is better and as timeless as ever with the addition of chocolate and the subtraction of fat. Bon appetit!*

| | | | |
|---|---|---|---|
| 2 | LARGE EGGS | ⅛ | TEASPOON SALT |
| 2 | LARGE EGG WHITES | ¼ | TEASPOON CINNAMON |
| ¾ | CUP FAT-FREE MILK | 10 | 1-INCH-THICK SLICES FRENCH BREAD |
| 3 | TABLESPOONS SUGAR | | OPTIONAL: POWDERED SUGAR |
| 2 | TABLESPOONS UNSWEETENED COCOA POWDER (NOT DUTCH PROCESS) | | OPTIONAL: 1 RECIPE CHOCOLATE FUDGE SAUCE (SEE PAGE 206) |
| ¼ | TEASPOON VANILLA EXTRACT | | |

In a medium bowl beat the eggs, egg whites, milk, sugar, cocoa powder, vanilla, salt, and cinnamon with an electric mixer set on medium speed until smooth.

Heat a nonstick griddle or nonstick skillet over medium heat.

Dip bread in egg mixture. Place on griddle. Cook about 4 minutes on each side. Serve immediately with powdered sugar and chocolate sauce, if desired. **Makes 10 servings.**

NUTRITION PER SERVING (1 SLICE):
CALORIES 217; FAT 3.1G (POLY .59G, MONO 1.2G, SAT .83G); PROTEIN 9G;
CHOLESTEROL 42.7MG; CARBOHYDRATE 39G.

# Bittersweet Chocolate Waffles

## WITH BERRY COMPOTE

*These double-chocolate treats make ordinary waffles taste ho-hum. They are extra-wonderful with the luscious berry compote spooned alongside.*

---

1   12-OUNCE BAG FROZEN MIXED BERRIES, THAWED, UNDRAINED

¼   CUP PLUS 1 TABLESPOON PACKED LIGHT BROWN SUGAR, DIVIDED USE

½   CUP ALL-PURPOSE FLOUR

½   CUP WHOLE WHEAT PASTRY FLOUR (OR ALL-PURPOSE FLOUR)

¼   CUP UNSWEETENED COCOA POWDER (NOT DUTCH PROCESS)

1¼  TEASPOONS BAKING POWDER

¼   TEASPOON BAKING SODA

⅛   TEASPOON SALT

2   OUNCES BITTERSWEET CHOCOLATE, FINELY CHOPPED

3   TABLESPOONS UNSALTED BUTTER

1   LARGE EGG

2   LARGE EGG WHITES

1   CUP PLUS 3 TABLESPOONS 1% LOW-FAT MILK

1   TEASPOON VANILLA EXTRACT

To make compote, combine thawed berries and their juices along with 1 tablespoon brown sugar in a medium saucepan. Cook over medium-high heat, breaking up berries slightly with spoon, for 5 minutes. Cool to room temperature while preparing waffles.

In a large bowl whisk the flours, cocoa powder, baking powder, baking soda, and salt. Whisk in remaining ¼ cup brown sugar. In a small, heavy-bottomed saucepan stir chocolate and butter over medium-low heat until melted. Pour into medium bowl. Whisk in eggs and egg whites; whisk in milk and vanilla. Make a well in the center of the dry ingredients. Gradually whisk in milk mixture.

Preheat oven to 350°F. Following manufacturer's instructions, make waffles with the batter (waffles will be somewhat soft when removed from pan). Cool waffles.

Cut waffles into large triangles. Place on baking sheet. Bake waffles until they begin to crisp around the edges, about 5 minutes.

Serve the warm waffle triangles with the berry compote. **Makes 10 servings.**

**Cook's Notes:** The waffles and the compote can be made 1 day ahead. Store chilled in airtight container. The waffles may also be frozen, in an airtight container for up to 1 month.

NUTRITION PER SERVING (1 WAFFLE AND 3 TABLESPOONS COMPOTE):
CALORIES 166; FAT 6.9G (POLY .37G, MONO 2.6G, SAT 3.5G);
PROTEIN 5.2G; CHOLESTEROL 32.3MG; CARBOHYDRATE 23G.

# Silver Dollar Chocolate Pancakes

## WITH RASPBERRY SAUCE

*If you have a chocolate lover in the family (who doesn't?), make these pancakes for an extra-special birthday morning treat. Leftover pancakes may be tightly wrapped and frozen for later use. To reheat, place five pancakes on a microwave-safe plate in a circular pattern; cover with wax paper and microwave on high for 1 minute or until warm. Yum!*

| | | | |
|---|---|---|---|
| 1 | RECIPE RASPBERRY SAUCE (SEE BELOW) | 1 | TEASPOON BAKING POWDER |
| 1 | CUP ALL-PURPOSE FLOUR | 1 | TEASPOON BAKING SODA |
| ½ | CUP WHOLE WHEAT PASTRY FLOUR (OR ALL-PURPOSE FLOUR) | 2 | CUPS LOW-FAT BUTTERMILK |
| ⅓ | CUP PACKED LIGHT BROWN SUGAR | 1 | LARGE EGG, LIGHTLY BEATEN |
| ½ | CUP UNSWEETENED COCOA POWDER (NOT DUTCH PROCESS) | 2 | LARGE EGG WHITES, LIGHTLY BEATEN |
| | | ¼ | CUP CANOLA OIL |
| | | 2 | TABLESPOONS HONEY |

Prepare the Raspberry Sauce.

In a large bowl whisk the flours, brown sugar, cocoa powder, baking powder, and baking soda until blended. In a medium bowl whisk the buttermilk, egg, egg whites, oil, and honey; add all at once to flour mixture. Stir just until moistened.

Pour about 1 tablespoon batter onto preheated nonstick griddle or nonstick skillet. Cook over medium heat until bubbles appear on surface of pancakes; turn and cook just until set.

For each serving, serve 5 pancakes topped with 3 tablespoons raspberry sauce. **Makes 8 servings.**

## RASPBERRY SAUCE

| | |
|---|---|
| ¼ | CUP WATER |
| 2 | TABLESPOONS SEEDLESS RASPBERRY JAM |
| 1½ | CUPS FRESH OR FROZEN (THAWED) RASPBERRIES |
| 1 | TEASPOON FRESH LEMON JUICE |

Combine the water and jam in a small saucepan, and bring to a boil. Cook for 1 minute over medium heat, stirring until the jam dissolves. Combine the raspberry syrup, raspberries, and lemon juice in a blender. Purée until smooth. Strain through a mesh sieve; discard seeds. Cover and chill.

NUTRITION PER SERVING (5 PANCAKES AND 3 TABLESPOONS SAUCE):
CALORIES 269; FAT 9.2G (POLY 2.4G, MONO 4.7G, SAT 1.5G);
PROTEIN 7.7G; CHOLESTEROL 28.9MG; CARBOHYDRATE 43G.

# CHOCOLATE-CARDAMOM
## French Toast Casserole

*Thanks to cardamom, pistachios, and chocolate, this otherwise traditional brunch bake has a quietly exotic aroma and flavor.*

| | |
|---|---|
| 1 CUP PACKED LIGHT BROWN SUGAR | 2 TABLESPOONS SUGAR |
| ¼ CUP (½ STICK) BUTTER, MELTED | 1 TEASPOON GROUND CARDAMOM |
| 2 TABLESPOONS HONEY | 1 TEASPOON VANILLA EXTRACT |
| ⅓ CUP CHOPPED PISTACHIOS | 1 CUP EGG SUBSTITUTE |
| 2 OUNCES BITTERSWEET CHOCOLATE, CHOPPED | 12 (1-INCH-THICK) SLICES FRENCH BREAD |
| 1½ CUPS FAT-FREE MILK | (ABOUT 1 POUND) |

Spray a 13 x 9-inch baking dish with nonstick cooking spray. In a medium bowl combine the brown sugar, butter, and honey; pour into prepared pan. Sprinkle pistachios and chocolate over brown sugar mixture.

In a medium bowl whisk the milk, sugar, cardamom, vanilla, and egg substitute until blended. Arrange bread slices over pistachios and chocolate in dish; pour egg mixture over bread. Cover and refrigerate 1 hour or up to overnight.

Preheat oven to 350°F.

Carefully turn bread slices over to absorb excess egg mixture. Let stand at room temperature 20 minutes.

Bake for 30–35 minutes or until lightly browned. **Makes 12 servings.**

NUTRITION PER SERVING (1/12 OF CASSEROLE):
CALORIES 367; FAT 9.5G (POLY 1.4G, MONO 3.0G, SAT 3.2G);
PROTEIN 10G; CHOLESTEROL 11.2MG; CARBOHYDRATE 62G.

# Oven-Puffed Pancake

## WITH CHOCOLATE & FRUIT

*My parents regularly made a variation of this yummy, puffy pancake on Saturday mornings (and still do). This version has a fraction of the fat, cholesterol and calories, but is every bit as delicious, especially with the additions of cocoa powder, bittersweet chocolate, and fresh berries.*

| | |
|---|---|
| 2 TABLESPOONS POWDERED SUGAR | ¼ TEASPOON SALT |
| 1 TABLESPOON UNSWEETENED COCOA POWDER (NOT DUTCH PROCESS) | 1 LARGE EGG |
| 1 OUNCE BITTERSWEET CHOCOLATE, FINELY CHOPPED OR GRATED | 1 LARGE EGG WHITE |
| ½ CUP ALL-PURPOSE FLOUR | 1 TEASPOON VANILLA EXTRACT |
| ½ CUP FAT-FREE MILK | 1 TABLESPOON UNSALTED BUTTER |
| | 2 CUPS ASSORTED FRESH BERRIES |

Preheat oven to 425°F.

Sift the powdered sugar and cocoa powder into a small bowl; stir in chocolate and set aside.

In a medium bowl whisk the flour, milk, salt, egg, egg white, and vanilla until blended.

Melt the butter in a 10-inch cast-iron skillet over medium heat. Pour batter into skillet and cook 1 minute (do not stir).

Transfer skillet to oven and bake 16–18 minutes or until puffed and golden. Sprinkle with the chocolate-cocoa mixture and bake 1 minute longer. Cut into quarters; serve immediately with fresh berries. **Makes 4 servings.**

NUTRITION PER SERVING (¼ OF PANCAKE):
CALORIES 183; FAT 6.0G (POLY .62G, MONO 1.7G, SAT 3.0G);
PROTEIN 6.3G; CHOLESTEROL 61MG; CARBOHYDRATE 28G.

# Orange Crêpes

## WITH DARK CHOCOLATE DRIZZLE

*These beautiful crêpes are great for entertaining (brunch anyone?), since the rich, chocolate sauce and tart sweet oranges will satisfy one and all. The crêpe batter should be made at least 1 hour before it is to be used; this allows the flour particles to expand in the liquid and insures a tender, light, thin crêpe.*

| | |
|---|---|
| 1 CUP ALL-PURPOSE FLOUR | 2 TEASPOONS GRATED ORANGE ZEST |
| 2 TEASPOONS SUGAR | ⅓ CUP CANNED FAT-FREE EVAPORATED MILK |
| ¼ TEASPOON SALT | 1 TABLESPOON HONEY |
| 1 CUP 1% LOW-FAT MILK | 3 OUNCES BITTERSWEET CHOCOLATE, |
| ½ CUP WATER | CHOPPED |
| 2 TEASPOONS BUTTER, MELTED | 2 11-OUNCE CANS MANDARIN ORANGES, |
| 2 LARGE EGGS | WELL-DRAINED |

For the crêpes, combine the flour, sugar, and salt in a small bowl. In a blender combine the milk, water, melted butter, eggs, and orange zest. Add the flour mixture to milk mixture, and process until smooth. Cover batter; chill for 1 hour.

For the sauce, combine the evaporated milk and honey in a small saucepan over medium heat. Bring to a simmer and cook 3 minutes, stirring frequently (do not boil). Remove from heat. Add chocolate, stirring until smooth.

Heat an 8-inch nonstick crêpe pan or skillet over medium heat. Pour a scant ¼ cup batter into pan; quickly tilt pan in all directions so batter covers pan with a thin film. Cook about 1 minute. Carefully lift the edge of the crêpe with a spatula to test for doneness. The crêpe is ready to turn when it can be shaken loose from the pan and the underside is lightly browned. Turn crêpe over, and cook for 30 seconds or until center is set.

Place crêpe on a towel; cool completely. Repeat procedure with the remaining batter, stirring batter between crêpes. Stack crêpes between single layers of wax paper to prevent sticking (makes 12 crêpes).

Fold each crêpe in half; fold in half again. Place 2 crêpes on each of 6 plates. Top each serving with an equal amount of mandarin oranges; drizzle with chocolate sauce. **Makes 6 servings.**

NUTRITION PER SERVING (2 CRÊPES WITH TOPPINGS):
CALORIES 247; FAT 7.8G (POLY .52G, MONO 2.5G, SAT 4.1G);
PROTEIN 8G; CHOLESTEROL 76.5MG; CARBOHYDRATE 39G.

# No-Bake Energy Bars

## WITH TOASTED OATMEAL, ALMONDS, & CHOCOLATE

*The richness of almonds and chocolate makes these treats taste anything but "light." A kiss of honey and brown sugar adds a sweet touch.*

1 CUP QUICK-COOKING OATS

1 TABLESPOON UNSALTED BUTTER

¼ CUP HONEY

¼ CUP PACKED DARK BROWN SUGAR

¼ CUP SHELLED ROASTED, SALTED SUN-
    FLOWER SEEDS

⅓ CUP ROASTED, LIGHTLY SALTED ALMONDS,
    CHOPPED

2 TABLESPOONS FLAXSEED MEAL

1½ CUPS CRISP RICE CEREAL (E.G., RICE
    KRISPIES®)

2½ OUNCES BITTERSWEET CHOCOLATE,
    CHOPPED

Spread the oatmeal evenly in a large nonstick skillet. Toast the oatmeal over medium heat until golden brown and fragrant. Remove from heat.

In a large saucepan, melt the butter, honey, and brown sugar over medium- high heat. Bring mixture to a boil, then boil 1 minute, stirring constantly. Remove pan from heat and stir in the toasted oats, sunflower seeds, almonds, flaxseed meal, crisp rice cereal, and chocolate until very well-coated.

Immediately press mixture into an ungreased 8-inch square pan using a large square of wax paper. Let stand until completely cooled and firm. Cut into 12 bars. **Makes 12 servings.**

NUTRITION PER SERVING (1 BAR):
CALORIES 174; FAT 8.9G (POLY 2.0G, MONO 3.7G, SAT 2.4G);
PROTEIN 4G; CHOLESTEROL 2.7MG; CARBOHYDRATE 23G.

# Chocolate Cinnamon Rolls

*The most delectable cinnamon roll I ever tasted was in a small bakery in Carmel, California. In addition to an over-the-top cream cheese icing, they were loaded with chunks of high-quality bittersweet chocolate. My enlightened version of the same treat will still knock your socks off.*

1 PACKAGE (ABOUT 2¼ TEASPOONS) DRY
   YEAST

2 TABLESPOONS SUGAR

1¼ CUPS WARM FAT-FREE MILK (105° TO
   115°)

¼ CUP (½ STICK) UNSALTED BUTTER,
   MELTED

2 TEASPOONS VANILLA EXTRACT, DIVIDED USE

1 LARGE EGG, LIGHTLY BEATEN

4 CUPS BREAD FLOUR, DIVIDED USE

⅓ CUP UNSWEETENED COCOA POWDER (NOT
   DUTCH PROCESS)

½ TEASPOON SALT

1 LARGE EGG WHITE, LIGHTLY BEATEN

¼ CUP FIRMLY PACKED LIGHT BROWN SUGAR

1 TEASPOON GROUND CINNAMON

1 OUNCE BITTERSWEET CHOCOLATE, VERY
   FINELY CHOPPED

1 CUP POWDERED SUGAR

2 TABLESPOONS FAT-FREE MILK

In a large bowl dissolve the yeast and sugar in the milk; let stand 5 minutes. Add melted butter, 1 teaspoon vanilla, and egg; stir well. Add 3½ cups flour, cocoa powder, and salt. Stir with a wooden spoon to form a soft dough.

Turn dough out onto a lightly floured surface and knead until smooth and elastic (about 10 minutes). Add enough of the remaining flour, 1 tablespoon at a time, to prevent dough from sticking to hands.

Place dough in a large bowl coated with nonstick cooking spray, turning to coat top. Cover and let rise in a warm draft-free place for 45 minutes or until doubled in bulk. Punch dough down.

Turn dough out onto a lightly floured surface; roll into a 16 x 8-inch rectangle. Brush egg white over entire surface. Combine brown sugar and cinnamon in a small cup; sprinkle evenly over dough. Sprinkle with chocolate.

Starting at long side, roll up dough tightly, jelly roll fashion; pinch seam to seal (do not seal ends of roll). Cut roll into 16 (1-inch) slices, using string or dental floss. Arrange slices, cut sides up, in a 13 x 9-inch baking pan coated with nonstick cooking spray. Cover and let rise 30 minutes or until doubled in bulk.

Preheat oven to 350°F.

Bake rolls for 18–20 minutes until hollow-sounding when tapped. Transfer pan to wire rack and cool 15 minutes. In a small bowl combine the powdered sugar, 2 tablespoons milk, and remaining 1 teaspoon vanilla until smooth. Drizzle over rolls. Serve warm or cool to room temperature. **Makes 16 rolls.**

NUTRITION PER SERVING (1 ROLL):
CALORIES 223; FAT 4.6G (POLY .43G, MONO 1.2G, SAT 2.5G);
PROTEIN 5.9G; CHOLESTEROL 21.2MG; CARBOHYDRATE 40G.

# Chocolate Energy Fruit Chews

*I predict you will make these on-the-go energy bites again and again—and you can vary the dried fruit combinations to suit your taste. Kids love them, too, so be sure to keep a separate stash just for yourself. For extra protein and nutrition as well as flavor, roll the balls in finely chopped nuts.*

| | |
|---|---|
| 1¼ CUPS DRIED FIGS, TRIMMED OF STEMS | 2 TABLESPOONS ORANGE JUICE |
| 1¼ CUPS DRIED APRICOTS | ½ CUP UNSWEETENED COCOA POWDER (NOT |
| 1¼ CUPS DRIED CRANBERRIES | DUTCH PROCESS) |
| 2 TABLESPOONS HONEY | |

Process the figs, apricots, and cranberries in a food processor until very finely chopped (mixture should resemble a paste).

Transfer fruit mixture to a medium bowl. Add the honey, orange juice, and cocoa powder. Mix with a wooden spoon or hands until well blended. Cover. Refrigerate until cold, at least 2 hours. Roll into 36 1¼-inch balls. **Makes 36 fruit chews.**

**Cook's Note:** Store, tightly covered, in the refrigerator for up to 1 week.

NUTRITION PER SERVING (1 FRUIT CHEW):
CALORIES 34; FAT .26G (POLY .04G, MONO .07G, SAT .11G);
PROTEIN .6G; CHOLESTEROL 0MG; CARBOHYDRATE 9G.

# DOUBLE CHOCOLATE
# *Health-Nut Bars*

*If you are a fan of oatmeal cookies, you will come to love breakfast on the run with these bars. Sweet with chocolate and crunchy with seeds and nuts, they're also easy to prepare. Enjoy as a breakfast treat or snack.*

| | |
|---|---|
| 2 CUPS OLD-FASHIONED ROLLED OATS | ½ TEASPOON SALT |
| ½ CUP RAW SUNFLOWER SEEDS | 2 TABLESPOONS UNSWEETENED COCOA POW- |
| 1 CUP SLICED ALMONDS | DER (NOT DUTCH PROCESS) |
| ½ CUP TOASTED WHEAT GERM | 2 TEASPOONS VANILLA EXTRACT |
| ½ CUP HONEY | 2 OUNCES BITTERSWEET CHOCOLATE, |
| ¼ CUP PACKED DARK BROWN SUGAR | CHOPPED INTO CHUNKS |
| 2 TABLESPOONS UNSALTED BUTTER | |

Preheat oven to 350°F. Spray a 9-inch square glass baking dish with nonstick cooking spray.

Spread the oats, sunflower seeds, almonds, and wheat germ onto a cookie sheet. Place in the oven and toast for 15 minutes, stirring occasionally. Remove from oven and reduce temperature to 300°F.

While the oats toast, combine the honey, brown sugar, butter, salt, and cocoa in a medium saucepan. Cook and stir over medium heat until the brown sugar has completely dissolved. Remove from heat and stir in the vanilla. Immediately add the oat mixture and chocolate to the liquid mixture, stirring to combine.

Turn mixture out into the prepared baking dish. Using a spatula or a large square of wax paper, press down evenly.

Bake 23–25 minutes until just set. Transfer pan to a wire cooling rack. Cool completely. Cut into 16 squares and store in an airtight container for up to 1 week. **Makes 16 servings.**

NUTRITION PER SERVING (1 SQUARE):
CALORIES 193; FAT 9.8G (POLY 2.4G, MONO 3.9G, SAT 2.3G);
PROTEIN 5.4G; CHOLESTEROL 4MG; CARBOHYDRATE 25G.

# CHERRY-CHOCOLATE CHUNK

# *Granola Bars*

*Decked out with plenty of chocolate and tart-sweet dried cherries, these bars will spoil you for all other granola bars. Not too sweet, they make a great breakfast with a glass of milk, or a good snack eaten plain.*

| | | | |
|---|---|---|---|
| ¾ | CUP ALL-PURPOSE FLOUR | 1 | CUP DRIED TART CHERRIES OR |
| 1½ | CUPS PACKED DARK BROWN SUGAR | | CRANBERRIES |
| ¼ | CUP SUGAR | ¾ | CUP PLAIN FAT-FREE YOGURT |
| 2 | TABLESPOONS TOASTED WHEAT GERM | 2 | TABLESPOONS UNSWEETENED APPLESAUCE |
| 2 | TABLESPOONS NONFAT DRY MILK | 1 | TABLESPOON CANOLA OIL |
| ¼ | TEASPOON BAKING SODA | 1 | TEASPOON VANILLA EXTRACT |
| ¼ | TEASPOON SALT | 1 | LARGE EGG, LIGHTLY BEATEN |
| 3½ | CUPS QUICK-COOKING OATS | | |
| 6 | OUNCES BITTERSWEET CHOCOLATE, CHOPPED INTO CHUNKS | | |

Preheat oven to 350°F. Spray a 13 x 9-inch baking pan with nonstick cooking spray.

In a large bowl combine the flour, brown sugar, sugar, wheat germ, dry milk, baking soda, salt, oats, chocolate, and cherries until blended; set aside.

In a small bowl combine the yogurt, applesauce, oil, and vanilla until blended. Gradually stir in lightly beaten egg.

Gradually add the yogurt mixture to the dry ingredients. Stir until the dry ingredients are evenly coated with the yogurt mixture (the mixture will be very stiff). Using a spatula or a large square of wax paper, evenly spread and press the mixture into the prepared pan.

Bake 32–37 minutes or until the top and edges are golden brown. Transfer pan to wire rack and cool completely. Cut into 36 small squares or bars. **Makes 36 bars.**

»ⓒ» **Cook's Note:** Individually wrap the granola bars in foil or plastic wrap. Seal in a ziplock plastic bag. Freeze the granola bars and take one out in the morning for a healthy, yummy snack later in the day. (It only takes about 1 hour for the granola bar to thaw.)

NUTRITION PER SERVING ( 1 BAR):
CALORIES 146; FAT 3.2G (POLY .59G, MONO .85G, SAT .28G);
PROTEIN 4G; CHOLESTEROL 6.3MG; CARBOHYDRATE 26G.

# CASHEW-CHOCOLATE

## Kashi Bars

*You've never had a cereal bar quite like this one: dark chocolate, sesame, ginger, and cashews co-alesce in a crisp-chewy base. It's a breakfast treat worth getting up for—or stow one away for a midmorning energy boost.*

3¼ CUPS PUFFED WHOLE GRAIN CEREAL (SUCH
   AS KASHI)
½  CUP ROASTED, LIGHTLY SALTED CASHEWS,
   COARSELY CHOPPED
2  OUNCES BITTERSWEET CHOCOLATE,
   CHOPPED

⅓  CUP CREAMY REDUCED-FAT PEANUT BUTTER
½  CUP HONEY
1¼ TEASPOONS GROUND GINGER
1  TEASPOON DARK TOASTED SESAME OIL
1  TEASPOON VANILLA EXTRACT

Preheat oven to 350°F. Spray a 9-inch square metal baking pan with nonstick cooking spray.

In a medium bowl combine the cereal, cashews, and chocolate.

Combine the peanut butter and honey in a small, heavy-bottomed saucepan. Bring to a boil, whisking constantly until mixture bubbles vigorously and thickens slightly, about 1 minute. Remove from heat and stir in ginger, sesame oil, and vanilla.

Immediately pour peanut butter mixture over cereal mixture in bowl; stir to blend. Transfer mixture to prepared pan. Use a large square of wax paper to press firmly and evenly into pan so that mixture is compacted.

Bake 10–12 minutes until just golden around edges. Transfer pan to a wire rack and cool completely. Cut into 18 bars. **Makes 18 bars.**

NUTRITION PER SERVING (1 BAR):
CALORIES 108; FAT 5.0G (POLY .98G, MONO 2.4G, SAT 1.4G);
PROTEIN 3G; CHOLESTEROL OMG; CARBOHYDRATE 15G.

# Crispy Bars

*Here's a fresh, fun spin on crispy rice bars—which never went out of style in my book. These are as pretty as they are healthful and delicious thanks to the dried fruit and green pepitas. Look for pepitas in the bulk or natural food section of your supermarket.*

| | |
|---|---|
| ½ CUP PEPITAS (RAW GREEN PUMPKINSEEDS) | ⅛ TEASPOON SALT |
| ¼ CUP (½ STICK) UNSALTED BUTTER | 5 CUPS CRISPY RICE CEREAL (E.G., RICE |
| 4½ CUPS MINIATURE MARSHMALLOWS | KRISPIES) |
| 1 TEASPOON VANILLA EXTRACT | ⅔ CUP DRIED TROPICAL FRUIT BITS |
| 1 TEASPOON GROUND GINGER | 2 OUNCES BITTERSWEET CHOCOLATE, |
| | CHOPPED |

Heat a large nonstick skillet over medium-high heat. Coat pan with nonstick cooking spray. Add pepitas; cook 4 minutes or until seeds begin to pop and lightly brown, stirring frequently. Remove from heat; cool.

Spray a 13 x 9-inch baking dish with nonstick cooking spray; set aside. Melt butter in a large saucepan over medium heat. Stir in marshmallows; cook 2 minutes or until melted and smooth, stirring constantly. Remove from heat; stir in vanilla, ginger, and salt. Stir in cereal, dried fruit, chocolate, and pepitas.

Evenly press cereal mixture into prepared dish using a large square of wax paper. Cool completely. Cut into 16 bars. **Makes 16 bars.**

NUTRITION PER SERVING (1 BAR):
CALORIES 170; FAT 6.6G (POLY 1.1G, MONO 2.3G, SAT 2.6G);
PROTEIN 2G; CHOLESTEROL 8.1MG; CARBOHYDRATE 28G.

# Chocolate Gorp

*Consider yourself forewarned: this handy snack is deliciously addictive. Great for energy on the go, it is also delicious sprinkled over yogurt for breakfast or dessert.*

| | |
|---|---|
| ¼  CUP CREAMY REDUCED-FAT PEANUT BUTTER | 32  FAT-FREE PRETZEL MINI-TWISTS, BROKEN |
| ¼  CUP HONEY | INTO SMALL PIECES |
| 1  TABLESPOON UNSWEETENED COCOA POWDER | 1  CUP PACKAGED MIXED DRIED FRUIT BITS |
| (NOT DUTCH PROCESS) | 2  OUNCES BITTERSWEET CHOCOLATE, |
| 1  CUP LOW-FAT GRANOLA | CHOPPED |

Preheat oven to 300°F.

Combine peanut butter and honey in a small microwave-safe bowl. Microwave on high 30 seconds or until hot; add cocoa powder and stir well. Place granola and pretzels in a large bowl; pour peanut butter mixture over granola mixture, stirring to coat.

Spread mixture in a single layer on a jelly roll pan coated with nonstick cooking spray.

Bake 25 minutes, stirring twice. Stir in dried fruit bits and chocolate; return pan to oven. Turn oven off; cool mixture in closed oven 30 minutes. Remove from oven; cool completely. **Makes 7 servings.**

NUTRITION PER SERVING (½ CUP):
CALORIES 154; FAT 4.1G (POLY .67G, MONO 1.1G, SAT 2.3G);
PROTEIN 2G; CHOLESTEROL 0MG; CARBOHYDRATE 30G.

SALTY-SWEET

# *Chocolate Popcorn*

*This crunchy old-time favorite is made new with a salty-sweet, honey-cocoa coating and just enough butter to add great taste but little fat or calories. It's an ideal gift for families, because both adults and children will eat it by the handful. For a gift, place the popcorn in glass jars tied with ribbon. And for immediate eating, put the popcorn in a cellophane-lined basket or box, and set it out for everyone to enjoy.*

| | |
|---|---|
| 8 CUPS AIR-POPPED POPCORN (POPPED WITHOUT SALT OR FAT) | 2 TABLESPOONS UNSWEETENED COCOA POWDER (NOT DUTCH PROCESS) |
| ½ CUP HONEY | ½ TEASPOON SALT |
| 1 TABLESPOON BUTTER | OPTIONAL: ½ TEASPOON CINNAMON |

Preheat oven to 300°F. Spray a 15 x 10-inch jelly roll pan or other large rimmed baking pan with nonstick cooking spray. Place popcorn in a large metal or glass bowl lightly sprayed with nonstick cooking spray.

Combine the honey, butter, cocoa powder, salt, and cinnamon, if desired, in a saucepan over medium heat. Bring to a boil, stirring just until combined. Cook, without stirring, for 2 minutes. Pour honey mixture over popcorn in a steady stream, stirring to coat.

Spread popcorn mixture in an even layer into prepared pan. Bake 15 minutes. Remove from oven, and cool completely in pan. Store in an airtight container. **Makes 16 servings.**

NUTRITION PER SERVING (½ CUP):
CALORIES 55; FAT 1G (POLY .11G, MONO .39G, SAT .46G);
PROTEIN .6G; CHOLESTEROL 2MG; CARBOHYDRATE 12G.

# *Banana Bites*

*Getting a delicious dose of daily cocoa is as easy as sprinkling it on ripe bananas along with a few teaspoons of toasted coconut.*

4   TEASPOONS UNSWEETENED COCOA POW-
    DER (NOT DUTCH PROCESS)

4   TEASPOONS TOASTED UNSWEETENED
    COCONUT

2   MEDIUM BANANAS, PEELED, THEN SLICED
    INTO 6 SLICES ON THE BIAS

Place the cocoa powder and coconut on two separate small plates. Roll each banana slice in the cocoa, shake off the excess, then dip in the coconut. Eat immediately. **Makes 4 servings.**

NUTRITION PER SERVING (½ OF A BANANA):
CALORIES 66; FAT 1.1G (POLY .06G, MONO .12 G, SAT .78G);
PROTEIN 1.0G; CHOLESTEROL 0MG; CARBOHYDRATE 15.2G.

# SPICED CHOCOLATE-CHIP

# *Pumpkin Bread*

*Dense, moist, and delicious, this spicy bread is great as a quick snack or toasted, with a glass of milk, for breakfast. And the pumpkin packs it with tremendous nutrition: naturally low in calories and fat, pumpkin contains a wide variety of vitamins and minerals, is rich in vitamin A, and is an excellent source of fiber.*

| | |
|---|---|
| 1½ CUPS ALL-PURPOSE FLOUR | ½ TEASPOON SALT |
| 1½ CUPS WHOLE WHEAT PASTRY FLOUR (OR ALL-PURPOSE FLOUR) | ¼ TEASPOON GROUND NUTMEG |
| | ⅔ CUP CANOLA OIL |
| 2 CUPS PACKED LIGHT BROWN SUGAR | 3 LARGE EGGS, LIGHTLY BEATEN |
| 2 TEASPOONS BAKING SODA | 1 15-OUNCE CAN SOLID-PACK PUMPKIN |
| 1 TEASPOON BAKING POWDER | 6 OUNCES BITTERSWEET CHOCOLATE, FINELY CHOPPED |
| 1 TEASPOON CINNAMON | |
| 1 TEASPOON GROUND GINGER | |

Preheat oven to 350°F. Spray two 9 x 5-inch loaf pans with nonstick cooking spray.

In a large bowl whisk the flours, brown sugar, baking soda, baking powder, cinnamon, ginger, salt, and nutmeg. In a medium bowl whisk the canola oil, eggs, and pumpkin until smooth. Make a well in the center of the flour mixture. Add egg mixture to the well, stirring just until moist. Fold in chocolate. Spoon batter into the prepared pans.

Bake 1 hour or until a wooden pick inserted in the center comes out clean. Transfer pans to wire racks and cool 10 minutes; remove from pans. Cool loaves completely. **Makes 32 slices, 16 per loaf.**

NUTRITION PER SERVING (1 SLICE):
CALORIES 154; FAT 6.8G (POLY 1.5G, MONO 3.4G, SAT 1.5G);
PROTEIN 2.5G; CHOLESTEROL 19.8MG; CARBOHYDRATE 22G.

# MARBLED-CHOCOLATE

# *Banana Bread*

*Bananas are a standard in my kitchen. I often buy extra bananas and let them get almost black just to make this bread—very ripe bananas make the very best bread. Overripe bananas can be peeled, mashed, and frozen, then defrosted whenever you want to bake up a batch.*

| | |
|---|---|
| 1 CUP ALL-PURPOSE FLOUR | ¼ CUP (½ STICK) UNSALTED BUTTER, SOFTENED |
| 1 CUP WHOLE WHEAT PASTRY FLOUR (OR ALL-PURPOSE FLOUR) | 1½ CUPS MASHED RIPE BANANA (ABOUT 3 BANANAS) |
| ¾ TEASPOON BAKING SODA | |
| ½ TEASPOON SALT | ½ CUP EGG SUBSTITUTE |
| ⅛ TEASPOON NUTMEG | ⅓ CUP PLAIN FAT-FREE YOGURT |
| 1 CUP SUGAR | 3 OUNCES BITTERSWEET CHOCOLATE, CHOPPED |

Preheat oven to 350°F.

In a medium bowl whisk the flours, baking soda, salt, and nutmeg until blended.

Place the sugar and butter in a large bowl; beat with a mixer at medium speed until well blended (about 1 minute). Add banana, egg substitute, and yogurt, beating until blended. Add the flour mixture with a wooden spoon, stirring until just blended.

Place chocolate in a medium microwave-safe bowl, and microwave on HIGH 1 minute or until almost melted, stirring until smooth. Cool slightly. Add 1 cup batter to chocolate, stirring until well combined. Spoon chocolate batter alternately with plain batter into an 8½ x 4½-inch loaf pan coated with nonstick cooking spray. Swirl batters together using a knife.

Bake 1 hour and 15 minutes or until a wooden pick inserted in center comes out clean. Cool 10 minutes in pan on a wire rack; remove from pan. Cool completely on wire rack. **Makes 1 loaf, 16 slices.**

NUTRITION PER SERVING (1 SLICE):
CALORIES 185; FAT 5.4G (POLY .38G, MONO 2.0G, SAT 2.8G);
PROTEIN 3.4G; CHOLESTEROL 8.2MG; CARBOHYDRATE 32G.

# Date-Nut Bread

*Cocoa works as a clandestine ingredient here, enhancing the deep, rich flavor of the dates and brown sugar. Serve one of these loaves the day you make them. Wrap the others in foil—it freezes beautifully—so that you'll have them on hand for unexpected company or for future quick breakfasts and snacks.*

| | |
|---|---|
| 2 CUPS CHOPPED PITTED DATES | 1 LARGE EGG |
| 2 TEASPOONS BAKING SODA | 2 CUPS ALL-PURPOSE FLOUR |
| 2 CUPS BOILING WATER | 1 CUP WHOLE WHEAT PASTRY FLOUR (OR |
| 2 CUPS PACKED DARK BROWN SUGAR | ALL-PURPOSE FLOUR) |
| 1 TABLESPOON VEGETABLE SHORTENING | ½ CUP UNSWEETENED COCOA POWDER (NOT |
| 1 TEASPOON SALT | DUTCH PROCESS) |
| 1 TEASPOON VANILLA EXTRACT | 1 CUP CHOPPED PECANS, TOASTED |

Combine the dates and baking soda in a medium bowl. Pour water over the date mixture. Stir and let cool.

Preheat oven to 350°F. Spray three 8½-inch loaf pans with nonstick cooking spray.

In a large bowl place the brown sugar, vegetable shortening, salt, vanilla, and egg. Beat with a mixer at medium speed until well blended. In a medium bowl whisk the flours and cocoa powder.

Add flour and date mixture alternately to sugar mixture, beginning and ending with the flour mixture. Stir in pecans. Pour batter into prepared pans.

Bake 40–45 minutes or until a wooden pick inserted in the center comes out clean. Cool 10 minutes in pans on wire racks. Remove from pans. Cool completely. **Makes 3 loaves, 16 slices per loaf.**

NUTRITION PER SERVING (1 SLICE):
CALORIES 75; FAT 2.2G (POLY .61G, MONO 1.1G, SAT .32G);
PROTEIN 1.5G; CHOLESTEROL 4.4MG; CARBOHYDRATE 13.5G.

# Chocolate Zucchini Bread

*Chocolate and cocoa powder turn this traditional zucchini bread into an addictive breakfast or snack. It's a great way to sneak some vegetables into your diet (or your kids' diets) at the start of the day.*

1½ CUPS WHOLE WHEAT PASTRY FLOUR (OR ALL-PURPOSE FLOUR)

½ CUP ALL-PURPOSE FLOUR

⅓ CUP UNSWEETENED COCOA POWDER (NOT DUTCH PROCESS)

½ TEASPOON BAKING POWDER

½ TEASPOON BAKING SODA

½ TEASPOON SALT

3 LARGE EGGS, LIGHTLY BEATEN

1½ CUPS SUGAR

¾ CUP UNSWEETENED APPLESAUCE

¼ CUP CANOLA OIL

1 TEASPOON VANILLA EXTRACT

1 OUNCE UNSWEETENED CHOCOLATE, MELTED

2 CUPS GRATED ZUCCHINI (ABOUT 1 MEDIUM-LARGE ZUCCHINI)

OPTIONAL: ⅓ CUP CHOPPED PECANS, TOASTED

Preheat oven to 325°F. Spray two 8½ x 4½-inch loaf pans with nonstick cooking spray.

In a large bowl whisk the flours, cocoa powder, baking powder, baking soda, and salt.

In another large bowl whisk the eggs, sugar, applesauce, oil, vanilla, and melted chocolate until blended.

Add the wet ingredients to the dry ingredients and stir with a rubber spatula until just blended. Fold in the zucchini and pecans, if using. Spoon the batter into the prepared pans, smoothing the tops.

Bake the loaves 55–60 minutes or until a skewer inserted in the center comes out clean. Let cool in pans on a wire rack 10 minutes. Invert loaves onto rack and cool completely. **Makes 16 servings (8 slices per loaf).**

NUTRITION PER SERVING (1 SLICE):
CALORIES 193; FAT 5.7G (POLY 1.3G, MONO 2.7G, SAT 1.3G);
PROTEIN 3.5G; CHOLESTEROL 40MG; CARBOHYDRATE 34G.

# 2. *Chocolate Cookies*

## AND OTHER PETITE TREATS

CHOCOLATE-CHOCOLATE CHUNKERS, JUMBO BROWNIE ROUNDS, CHOCOLATE CRACKLES, MEXICAN CHOCOLATE THINS, BAKEHOUSE CHOCOLATE CHIPPERS, MULTIGRAIN CHOCOLATE CHIP COOKIES, OATMEAL COOKIES WITH CHOCOLATE & CHERRIES, MUDSLIDE COOKIES, CHOCOLATE THUMBPRINTS, CHEWY CHOCOLATE-APRICOT COOKIES, CHOCOLATE TRUFFLE-TOP SUGAR COOKIES, BLACK-AND-WHITE COOKIES, CHOCOLATE MADELEINES, CHEWY CHOCOLATE-COCONUT MACAROONS, CHOCOLATE GINGERSNAPS, CHOCOLATE-CINNAMON ICEBOX COOKIES, DOUBLE DARK CHOCOLATE BISCOTTI, MOCHA BISCOTTI, GINGER-CHOCOLATE FLECKED BISCOTTI, CHAI-CHOCOLATE CHIP BISCOTTI, MOCHA-CHIP CRISPY RICE BARS, CHOCOLATE-TOPPED PEANUT BUTTER CRISPY RICE BARS, CHOCOLATE-OATMEAL NO-BAKES, EASY BITTERSWEET CHOCOLATE TRUFFLES (WITH VARIATIONS), DECADENT DAIRY-FREE BITTERSWEET CHOCOLATE TRUFFLES, DATE-NUT COCOA "TRUFFLES", MINI TRIPLE-CHOCOLATE CHEESECAKES, MOCHA MERINGUE KISSES, BITTERSWEET CHOCOLATE-FLECKED MERINGUE COOKIES, ENGLISH TOFFEE PUFFS, CHOCOLATE-CHUNK PECAN BARS, BUTTERSCOTCH-CHOCOLATE CHUNK BARS, CRANBERRY-CHOCOLATE BARS WITH ORANGE & PISTACHIOS, CHOCOLATE-CHERRY STREUSEL BARS, BITTERSWEET CHOCOLATE-STUDDED BLONDIES, CHOCOLATE-COVERED RAISIN BARS, AND MORE...

# Chocolate-Chocolate Chunkers

*Nothing beats cookies fresh from the oven, especially double-chocolate cookies. And you get the pleasure of filling your house with their warm, sweet scent as they bake.*

¼ CUP (½ STICK) UNSALTED BUTTER, SOFTENED

½ CUP PACKED DARK BROWN SUGAR

¼ CUP SUGAR

¼ CUP CANOLA OIL

1 LARGE EGG

1 TEASPOON VANILLA

½ CUP ALL-PURPOSE FLOUR

½ CUP WHOLE WHEAT PASTRY FLOUR (OR ALL-PURPOSE FLOUR)

¼ CUP UNSWEETENED COCOA POWDER (NOT DUTCH PROCESS)

¼ TEASPOON SALT

4 OUNCES BITTERSWEET CHOCOLATE, COARSELY CHOPPED

Preheat oven to 350°F.

In a large bowl beat the butter and sugars with an electric mixer set on medium speed until well combined. Add the oil and egg and beat until creamy. Mix in vanilla.

In a medium bowl whisk the flours, cocoa powder, and salt. Add flour mixture to the bowl of wet ingredients, mixing until well blended. Stir in the chopped chocolate until combined.

Drop dough by heaping tablespoons 2 inches apart onto an ungreased cookie sheet.

Bake 11–13 minutes until set at edges. Transfer cookies to wire rack with spatula. Cool completely. **Makes 2 dozen cookies.**

NUTRITION PER SERVING (1 COOKIE):
CALORIES 104; FAT 6.3G (POLY .86G, MONO 2.9G, SAT 2.3G);
PROTEIN 1.4G; CHOLESTEROL 14.2MG; CARBOHYDRATE 12G.

# Jumbo Brownie Rounds

*These taste like brownies, in cookie form. You'll love the texture: not quite as dense as regular brownies, they have crispy edges and crackles coupled with appealingly fudgy interiors. Smaller than the average brownie, they have a sophistication that the former lack—perfect with a skim espresso drink.*

| | |
|---|---|
| 1¼ CUPS ALL-PURPOSE FLOUR | 6 OUNCES BITTERSWEET CHOCOLATE, |
| ½ CUP WHOLE WHEAT PASTRY FLOUR (OR | CHOPPED |
| ALL-PURPOSE FLOUR) | ¼ CUP (½ STICK) UNSALTED BUTTER |
| ¾ CUP POWDERED SUGAR | 1 CUP PACKED LIGHT BROWN SUGAR |
| ⅓ CUP UNSWEETENED COCOA POWDER (NOT | 1 LARGE EGG |
| DUTCH PROCESS) | 2 LARGE EGG WHITES |
| 1¾ TEASPOONS BAKING POWDER | 2 TABLESPOONS HONEY |
| ¼ TEASPOON BAKING SODA | 1 TABLESPOON FAT-FREE MILK |
| ¼ TEASPOON SALT | 2 TEASPOONS VANILLA EXTRACT |

In a medium bowl whisk the flours, powdered sugar, cocoa powder, baking powder, baking soda, and salt; set aside.

Place the chocolate and butter in a large microwavable bowl. Microwave on MEDIUM until chocolate melts, stopping every 30 seconds to stir. Let cool 5 minutes. Stir in the brown sugar, egg, egg whites, honey, milk, and vanilla until blended and smooth. Add the flour mixture, stirring with a wooden spoon until just blended. Chill 15 minutes.

Preheat oven to 350°F. Spray cookie sheets with nonstick cooking spray.

Drop dough by heaping tablespoonfuls 2 inches apart onto prepared cookie sheets. Bake 11–13 minutes until just set at edges.

Remove from oven and let cool on sheets 1 minute. Transfer cookies to wire rack with spatula. Cool completely. **Makes 2½ dozen large cookies.**

NUTRITION PER SERVING (1 COOKIE):
CALORIES 119; FAT 3.8G (POLY .15G, MONO .8G, SAT 1.1G);
PROTEIN 2G; CHOLESTEROL 11.4MG; CARBOHYDRATE 21G.

# Chocolate Crackles

*It's a good idea to have a napkin handy when eating these crackle-top chocolate cookies—the powdered-sugar coating can get all over the place. But they are so very worth the mess!*

| | |
|---|---|
| 1 CUP ALL-PURPOSE FLOUR | ⅛ TEASPOON BAKING SODA |
| ⅓ CUP WHOLE WHEAT PASTRY FLOUR (OR ALL-PURPOSE FLOUR) | ¼ TEASPOON SALT |
| | ¼ CUP (½ STICK) UNSALTED BUTTER |
| ⅓ CUP PACKED LIGHT BROWN SUGAR | 3 LARGE EGG WHITES |
| ½ CUP UNSWEETENED COCOA POWDER (NOT DUTCH PROCESS) | 1 TEASPOON VANILLA EXTRACT |
| | ½ CUP POWDERED SUGAR |
| 1 TEASPOON BAKING POWDER | |

Preheat oven to 350°F. Spray cookie sheets with nonstick cooking spray.

In a medium bowl whisk the flours, brown sugar, cocoa powder, baking powder, baking soda, and salt.

Cut in the butter to the flour mixture with a pastry cutter or your fingers until mixture has the texture of fresh breadcrumbs. Add the egg whites and vanilla, stirring with a wooden spoon until just blended.

Place the powdered sugar in a shallow dish. Shape and roll dough into 1½-inch balls. Roll balls in the sugar to coat. Place balls 2 inches apart onto prepared cookie sheets.

Bake 11–13 minutes until just set at edges. Remove from oven and let cool on sheets 1 minute. Transfer cookies to wire rack with spatula. Cool completely. **Makes 2 dozen cookies.**

NUTRITION PER SERVING (1 COOKIE):
CALORIES 69; FAT 2.3G (POLY .12G, MONO .59G, SAT 1.4G);
PROTEIN 2G; CHOLESTEROL 11.7MG; CARBOHYDRATE 12G.

# Mexican Chocolate Thins

*Crisp at the edges and chewy at the center, these slender cookies have a distinct Mexican flavor profile thanks to a pinch of cinnamon, a touch of almond, and a kick of cayenne.*

| | |
|---|---|
| 1 CUP ALL-PURPOSE FLOUR | 5 TABLESPOONS BUTTER |
| 1 CUP WHOLE WHEAT PASTRY FLOUR (OR ALL-PURPOSE FLOUR) | 7 TABLESPOONS UNSWEETENED COCOA POWDER (NOT DUTCH PROCESS) |
| ½ TEASPOON CINNAMON | ⅔ CUP SUGAR |
| ¼ TEASPOON BAKING SODA | ⅓ CUP PACKED DARK BROWN SUGAR |
| ⅛ TEASPOON CAYENNE PEPPER | ⅓ CUP PLAIN LOW-FAT YOGURT |
| ⅛ TEASPOON SALT | ½ TEASPOON ALMOND EXTRACT |

Preheat oven to 350°F. Spray two cookie sheets with nonstick cooking spray; set aside.

Whisk the flours, cinnamon, soda, cayenne, and salt in a small bowl; set aside.

Melt the butter in a large saucepan over medium heat. Remove from heat and stir in the cocoa powder and sugars (mixture will resemble coarse sand). Add the yogurt and almond extract, stirring to combine. Add flour mixture, stirring until moist.

Drop by level tablespoons 2 inches apart onto prepared sheets.

Bake 8–10 minutes or until almost set. Cool on sheets 2–3 minutes or until firm. Transfer cookies to wire rack with spatula. Cool completely. **Makes 2 dozen cookies.**

NUTRITION PER SERVING (1 COOKIE):
CALORIES 79; FAT 2.7G (POLY .12G, MONO .71G, SAT 1.7G);
PROTEIN 1G; CHOLESTEROL 6.6MG; CARBOHYDRATE 14G.

# Bakehouse Chocolate Chippers

*If any cookie can make you feel like a kid again, it's a chocolate chipper still warm from the oven. You'll make this enlightened version again and again, not because it's low-fat, but because the results are so darn good.*

| | | | |
|---|---|---|---|
| ¾ | CUP ALL-PURPOSE FLOUR | 1 | CUP PACKED LIGHT BROWN SUGAR |
| ¾ | CUP WHOLE WHEAT PASTRY FLOUR (OR ALL-PURPOSE FLOUR) | ¼ | CUP (½ STICK) UNSALTED BUTTER |
| 1 | TEASPOON BAKING SODA | 1 | TEASPOON VANILLA EXTRACT |
| ¼ | TEASPOON GROUND CINNAMON | 1 | LARGE EGG (AT ROOM TEMPERATURE) |
| ¼ | TEASPOON SALT | 2 | TABLESPOONS LIGHT-COLORED CORN SYRUP |
| | | ¾ | CUP BITTERSWEET CHOCOLATE CHIPS |

Preheat oven to 375°F. Spray 2 cookie sheets with nonstick cooking spray.

In a medium bowl whisk the flours, baking soda, cinnamon, and salt; set aside.

Beat the brown sugar, butter, and vanilla with an electric mixer set at medium speed until well blended (about 5 minutes). Add the egg and corn syrup; beat until just blended.

With a wooden spoon, mix the flour mixture and chocolate chips into sugar mixture until just blended.

Drop dough by level tablespoonfuls 1 inch apart onto prepared sheets.

Bake 10–11 minutes or until golden (do not overbake; cookies may still look slightly soft at the center). Cool on sheets 5 minutes. Transfer cookies to wire racks with spatula. Cool completely. Store loosely covered. **Makes 2 dozen cookies.**

NUTRITION PER SERVING (1 COOKIE):
CALORIES 112; FAT 3.8G (POLY .2G, MONO 1.1G, SAT 2.2G);
PROTEIN 1G; CHOLESTEROL 13.9MG; CARBOHYDRATE 19G.

**Variations**

**Mocha Chippers:** Prepare as directed but add 2 teaspoons instant espresso powder to the dough along with the corn syrup and egg.

**Peppermint Chippers:** Prepare as directed but substitute 1 teaspoon pure peppermint extract for the vanilla.

**Double Ginger Chippers:** Prepare as directed but add 1½ teaspoons ground ginger to the flour mixture and 3 tablespoons minced crystallized ginger to the dough along with the chocolate chips.

**Cranberry-Maple Chippers:** Prepare as directed but substitute pure maple syrup for the corn syrup and maple extract for the vanilla. Add 3 tablespoons chopped dried cranberries.

# Multigrain Chocolate-Chip Cookies

*Classic chocolate chippers get several new-fashioned, whole grain twists—whole wheat flour, flaxseed meal, and oats—that add as much flavor as they do good health. Note that the dough needs to be chilled for several hours or overnight before baking. This allows the flours and oats to better absorb the liquid components of the dough, yielding tender cookies.*

| | |
|---|---|
| ¾ CUP ALL-PURPOSE FLOUR | ¾ CUP PACKED DARK BROWN SUGAR |
| ¾ CUP WHOLE WHEAT FLOUR | 5 TABLESPOONS UNSALTED BUTTER, |
| ¾ CUP OLD-FASHIONED OATS | SOFTENED |
| 2 TABLESPOONS FLAXSEED MEAL | 3 TABLESPOONS HONEY |
| ½ TEASPOON BAKING POWDER | ¾ TEASPOON VANILLA EXTRACT |
| ¼ TEASPOON BAKING SODA | 1 LARGE EGG |
| ¼ TEASPOON SALT | 1 LARGE EGG WHITE |
| ¾ CUP BITTERSWEET CHOCOLATE CHIPS | |

In a medium bowl combine the flours, oats, flaxseed meal, baking powder, baking soda, salt, and chocolate chips.

Beat the brown sugar and butter in a large bowl with an electric mixer at medium speed until light and fluffy. Beat in the honey, vanilla, egg, and egg white. With mixer set on low speed, beat the flour mixture into the sugar mixture until well blended. Cover and refrigerate overnight.

Preheat oven to 350°F. Spray 2 cookie sheets with nonstick cooking spray.

Drop batter by tablespoonfuls onto prepared sheets.

Bake 10–12 minutes until set at edges. Cool 2 minutes on sheets. Transfer to wire racks with spatula. Cool completely. **Makes 3 dozen cookies.**

NUTRITION PER SERVING (1 COOKIE):
CALORIES 90; FAT 3.3G (POLY .38G, MONO .94G, SAT 1.8G);
PROTEIN 2G; CHOLESTEROL 10.1MG; CARBOHYDRATE 14G.

# Oatmeal Cookies

## WITH CHOCOLATE & CHERRIES

*These hearty cookies are a staple at my house. Adding dried cherries and chocolate chips turns classic oatmeal cookies into something new. They are exceptional travelers for lunchboxes, care packages, and in backpacks for long hikes.*

| | |
|---|---|
| 1 CUP WHOLE WHEAT FLOUR | ¼ CUP REDUCED-FAT SOUR CREAM |
| ¼ CUP ALL-PURPOSE FLOUR | 1 TEASPOON VANILLA EXTRACT |
| ¾ CUP OLD-FASHIONED OATS | 2 LARGE EGG WHITES |
| 1 TEASPOON BAKING SODA | 5 OUNCES BITTERSWEET CHOCOLATE, |
| ½ TEASPOON SALT | CHOPPED |
| 1½ CUPS PACKED BROWN SUGAR | ½ CUP SWEETENED DRIED CHERRIES OR |
| ¼ CUP (½ STICK) UNSALTED BUTTER, | CRANBERRIES, COARSELY CHOPPED |
| SOFTENED | |

Preheat oven to 350°F. Line 2 cookie sheets with parchment paper.

In a medium bowl combine the flours, oats, baking soda, and salt. In a large bowl place brown sugar, butter, and sour cream; beat with a mixer at high speed until smooth. Add vanilla and egg whites; beat well. Gradually add flour mixture, stirring until blended. Fold in chocolate and cherries.

Drop dough by tablespoonfuls 2 inches apart onto the prepared sheets.

Bake 13–15 minutes or until edges of cookies are browned. Cool on sheets 5 minutes. Transfer cookies to wire rack with a spatula. Cool completely. **Makes 4 dozen cookies.**

NUTRITION PER SERVING (1 COOKIE):
CALORIES 75; FAT 2.3G (POLY .14G, MONO .51G, SAT .75G);
PROTEIN 1G; CHOLESTEROL 3.1MG; CARBOHYDRATE 13G.

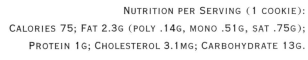

# Mudslide Cookies

*You may not associate mud with cookies, but the name for these classic chocolate cookies actually gets its unlikely moniker from the color—the same as the deep, rich soil that lines Old Man River.*

1½ TABLESPOONS BUTTER

2 OUNCES UNSWEETENED CHOCOLATE, FINELY CHOPPED

4 OUNCES BITTERSWEET CHOCOLATE, FINELY CHOPPED, DIVIDED USE

1 TABLESPOON INSTANT ESPRESSO POWDER

1 TABLESPOON HOT WATER

1 TEASPOON VANILLA EXTRACT

¾ CUP ALL-PURPOSE FLOUR

¾ CUP WHOLE WHEAT PASTRY FLOUR (OR ALL-PURPOSE FLOUR)

½ CUP UNSWEETENED COCOA POWDER (NOT DUTCH PROCESS)

1¾ TEASPOONS BAKING POWDER

¼ TEASPOON BAKING SODA

⅛ TEASPOON SALT

2½ CUPS SUGAR

4 LARGE EGG WHITES

2 LARGE EGGS

Preheat oven to 350°F. Line 2 cookie sheets with parchment paper.

Place the butter, unsweetened chocolate, and 2 ounces bittersweet chocolate into a microwave-safe bowl; microwave on HIGH 1 minute or until chocolate is almost melted. Stir until smooth; set aside momentarily.

In a small cup dissolve the espresso powder in the hot water; add to chocolate mixture, along with the vanilla.

In a medium bowl whisk the flours, cocoa powder, baking powder, baking soda, and salt. Combine sugar, egg whites, and eggs in a large bowl; beat with a mixer at high speed 6 minutes or until thick and pale. Gently stir one-fourth of egg mixture into chocolate mixture; stir chocolate mixture into remaining egg mixture. Stir in flour mixture and remaining 2 ounces bittersweet chocolate.

Drop dough by rounded teaspoonfuls 2 inches apart onto prepared cookie sheets. With moist hands, gently press dough into ¼-inch-thick rounds.

Bake 13–15 minutes or until just set. Cool 1 minute. Transfer cookies to wire rack with spatula. Cool completely. **Makes 3 dozen cookies.**

NUTRITION PER SERVING (1 COOKIE):
CALORIES 110; FAT 2.9G (POLY .15G, MONO .90G, SAT 1.6G);
PROTEIN 2G; CHOLESTEROL 13.0MG; CARBOHYDRATE 21G.

# Chocolate Thumbprints

*Dainty thumbprint cookies filled with preserves and dusted with a veil of powdered sugar look as if they belong on a restaurant's petits fours plate.*

| | |
|---|---|
| 1 CUP ALL-PURPOSE FLOUR | ½ CUP SUGAR |
| ½ CUP WHOLE WHEAT PASTRY FLOUR (OR ALL-PURPOSE FLOUR) | ¼ CUP FIRMLY PACKED LIGHT BROWN SUGAR |
| ⅓ CUP UNSWEETENED COCOA POWDER (NOT DUTCH PROCESS) | 1 LARGE EGG |
| | 2 TABLESPOONS LIGHT-COLORED CORN SYRUP |
| ½ TEASPOON BAKING POWDER | 1 TEASPOON VANILLA EXTRACT |
| ¼ TEASPOON BAKING SODA | ½ TEASPOON ALMOND EXTRACT |
| ¼ TEASPOON SALT | ¼ CUP SEEDLESS RASPBERRY PRESERVES (OR OTHER FRUIT JAM OF CHOICE) |
| ¼ CUP (½ STICK) UNSALTED BUTTER, SOFTENED | OPTIONAL: 2 TABLESPOONS POWDERED SUGAR |

Preheat oven to 375°F. Line 2 cookie sheets with parchment paper.

In a medium bowl whisk the flours, cocoa powder, baking powder, baking soda, and salt.

In a large bowl beat the butter, sugar, and brown sugar with an electric mixer set on medium speed until smooth and blended. Beat in the egg, corn syrup, vanilla, and almond extract until blended. Mix in the flour mixture with a wooden spoon until a soft dough forms.

Shape and roll dough into 1½-inch balls. Place balls 2 inches apart onto prepared cookie sheets. Make indentations in the center of each cookie using your thumb or the back of a round ¼-teaspoon measuring spoon. Fill with a scant ¼-teaspoon jam.

Bake for 13–15 minutes until just set at edges. Transfer cookies to wire rack with spatula. Cool completely. If desired, sprinkle tops with powdered sugar. **Makes 2 dozen cookies.**

NUTRITION PER SERVING (1 COOKIE):
CALORIES 88; FAT 2.4G (POLY .15G, MONO .65G, SAT 1.4G);
PROTEIN 1G; CHOLESTEROL 13.9MG; CARBOHYDRATE 17G.

# CHEWY CHOCOLATE-APRICOT

# *Cookies*

*Pure chocolate—in the form of cocoa powder and bittersweet chocolate—combines with sophisticated apricot and a delicate accent of almond to give these cookies a cosmopolitan air.*

| | |
|---|---|
| ½ CUP ALL-PURPOSE FLOUR | 1 CUP SUGAR |
| ½ CUP WHOLE WHEAT PASTRY FLOUR (OR ALL-PURPOSE FLOUR) | ⅓ CUP UNSALTED BUTTER, SOFTENED |
| ⅓ CUP UNSWEETENED COCOA POWDER (NOT DUTCH PROCESS) | ½ TEASPOON ALMOND EXTRACT |
| ½ TEASPOON BAKING POWDER | 1 LARGE EGG |
| ¼ TEASPOON BAKING SODA | ⅔ CUP MINCED DRIED APRICOTS |
| ¼ TEASPOON SALT | 2½ OUNCES BITTERSWEET CHOCOLATE, CHOPPED |

Preheat oven to 350°F. Spray 2 cookie sheets with nonstick cooking spray.

In a medium bowl whisk the flours, cocoa powder, baking powder, baking soda, and salt until well blended.

Place the sugar and butter in a large bowl; beat with a mixer at high speed until well blended. Beat in the almond extract and egg. With mixer on low speed, gradually add flour mixture. Beat just until combined. Fold in apricots and chocolate.

Drop by tablespoonfuls 2 inches apart onto prepared sheets.

Bake 11–13 minutes or just until set. Remove from oven and cool on pans 5 minutes. Transfer cookies to wire rack with spatula. Cool completely. **Makes 2½ dozen cookies.**

NUTRITION PER SERVING (1 COOKIE):
CALORIES 82; FAT 3.0G (POLY .13G, MONO .73G, SAT 1.3G);
PROTEIN 1G; CHOLESTEROL 12.2MG; CARBOHYDRATE 14G.

# *Sugar Cookies*

*These dramatic sugar cookies—part cookies, part candies thanks to their truffle-like topping—are favorites among friends and family. I think they deserve a wider audience.*

| | |
|---|---|
| 1 CUP ALL-PURPOSE FLOUR | 1¼ TEASPOONS VANILLA EXTRACT, DIVIDED USE |
| ¼ TEASPOON BAKING SODA | 1 CUP POWDERED SUGAR, SIFTED |
| ⅛ TEASPOON SALT | 1 TABLESPOON UNSWEETENED COCOA POWDER |
| ¼ CUP (½ STICK) UNSALTED BUTTER, SOFTENED | 1 TABLESPOON FAT-FREE MILK |
| ⅔ CUP SUGAR | 1 OUNCE BITTERSWEET CHOCOLATE, CHOPPED |
| 1 LARGE EGG WHITE | |

Whisk the flour, baking soda, and salt in a medium bowl.

In a large bowl beat the butter with an electric mixer at medium speed until light and fluffy. Gradually add the sugar, beating until well blended. Add the egg white and 1 teaspoon of the vanilla, beating well. Add the flour mixture, stirring with a wooden spoon until well blended.

Turn dough out onto wax paper; shape into a 6-inch log. Wrap log in wax paper and freeze for 3 hours or until very firm.

Preheat oven to 350°F. Spray 2 cookie sheets with nonstick cooking spray.

Cut log into twenty-four ¼-inch slices. Place the slices 1 inch apart on prepared cookie sheets. Bake 8–10 minutes. Transfer cookies to wire rack with spatula. Cool completely.

Whisk powdered sugar and cocoa in a small bowl. Add milk and remaining ¼ teaspoon vanilla until blended and smooth. Spread over cookies to within ¼ inch of edges.

Place bittersweet chocolate in separate heavy-duty ziplock plastic bag; seal. Microwave chocolate on HIGH for 1 minute or until chocolate is soft. Knead the bag until smooth. Snip a tiny hole in corner of bags, then drizzle chocolate over the frosted cookies so that they resemble truffles. **Makes 2 dozen cookies.**

NUTRITION PER SERVING (1 COOKIE):
CALORIES 84; FAT 2.4G (POLY .10G, MONO .58G, SAT 1.2G);
PROTEIN 1G; CHOLESTEROL 5.2MG; CARBOHYDRATE 15G.

# Black-and-White Cookies

*I admit, these cookies always bring a smile to my face—they remind me of a favorite episode from the TV show* Seinfeld, *in which Jerry ponders the power of the black & white cookie to bring about racial harmony and world peace. Jerry may have been a bit delusional on the subject, but these cheerful cookies, half dipped in white and cocoa icing, are incredibly appealing to one and all.*

| | |
|---|---|
| ⅔ CUP UNSWEETENED APPLESAUCE | 2 LARGE EGG WHITES |
| 1½ CUPS ALL-PURPOSE FLOUR | 1½ CUPS POWDERED SUGAR, DIVIDED USE |
| 1½ TEASPOONS BAKING POWDER | 3 TABLESPOONS 2% REDUCED-FAT MILK, DIVIDED USE |
| ½ TEASPOON SALT | |
| 1 CUP SUGAR | ¼ TEASPOON ALMOND EXTRACT |
| ¼ CUP (½ STICK) UNSALTED BUTTER, SOFTENED | 2 TABLESPOONS UNSWEETENED COCOA POWDER (NOT DUTCH PROCESS) |
| 1½ TEASPOONS VANILLA EXTRACT | |

Preheat oven to 375°F. Line 2 cookie sheets with parchment paper. Place applesauce in a fine sieve and let drain 15 minutes.

In a medium bowl whisk the flour, baking powder, and salt.

In a large bowl beat the drained applesauce, sugar, and butter with an electric mixer at medium speed for 2 minutes until well blended. Beat in vanilla and egg whites. Add the flour mixture; beat at low speed until blended.

Drop dough by tablespoonfuls 2 inches apart onto prepared cookie sheets.

Bake 9–11 minutes or until just set. Cool on sheets 2 minutes. Transfer cookies to wire rack with spatula. Cool completely.

Meanwhile, whisk ¾ cup powdered sugar, 1 tablespoon milk, and almond extract in a small bowl until smooth. Working with 1 cookie at a time, hold cookie over bowl and spread about 1 teaspoon white frosting over half of cookie (scrape excess frosting from edges). Let stand 10 minutes or until frosting is set.

In a separate small bowl, whisk the cocoa powder, remaining ¾ cup powdered sugar, and remaining 2 tablespoons milk until smooth. Working with 1 cookie at a time, hold cookie over bowl and spread about 1 teaspoon chocolate frosting over other half of cookie (scrape excess frosting from edges). Let stand 10 minutes or until frosting is set. **Makes 2 dozen cookies.**

NUTRITION PER SERVING (1 COOKIE):
CALORIES 114; FAT 2.2G (POLY .11G, MONO .55G, SAT 1.3G);
PROTEIN 1G; CHOLESTEROL 5.4MG; CARBOHYDRATE 23G.

# Chocolate Madeleines

*The understated, familiar flavor of these sweet and tender, shell-shaped cookies—they taste like little chocolate cakes—will take you straight back to your childhood.*

|   | |
|---|---|
| | NONSTICK BAKING SPRAY WITH FLOUR |
| 1 | LARGE EGG |
| 1 | LARGE EGG WHITE |
| ¾ | CUP SUGAR |
| 1 | CUP ALL-PURPOSE FLOUR |
| ¼ | CUP UNSWEETENED COCOA POWDER (NOT DUTCH PROCESS) |
| 1½ | TEASPOONS BAKING POWDER |
| ½ | TEASPOON BAKING SODA |

|   | |
|---|---|
| ¼ | TEASPOON SALT |
| ½ | CUP LOW-FAT BUTTERMILK |
| 3 | TABLESPOONS CANOLA OIL |
| 1 | TEASPOON VANILLA EXTRACT |
| ¼ | TEASPOON ALMOND EXTRACT |
| 1 | OUNCE BITTERSWEET CHOCOLATE, FINELY CHOPPED |
| 2 | TABLESPOONS POWDERED SUGAR |

Preheat oven to 400°F. Spray a standard-size madeleine pan with nonstick baking spray with flour.

In a medium glass bowl whisk the egg, egg white, and sugar. Set bowl over a medium saucepan of simmering water. Allow mixture to warm 5 minutes, whisking occasionally.

Whisk the flour, cocoa powder, baking powder, baking soda, and salt in a medium bowl until blended. In a small bowl whisk the buttermilk and oil until blended; set aside.

Remove the bowl with the egg mixture from pan. Beat with an electric mixer set on high speed 5 minutes until pale yellow and mixture holds a ribbon trail when lifted. Beat in vanilla and almond extracts. Using a rubber spatula, alternately fold the buttermilk mixture and flour mixture into dry ingredients. Fold in chopped chocolate.

Drop batter by tablespoonfuls into prepared pan, filling molds three-fourths full (batter will spread as it bakes).

Bake 12–15 minutes until tops of madeleines spring back when touched. Invert madeleines from pan onto wire rack. Cool completely. Clean pan and repeat procedure with remaining batter.

Sift powdered sugar over the cooled madeleines. **Makes 2 dozen madeleines.**

NUTRITION PER SERVING (1 MADELEINE):
CALORIES 76; FAT 2.6G (POLY .58G, MONO 1.3G, SAT .57G);
PROTEIN 1.5G; CHOLESTEROL 9.2MG; CARBOHYDRATE 12G.

# *Macaroons*

*These sweet treats can be made two days in advance. Just store them in an airtight container in the refrigerator.*

---

2   OUNCES UNSWEETENED CHOCOLATE, CHOPPED

½   CUP SIFTED CAKE FLOUR

2   TABLESPOONS UNSWEETENED COCOA POWDER (NOT DUTCH PROCESS)

⅛   TEASPOON SALT

2½ CUPS LIGHTLY PACKED FLAKED SWEETENED COCONUT

1   TEASPOON VANILLA EXTRACT

1   14-OUNCE CAN FAT-FREE SWEETENED CONDENSED MILK

Preheat oven to 250°F. Line a cookie sheet with parchment paper; secure with masking tape.

Place unsweetened chocolate in a small microwave-safe bowl. Microwave on HIGH for 1 minute or until almost melted. Remove from microwave; stir until chocolate is completely melted.

In a large bowl whisk the cake flour, cocoa powder, and salt. Add the coconut. Stir in the melted chocolate, vanilla, and sweetened condensed milk (the mixture will be stiff). Drop by level tablespoonfuls 2 inches apart onto prepared cookie sheet.

Bake 45 minutes or until edges of cookies are firm and center of cookies are soft, rotating cookie sheet once during baking time. Remove cookies from oven, and cool 10 minutes on sheet on a wire rack. Remove the cookies from the parchment paper. Transfer cookies to wire rack. Cool completely. **Makes 3 dozen cookies.**

NUTRITION PER SERVING (1 MACAROON):
CALORIES 77; FAT 3.2G (POLY .06G, MONO .37G, SAT 2.6G); PROTEIN 1G;
CHOLESTEROL .28MG; CARBOHYDRATE 5G.

# Chocolate Gingersnaps

*Molasses and holiday spices give these chocolate cookies seasonal charm. But don't save them for December—they're worth making year-round.*

| | |
|---|---|
| ½ CUP ALL-PURPOSE FLOUR | ⅛ TEASPOON GROUND CLOVES |
| ½ CUP WHOLE WHEAT PASTRY FLOUR (OR ALL-PURPOSE FLOUR) | ½ TEASPOON BAKING SODA |
| ¼ CUP UNSWEETENED COCOA POWDER (NOT DUTCH PROCESS), SIFTED | ¼ TEASPOON SALT |
| | ½ CUP PACKED DARK BROWN SUGAR |
| 2 TEASPOONS GROUND GINGER | ¼ CUP (½ STICK) UNSALTED BUTTER, SOFTENED |
| ½ TEASPOON GROUND CINNAMON | ¼ CUP DARK MOLASSES (NOT BLACKSTRAP) |
| | 1 LARGE EGG |

Whisk the flours, cocoa powder, ginger, cinnamon, cloves, baking soda, and salt in a medium bowl.

Place the brown sugar and butter in a separate medium bowl; beat with a mixer at medium speed 2 minutes or until creamy. Add the molasses, beating until smooth. Add the egg, beating until well combined. Add flour mixture to sugar mixture, stirring until well combined. Cover and chill dough 30 minutes.

Preheat oven to 350°F. Spray two cookie sheets with nonstick cooking spray.

Shape dough into 36 balls, about 1½ teaspoons each. Place 2 inches apart on prepared cookie sheets; flatten balls to ½-inch thickness with bottom of a glass.

Bake, one sheet at a time, 10 minutes (place other sheet of cookies in refrigerator while baking first batch). Move sheet to wire rack and cool 4 minutes. Transfer cookies to wire rack with spatula. Cool completely. **Makes 3 dozen cookies.**

**Cook's Note:** Store cookies in an airtight container at room temperature for up to 3 days.

NUTRITION PER SERVING (1 COOKIE):
CALORIES 46; FAT 1.5G (POLY .08G, MONO .42G, SAT .91G);
PROTEIN 1G; CHOLESTEROL 9.3MG; CARBOHYDRATE 8G.

# Icebox Cookies

*I love icebox cookies: I can slice and bake a few cookies at a time and refrigerate or freeze the remaining dough for later. The turbinado sugar (also called "raw" sugar) is worth acquiring. The large, amber-colored sugar crystals have a slight molasses flavor and plenty of sparkle. Find it in the baking aisle of the grocery store with all of the other sugars.*

| | |
|---|---|
| ¾ CUP ALL-PURPOSE FLOUR | ¼ CUP (½ STICK) UNSALTED BUTTER, SOFTENED |
| ¼ CUP UNSWEETENED COCOA POWDER (NOT DUTCH PROCESS) | ⅔ CUP PACKED LIGHT BROWN SUGAR |
| | 1 TEASPOON VANILLA EXTRACT |
| ¼ TEASPOON BAKING SODA | 1 LARGE EGG WHITE |
| ⅛ TEASPOON SALT | 2 TABLESPOONS TURBINADO SUGAR |

In a small bowl whisk the flour, cocoa powder, baking soda, and salt.

In a medium bowl beat the butter with an electric mixer set at medium speed until light and fluffy. Gradually add the brown sugar, beating at medium speed until mixture is well blended and resembles a grainy paste. Add the vanilla and egg white, beating well. Stir in the flour mixture with a wooden spoon until well blended.

Turn dough out onto wax paper; shape into a 6-inch log. Wrap the log in wax paper. Freeze log 3–4 hours or until very firm.

Preheat oven to 350°F. Spray a cookie sheet with nonstick cooking spray; set aside.

Remove log from freezer and roll in turbinado sugar, gently pressing to adhere. Cut log into 24 ¼-inch slices. Place slices 1 inch apart on prepared cookie sheet.

Bake cookies 8–10 minutes until just set. Transfer cookies to wire rack with spatula. Cool completely. **Makes 2 dozen cookies.**

**Variations**

**Double-Chocolate Icebox Cookies:** Add 2 ounces finely chopped bittersweet chocolate.

**Chocolate-Cinnamon Icebox Cookies:** Add 1 teaspoon ground cinnamon to the flour mixture.

**Chocolate-Peppermint Icebox Cookies:** Substitute 1 teaspoon of peppermint extract for the vanilla extract.

**Chocolate-Orange Icebox Cookies:** Add 1½ teaspoons freshly grated orange zest to the butter–brown sugar mixture.

NUTRITION PER SERVING (1 COOKIE): CALORIES 61; FAT 2.1G (POLY .09G, MONO .54G, SAT 1.3G); PROTEIN 1G; CHOLESTEROL 5.1MG; CARBOHYDRATE 11G.

# Biscotti

*Unlike many commercially available chocolate biscotti, these have a deep chocolate-y flavor. They can be varied with a wide range of additional flavors, such as a teaspoon of cinnamon, a couple of tablespoons of finely chopped candied ginger, a sprinkle of fresh orange zest, or a teaspoon of peppermint extract.*

| | |
|---|---|
| 1 CUP ALL-PURPOSE FLOUR | ¼ TEASPOON SALT |
| ⅔ CUP WHOLE WHEAT PASTRY FLOUR | 2 TABLESPOONS UNSALTED BUTTER, SOFTENED |
| (OR ALL-PURPOSE FLOUR) | ¾ CUP SUGAR |
| ½ CUP UNSWEETENED COCOA POWDER | 1 LARGE EGG |
| (NOT DUTCH PROCESS) | 1 LARGE EGG WHITE |
| ¾ TEASPOON BAKING SODA | 1 TEASPOON VANILLA EXTRACT |
| ½ TEASPOON BAKING POWDER | 3 OUNCES BITTERSWEET CHOCOLATE, CHOPPED |

Preheat oven to 350°F. Line a cookie sheet with parchment paper.

In a medium bowl combine the flours, cocoa powder, baking soda, baking powder and salt; set aside.

In a large bowl place the butter, sugar, egg, egg white, and vanilla. Beat with an electric mixer set on high speed until blended and smooth. Gradually add the flour mixture with a wooden spoon, stirring until well blended. Stir in the chopped chocolate.

Divide the dough in half. With lightly floured hands, shape each half into an 8x2x1-inch log. Place logs 3 inches apart on prepared cookie sheet.

Bake logs 20–25 minutes until log feels firm to the touch and the top develops several cracks. Using the parchment paper, carefully transfer logs to wire cooling racks. Cool 15 minutes. Reduce oven temperature to 275°F.

Transfer the cooled logs to a cutting board. Using a sharp serrated knife, cut each log into ¾-inch thick slices on the diagonal. Place biscotti, cut side down, on the cookie sheet (no need to re-line). Bake 30 minutes. Remove from oven. Let cool on sheets 10 minutes. Transfer biscotti to wire rack with spatula. Cool completely. **Makes 2 dozen biscotti.**

NUTRITION PER SERVING (1 BISCOTTO):
CALORIES 89; FAT 2.7G (POLY .14G, MONO .60G, SAT .84G);
PROTEIN 2G; CHOLESTEROL 12MG; CARBOHYDRATE 16G.

# Mocha Biscotti

*Anyone who's ever dropped into a local bakery for an afternoon pick-me-up can testify to the appeal of coffee and a biscotto. Here, biscotti with a touch of cinnamon get an extra jolt of flavor from instant espresso powder.*

| | | | |
|---|---|---|---|
| 1 | CUP ALL-PURPOSE FLOUR | ½ | TEASPOON BAKING SODA |
| 1 | CUP WHOLE WHEAT PASTRY FLOUR (OR | ½ | TEASPOON SALT |
| | ALL-PURPOSE FLOUR) | ½ | TEASPOON GROUND CINNAMON |
| 1 | CUP SUGAR | 2 | TEASPOONS INSTANT ESPRESSO POWDER |
| ⅓ | CUP CHOPPED WALNUTS | 2 | TEASPOONS HOT WATER |
| ¼ | CUP UNSWEETENED COCOA POWDER (NOT | 1 | TEASPOON VANILLA EXTRACT |
| | DUTCH PROCESS) | 2 | LARGE EGGS |
| ½ | TEASPOON BAKING POWDER | 1 | LARGE EGG WHITE |

Preheat oven to 350°F. Line a cookie sheet with parchment paper.

In a large bowl combine the flours, sugar, walnuts, cocoa powder, baking powder, baking soda, salt, and cinnamon. Combine espresso powder and hot water in a small bowl. Whisk in vanilla, eggs, and egg whites. Add egg mixture to flour mixture, stirring until well blended (the dough will be dry and crumbly).

Turn dough out onto a lightly floured surface; knead lightly 7 or 8 times. Divide the dough in half. Shape each portion into an 8-inch-long roll. Place rolls 6 inches apart on prepared sheet; flatten each roll to 1-inch thickness.

Bake 30 minutes. Using the parchment paper, carefully transfer logs to wire cooling racks. Cool for 10 minutes. Using a serrated knife, cut each roll diagonally into 12 ¾-inch slices. Place the slices, cut sides down, on cookie sheet (no need to reline).

Reduce the oven temperature to 325°F; bake 10 minutes. Turn cookies over; bake an additional 10 minutes (the cookies will be slightly soft in center but will harden as they cool). Transfer biscotti to wire rack with spatula. Cool completely. **Makes 2 dozen biscotti.**

NUTRITION PER SERVING (1 BISCOTTO):
CALORIES 88; FAT 1.7G (POLY .88G, MONO .36G, SAT .32G);
PROTEIN 2G; CHOLESTEROL 17.6MG; CARBOHYDRATE 17G.

# *Biscotti*

*This classic cookie combines two of my favorite sweets: spicy crystallized ginger and satiny-smooth bittersweet chocolate. The crisp, clean texture makes these the perfect accompaniment to hot tea or hot cocoa.*

| | | | |
|---|---|---|---|
| 2 | LARGE EGGS | 2 | TEASPOONS GROUND GINGER |
| 1 | LARGE EGG WHITE | ½ | TEASPOON BAKING POWDER |
| 2 | TEASPOONS GRATED LEMON ZEST | ½ | TEASPOON BAKING SODA |
| 1 | TEASPOON VANILLA EXTRACT | ½ | TEASPOON SALT |
| 1 | CUP ALL-PURPOSE FLOUR | 3 | OUNCES BITTERSWEET CHOCOLATE, FINELY CHOPPED |
| 1 | CUP WHITE WHOLE WHEAT FLOUR (NOT REGULAR WHOLE WHEAT FLOUR; SEE DESCRIPTION PAGE 12) | 2 | TABLESPOONS CHOPPED CRYSTALLIZED GINGER |
| 1 | CUP SUGAR | | |

Preheat oven to 350°F. Line a cookie sheet with parchment paper.

In a large bowl whisk the eggs, egg white, lemon zest, and vanilla.

In a medium bowl whisk the flours, sugar, ground ginger, baking powder, baking soda, and salt. Add to the egg mixture along with the chocolate and crystallized ginger. Stir with a wooden spoon until well blended.

Divide dough in half, and turn out onto prepared cookie sheet. Shape each portion of dough into a 12-inch-long roll; flatten to ½-inch thickness.

Bake logs 25 minutes. Using the parchment paper, carefully transfer logs to wire cooling racks. Cool for 10 minutes. Leave oven on.

Using a serrated knife, cut each roll diagonally into 18 ½-inch slices. Place slices, cut sides down, on cookie sheet. Bake 10 minutes. Turn cookies over; bake an additional 10 minutes (cookies will be slightly soft in center but will harden as they cool). Transfer biscotti to wire rack with spatula. Cool completely. **Makes 3 dozen biscotti.**

NUTRITION PER SERVING (1 BISCOTTO):
CALORIES 64; FAT 1.1G (POLY .09G, MONO .24G, SAT .10G);
PROTEIN 1G; CHOLESTEROL 11.9MG; CARBOHYDRATE 12G.

# Biscotti

*Chai tea spice—ginger, cinnamon, cardamom, and cloves—flavor these delicious, chocolate-studded biscotti. They are just the thing to enjoy with a spot of tea.*

---

1½ CUPS ALL-PURPOSE FLOUR

1¼ CUPS WHOLE WHEAT PASTRY FLOUR (OR ALL-PURPOSE FLOUR)

1 CUP PACKED LIGHT BROWN SUGAR

1 TABLESPOON LOOSE CHAI SPICE TEA OR ORANGE SPICE TEA (ABOUT 3 TEA BAGS)

2 TEASPOONS BAKING POWDER

2 TEASPOONS GROUND GINGER

1½ TEASPOONS CINNAMON

1 TEASPOON GROUND CARDAMOM

⅛ TEASPOON GROUND CLOVES

1 TABLESPOON CANOLA OIL

1 TABLESPOON ORANGE JUICE

3 LARGE EGGS

1 TEASPOON GRATED ORANGE ZEST

3 OUNCES BITTERSWEET CHOCOLATE, CHOPPED

Preheat oven to 350°F. Line a cookie sheet with parchment paper.

In a large bowl combine the flours, brown sugar, tea, baking powder, ginger, cinnamon, cardamom, and cloves.

In a small bowl combine the oil, orange juice, eggs, and orange zest. Add to the flour mixture, along with the chocolate, stirring until well blended (the dough will be dry and crumbly).

Turn dough out onto a lightly floured surface; knead lightly 7 or 8 times. Divide the dough in half. Shape each portion into an 8-inch-long roll. Place rolls 6 inches apart on prepared sheet; flatten each roll to 1-inch thickness.

Bake 30 minutes. Using the parchment paper, carefully transfer logs to wire cooling racks. Cool 10 minutes. Using a serrated knife, cut each roll diagonally into 12 ¾-inch slices. Place the slices, cut sides down, on cookie sheet.

Reduce the oven temperature to 325°F; bake 10 minutes. Turn cookies over; bake an additional 10 minutes (the cookies will be slightly soft in center but will harden as they cool). Transfer biscotti to wire rack with spatula. Cool completely. **Makes 2 dozen biscotti.**

NUTRITION PER SERVING (1 BISCOTTO):
CALORIES 118; FAT 2.6G (POLY .44G, MONO .69G, SAT .28G);
PROTEIN 3G; CHOLESTEROL 26.6MG; CARBOHYDRATE 22G.

# *Crispy Rice Bars*

*Who doesn't love crispy rice treats? By adding cocoa powder, flecks of dark chocolate, and a tiny jolt of espresso flavor, the kid-favorite is turned into a sophisticated and whimsical bite-size dessert.*

| | |
|---|---|
| 3 TABLESPOONS UNSALTED BUTTER | 6 CUPS OVEN-TOASTED RICE CEREAL (E.G., |
| 1 10.5-OUNCE BAG MINIATURE MARSHMAL- | RICE KRISPIES) |
| LOWS | 2 OUNCES BITTERSWEET CHOCOLATE, FINELY |
| 1 TEASPOON INSTANT ESPRESSO POWDER | CHOPPED |
| 2 TABLESPOONS UNSWEETENED COCOA POW- | |
| DER (NOT DUTCH PROCESS) | |

Spray a 13 x 9-inch baking pan with nonstick cooking spray; set aside.

Melt the butter in a large saucepan set over low heat. Add the marshmallows and espresso powder and continue stirring until melted and smooth. Mix in the cocoa powder until blended.

Remove saucepan from heat and stir in the cereal and chopped chocolate; toss until thoroughly coated. Using a large square of wax paper, evenly press cereal mixture into prepared pan. Cool slightly. Cut into 24 pieces. **Makes 2 dozen bars.**

NUTRITION PER SERVING (1 BAR):
CALORIES 83; FAT 2.3G (POLY .12G, MONO .56G, SAT 1.0G);
PROTEIN 1G; CHOLESTEROL 3.9MG; CARBOHYDRATE 16G.

# *Crispy Rice Bars*

*Part cookie, part candy, and entirely delicious, these no-bake cookies are reminiscent of s'mores.*

| | |
|---|---|
| ⅓ CUP CREAMY REDUCED-FAT PEANUT BUTTER | 6 CUPS OVEN-TOASTED RICE CEREAL (E.G., RICE KRISPIES) |
| 1 TABLESPOON UNSALTED BUTTER | 4 OUNCES BITTERSWEET CHOCOLATE, CHOPPED |
| 1 10.5-OUNCE BAG MINIATURE MARSHMALLOWS | |

Spray a 13 x 9-inch baking pan with nonstick cooking spray; set aside.

Combine the peanut butter and butter in a large microwave-safe bowl. Microwave on HIGH 45 seconds or until mixture melts. Add the marshmallows. Microwave on HIGH 1½ minutes or until smooth, stirring every 30 seconds.

Add cereal to peanut butter mixture; toss until thoroughly coated. Using a large square of wax paper, evenly press cereal mixture into prepared pan.

Place chopped chocolate in a small microwave-safe bowl. Microwave on HIGH 30 seconds or until chocolate melts. Spoon the melted chocolate into a small heavy-duty ziplock plastic bag; seal. Snip a tiny hole in 1 corner of bag; drizzle melted chocolate over cereal mixture. Cool slightly. Cut into 24 pieces. **Makes 2 dozen bars.**

NUTRITION PER SERVING (1 BAR):
CALORIES 103; FAT 3.2G (POLY .41G, MONO .92G, SAT .58G);
PROTEIN 2G; CHOLESTEROL 1.5MG; CARBOHYDRATE 18G.

# No-Bakes

*So easy and so good, variations of this great chocolate no-bake cookie abound. But traditional versions have up to an entire stick of butter per batch. My enlightened version has a mere two tablespoons, without any sacrifice of chocolate goodness.*

1   CUP PACKED LIGHT BROWN SUGAR

2   TABLESPOONS (¼ STICK) BUTTER

⅓   CUP FAT-FREE MILK

⅔   CUP UNSWEETENED COCOA POWDER (NOT
    DUTCH PROCESS), DIVIDED USE

1   TEASPOON VANILLA EXTRACT

1¼ CUPS QUICK-COOKING OATS

¼   CUP FINELY CHOPPED TOASTED PECANS

Combine the brown sugar, butter, and milk in a medium saucepan set over medium-high heat. Bring mixture to a boil. Lower heat to medium-low and simmer 3 minutes, stirring constantly.

Remove the saucepan from the heat and stir in ⅓ cup cocoa powder, vanilla, oats, and pecans until thoroughly blended. Transfer mixture to a medium bowl and chill, covered, 1 hour or until firm.

Sift the remaining ⅓ cup cocoa powder into a small shallow dish. Shape the chilled mixture into 1-inch balls and roll in the cocoa powder. Store cookies, in the refrigerator, in a covered container. **Makes 20 cookies.**

NUTRITION PER SERVING (1 COOKIE):
CALORIES 106; FAT 3.0G (POLY .59G, MONO 1.1G, SAT .94G);
PROTEIN 2G; CHOLESTEROL 3.1MG; CARBOHYDRATE 18G.

# Easy Bittersweet Chocolate Truffles

## (WITH VARIATIONS)

*Little bites of chocolate heaven, these truffles require little more than melting, beating, and rolling.*

| | |
|---|---|
| 3 OUNCES BITTERSWEET CHOCOLATE, CHOPPED | ½ CUP UNSWEETENED COCOA POWDER (NOT DUTCH PROCESS), DIVIDED USE |
| ½ OF AN 8-OUNCE PACKAGE REDUCED-FAT CREAM CHEESE (ALSO CALLED NEUFCHATEL), SOFTENED | 1 TEASPOON VANILLA EXTRACT |
| | 1¾ CUPS POWDERED SUGAR |

Line a cookie sheet with wax or parchment paper.

Place the chopped chocolate in a small microwave-safe bowl. Microwave on HIGH for 1 minute. Remove bowl from microwave and stir until chocolate is melted and smooth; set aside.

Place the cream cheese in a medium bowl and beat with electric mixer set on high speed until smooth. Add the melted chocolate. Beat until well blended, stopping to scrape sides of bowl with a rubber spatula. Stir in ¼ cup cocoa powder, vanilla, and 1 cup of the powdered sugar with a wooden spoon until incorporated. Mix in the remaining ¾ cup powered sugar (mixture will be fairly stiff).

Sift the remaining ¼ cup cocoa powder into a small shallow dish. Shape the truffle mixture into 1-inch balls and roll in the cocoa powder to coat. Place truffles on prepared cookie sheet and refrigerate until chilled. Store truffles, in the refrigerator, in a covered container. **Makes 2 dozen truffles.**

## Variations

**Espresso-Kahlua Truffles:** Dissolve 1½ teaspoons instant espresso powder in 1 tablespoon Kahlua or other coffee liqueur. Add to the cream cheese mixture along with the melted chocolate.

**Grand Marnier Truffles:** Add 1 teaspoon grated orange zest and 1 tablespoon Grand Marnier or other orange liqueur to the cream cheese mixture along with the melted chocolate.

**Peppermint Truffles:** Replace the vanilla extract with ¾ teaspoon pure peppermint extract.

**Almond Truffles:** Replace the vanilla extract with ¾ teaspoon pure almond extract. Shape each truffle around 1 whole, toasted almond.

**Exotic Spice Truffles:** Add ¼ teaspoon ground cardamom, ⅛ teaspoon ground cinnamon, and ⅛ teaspoon ground cloves.

NUTRITION PER SERVING (1 TRUFFLE):
CALORIES 66; FAT 2.2G (POLY .06G, MONO .47G, SAT .63G);
PROTEIN 1G; CHOLESTEROL 3MG; CARBOHYDRATE 12G.

# DECADENT DAIRY-FREE BITTERSWEET CHOCOLATE

*Truffles*

*A combination of nut oil and a bit of water takes the place of heavy cream in the base of these deeply dark and delicious truffles. Splurge on the very best chocolate and cocoa powder your budget can afford (although, truth be told, I've made these with the supermarket varieties and canola oil instead of the nut oil, and they still blew everyone away).*

| | |
|---|---|
| 6 OUNCES BITTERSWEET CHOCOLATE (PREFERABLY 70% COCOA), FINELY CHOPPED | 1¼ TEASPOONS VANILLA EXTRACT |
| ¼ CUP WALNUT, ALMOND, HAZELNUT, OR PISTACHIO OIL | ½ CUP UNSWEETENED COCOA POWDER (NOT DUTCH PROCESS), SIFTED |
| ⅓ CUP WATER | ½ CUP CHOPPED, LIGHTLY TOASTED NUTS (E.G., WALNUTS, ALMONDS, PECANS) |

Place the chocolate, oil, and water in a small microwave-safe bowl. Heat on HIGH in microwave 1 minute. Stir mixture, then microwave 1 minute longer, or until chocolate has melted. Whisk until smooth. Whisk in vanilla. Cover with plastic wrap and chill 6 hours or overnight.

Place cocoa and nuts on two separate small plates. Shape truffle mixture by heaping teaspoonfuls into ¾-inch balls. Roll in cocoa or chopped nuts. Chill until ready to serve. **Makes 30 small truffles.**

## Variations

**Cardamom-Pistachio Truffles:** Prepare as directed, adding ¼ teaspoon ground cardamom to the truffle base along with the vanilla. Use chopped, roasted pistachios for the nuts.

**Macadamia-Rum Truffles:** Prepare as directed, replacing 2 tablespoons of the water with dark rum and adding ¼ teaspoon ground ginger to the truffle base along with the vanilla. Use chopped, toasted macadamia nuts for the nuts.

NUTRITION PER SERVING (1 TRUFFLE):
CALORIES 59; FAT 5G (POLY 2.2G, MONO 1.2G, SAT 1.4G);
PROTEIN 1G; CHOLESTEROL 0MG; CARBOHYDRATE 4.5G.

# DATE-NUT COCOA

## "Truffles"

*These super-easy "truffles" are great during the holidays (especially if you are not a baker and still want to make festive treats from your kitchen). You can dress them up in cellophane bags with colorful ribbons for healthy chocolate gifts, or pop them into a ziplock plastic bag, and freeze for anytime sweet tooth attacks.*

---

2   CUPS PITTED DATES

½   CUP CHOPPED, LIGHTLY TOASTED ALMONDS

7   TABLESPOONS UNSWEETENED COCOA POW-
      DER (NOT DUTCH PROCESS), DIVIDED USE

2   TEASPOONS VANILLA EXTRACT

1   TEASPOON GROUND CINNAMON, DIVIDED
      USE

¼   TEASPOON ALMOND EXTRACT

PINCH OF SALT

½   CUP SWEETENED FLAKE COCONUT

2   TABLESPOONS SUGAR

Place dates in saucepan and add just enough water to cover. Bring to a boil, remove from heat, cover, and let stand 10 minutes. Drain, reserving 2 tablespoons liquid. Transfer to food processor and purée with reserved liquid until smooth.

Transfer mixture to medium bowl. Stir in the almonds, 3 tablespoons cocoa powder, vanilla, ½ teaspoon cinnamon, almond extract, and pinch of salt.

Spread the coconut on a small plate. Sift the sugar, remaining 4 tablespoons cocoa, and remaining ½ teaspoon cinnamon into a shallow bowl.

Using a kitchen teaspoon, scoop out a small amount of the date mixture and form into 1-inch balls. Roll in coconut, and then in the cocoa mixture. Serve immediately or store tightly covered in refrigerator for up to 2 weeks or in freezer up to 2 months. **Makes about 3 dozen truffles.**

NUTRITION PER SERVING (1 TRUFFLE):
CALORIES 50; FAT 1.5G (POLY .23G, MONO .65G, SAT .56G);
PROTEIN 1G; CHOLESTEROL 0MG; CARBOHYDRATE 10G.

# MINI TRIPLE-CHOCOLATE
# *Cheesecakes*

*I love making desserts in miniature for parties and get-togethers because it gives everyone a chance to get a sweet nibble at the end of a meal. So while an entire slice of cheesecake is often too much, there always seems to be room for a two- or three-bite mini cheesecake and a lovely cup of coffee.*

| | | | |
|---|---|---|---|
| 1 | CUP CHOCOLATE WAFER CRUMBS (ABOUT 22 COOKIES) | 3 | TABLESPOONS UNSWEETENED COCOA POWDER (NOT DUTCH PROCESS) |
| 2 | TABLESPOONS BUTTER, MELTED | 2 | LARGE EGG WHITES |
| 7 | TABLESPOONS SUGAR, DIVIDED USE | 1 | LARGE EGG |
| 6 | OUNCES (¾ OF AN 8-OUNCE PACKAGE) FAT-FREE CREAM CHEESE, SOFTENED | 1 | 8-OUNCE CARTON LOW-FAT SOUR CREAM |
| 4 | OUNCES (½ OF AN 8-OUNCE PACKAGE) REDUCED-FAT CREAM CHEESE, SOFTENED | 1 | TEASPOON VANILLA EXTRACT |
| | | 2 | OUNCES BITTERSWEET CHOCOLATE, FINELY CHOPPED |

Preheat oven to 325°F. Line the cups of 2 mini-muffin pans (48 cups total) with paper liners.

In a small bowl combine the chocolate crumbs, wafer butter, and 2 tablespoons sugar. Press about 1½ teaspoons crumb mixture into the bottom of each of the prepared mini muffin cups. Bake for 5 minutes. Transfer to wire rack. Keep oven on.

In a food processor place the cream cheeses, cocoa powder, egg whites, egg, sour cream, vanilla, and remaining 5 tablespoons sugar; process until smooth. Stir in the chocolate. Divide the filling evenly among prepared crusts.

Bake 10–12 minutes until just barely set (do not overbake). Transfer to a wire rack and cool completely. Remove mini cheesecakes from pans. Chill at least 1 hour before serving. Store, loosely covered, in refrigerator. **Makes 4 dozen cheesecakes.**

NUTRITION PER SERVING (1 MINI CHEESECAKE):
CALORIES 57; FAT 2.9G (POLY .18G, MONO .98G, SAT 1.5G);
PROTEIN 2G; CHOLESTEROL 9.8MG; CARBOHYDRATE 6.4G.

# Meringue Kisses

*Despite being low in fat, these charming cookies will satisfy any chocolate lover's craving.*

| | |
|---|---|
| ¼ CUP UNSWEETENED COCOA POWDER (NOT DUTCH PROCESS) | 1½ TABLESPOONS CORNSTARCH |
| 1 OUNCE UNSWEETENED CHOCOLATE, COARSELY CHOPPED | 3 LARGE EGG WHITES |
| | 2 TEASPOONS INSTANT ESPRESSO POWDER |
| ¼ CUP SIFTED POWDERED SUGAR | ⅔ CUP SUGAR |
| | 1 TEASPOON VANILLA EXTRACT |

Preheat oven to 325°F. Line a cookie sheet with parchment paper and secure with masking tape; set aside.

Pulse the cocoa powder and chocolate in a food processor 4 times or until the chocolate is finely chopped. Add the powdered sugar and cornstarch. Pulse 2-3 times or until mixture is well blended.

Beat the egg whites and espresso powder in a medium bowl with an electric mixer at high speed until foamy. Gradually add the sugar, 1 tablespoon at a time, beating mixture until stiff peaks form. Fold in the cocoa mixture and vanilla.

Spoon the egg-white mixture into a ziplock plastic bag, and seal. Carefully snip off 1 bottom corner of bag. Pipe the egg-white mixture into 24 portions onto prepared baking sheet, forming pointed mounds 2 inches wide and 1½ inches high.

Bake 30–35 minutes or until dry. Carefully remove the meringues from the paper. Transfer meringues to wire rack. Cool completely. **Makes 2 dozen kisses.**

»ⓔ• **Cook's Note:** Store kisses in an airtight container for up to 2 days.

NUTRITION PER SERVING (1 KISS):
CALORIES 39; FAT .76G (POLY .02G, MONO .24G, SAT .47G);
PROTEIN 1G; CHOLESTEROL 0MG; CARBOHYDRATE 8G.

# BITTERSWEET CHOCOLATE-FLECKED
## *Meringue Cookies*

*Unlike other meringue-type cookies, these have an almost fudge-like texture because of the flecks of bittersweet chocolate throughout. They are a snap to make, but you need to plan ahead because they need to cool in the oven for 1½ hours.*

| | |
|---|---|
| ⅓ CUP UNSWEETENED COCOA POWDER | ⅔ CUP SUGAR |
| ½ CUP PLUS 1 TABLESPOON POWDERED SUGAR, DIVIDED USE | 1 TEASPOON VANILLA EXTRACT |
| 5 LARGE EGG WHITES | 2 OUNCES BITTERSWEET CHOCOLATE, FINELY CHOPPED |
| ¼ TEASPOON CREAM OF TARTAR | |

Preheat oven to 300°F. Line 2 large cookie sheets with parchment paper; secure with masking tape.

Sift together cocoa powder and ½ cup powdered sugar into a medium bowl; set aside.

In a large bowl beat the egg whites and cream of tartar with an electric mixer at high speed until soft peaks form. Gradually add the sugar and then the cocoa mixture, 1 tablespoon at a time, beating until stiff peaks form. Beat in the vanilla. Fold in the chopped chocolate.

Drop dough by rounded tablespoonfuls onto prepared sheets to form 36 mounds.

Bake 30–35 minutes, rotating sheets after 15 minutes. Turn oven off. Cool meringues in closed oven 1½ hours or until dry. Carefully remove the meringues from the paper. Transfer meringues to wire rack. Cool completely. Sprinkle evenly with remaining 1 tablespoon powdered sugar. **Makes 3 dozen cookies.**

◉ **Cook's Note:** Store cooled cookies in an airtight container for up to 2 weeks.

NUTRITION PER SERVING (1 COOKIE):
CALORIES 34; FAT .63G (POLY .01G, MONO .12G, SAT .06G);
PROTEIN 1G; CHOLESTEROL .08MG; CARBOHYDRATE 7G.

# ENGLISH TOFFEE

*Puffs*

*Nicely chewy under their crumbly shell, these are delicious and easy to make. And the surprise of chocolate and toffee in each bite makes this a recipe worth memorizing. If you are unfamiliar with cream of tartar, it is a white powder added to egg whites to help them rise higher and stay fluffy.*

| | |
|---|---|
| 1 CUP POWDERED SUGAR, SIFTED | 4 LARGE EGG WHITES |
| ½ CUP UNSWEETENED COCOA POWDER (NOT DUTCH PROCESS) | ¼ TEASPOON CREAM OF TARTAR |
| 2 1.4-OUNCE CHOCOLATE-COVERED TOFFEE BARS (E.G., HEATH OR SKOR), CRUSHED | ⅓ CUP SUGAR |

Preheat oven to 350°F. Line a large cookie sheet with parchment paper; secure with masking tape.

In a small bowl mix the powdered sugar, cocoa powder, and candy bars until blended; set aside.

In a large metal bowl beat the egg whites and cream of tartar with an electric mixer set at high speed until soft peaks form. Gradually add the sugar, beating until glossy and stiff peaks form.

Fold half of cocoa mixture into egg whites (egg whites will deflate). Fold in remaining cocoa mixture until smooth. Drop the mixture by rounded tablespoonfuls onto prepared baking sheet.

Bake 15 minutes (do not overbake; puffs will be slightly soft in center). Use parchment paper to lift and transfer puffs to a wire rack. Cool completely. Carefully remove cookies from paper. **Makes 2 dozen puffs.**

NUTRITION PER SERVING (1 PUFF):
CALORIES 54; FAT 1.3G (POLY .05G, MONO .39G, SAT .76G);
PROTEIN 1G; CHOLESTEROL 1.7MG; CARBOHYDRATE 11G.

# Pecan Bars

*A sinfully rich cookie that's amazingly easy to prepare.*

---

1½ CUPS WHOLE WHEAT PASTRY FLOUR (OR
   ALL-PURPOSE FLOUR)

1 TEASPOON BAKING POWDER

½ TEASPOON BAKING SODA

¼ TEASPOON SALT

½ CUP GRANULATED SUGAR

½ CUP PACKED DARK BROWN SUGAR

¼ CUP (½ STICK) BUTTER, SOFTENED

1 TEASPOON VANILLA EXTRACT

1 LARGE EGG

⅓ CUP CHOPPED PECANS

2½ OUNCES BITTERSWEET CHOCOLATE,
   CHOPPED INTO CHUNKS

Preheat oven to 350°F. Spray a 9-inch square baking pan with nonstick cooking spray.

In a medium bowl whisk the flour, baking powder, baking soda, and salt.

In a large bowl beat the sugars and butter with an electric mixer at medium speed for 3 minutes or until well combined. Beat in the vanilla and egg until combined. Stir in the flour mixture until well combined. Stir in pecans and chocolate. Spread mixture evenly in prepared pan.

Bake 25–30 minutes until just set. Transfer pan to wire rack and cool in pan 10 minutes. Cut into 16 bars while still warm. Cool completely. **Makes 16 bars.**

NUTRITION PER SERVING (1 BAR):
CALORIES 152; FAT 6.6G (POLY .75G, MONO 2.8G, SAT 2.7G);
PROTEIN 2G; CHOLESTEROL 21.3MG; CARBOHYDRATE 22G.

# *Bars*

*These cookies remind me of a no-bake cookie from my childhood, made with graham crackers, marshmallows, butterscotch baking chips, and about a cup of butter. This is a decidedly grown-up version—far less sweet and less fat—but still yummy. And yes, kids will still love them, too.*

| | |
|---|---|
| ½ CUP WHOLE WHEAT PASTRY FLOUR (OR ALL-PURPOSE FLOUR) | 2 OUNCES BITTERSWEET CHOCOLATE, CHOPPED |
| 1 CUP REDUCED-FAT GRAHAM CRACKER CRUMBS (ABOUT 5 COOKIE SHEETS) | 1 TABLESPOON CANOLA OIL |
| ⅔ CUP PACKED LIGHT BROWN SUGAR | 1½ TEASPOONS VANILLA EXTRACT |
| ⅓ CUP QUICK-COOKING OATS | 2 LARGE EGG WHITES |
| 1 TEASPOON BAKING POWDER | 1 TABLESPOON POWDERED SUGAR |

Preheat oven to 350°F. Spray an 8-inch square baking pan with nonstick cooking spray.

In a medium bowl whisk the flour, graham cracker crumbs, brown sugar, oats, baking powder, and chocolate.

In a small bowl whisk the oil, vanilla, and egg whites; add to the flour mixture, stirring just until blended. Using a large square of wax paper, press the batter evenly into prepared pan.

Bake 16–18 minutes or until a wooden pick inserted in the center comes out clean. Cool in pan on a wire rack. Sift powdered sugar over top. Cut into 16 pieces while still warm. **Makes 16 bars.**

NUTRITION PER SERVING (1 BAR):
CALORIES 89; FAT 2.5G (POLY .35G, MONO 1G, SAT .82G);
PROTEIN 1.5G; CHOLESTEROL 0MG; CARBOHYDRATE 16G.

# Cranberry-Chocolate Bars
## WITH ORANGE & PISTACHIOS

*Country cookie meets city flavors: the dough is revved up with the fresh flavors of orange and cranberry and the delicate nuttiness of pistachios. Don't worry about finding unsalted pistachio nuts; the salted ones add an extra contrast to the sweet cookies.*

| | |
|---|---|
| 3 TABLESPOONS UNSALTED BUTTER | ½ TEASPOON BAKING POWDER |
| 2 TABLESPOONS PACKED LIGHT BROWN SUGAR | 1 LARGE EGG |
| ¾ CUP PLUS 2 TABLESPOONS SUGAR, DIVIDED USE | 1 LARGE EGG WHITE |
| ⅔ CUP WHOLE WHEAT PASTRY FLOUR (OR ALL-PURPOSE FLOUR) | 1 TEASPOON GRATED ORANGE ZEST |
| | ¼ CUP FRESH ORANGE JUICE |
| 3 TABLESPOONS UNSWEETENED COCOA POWDER (NOT DUTCH PROCESS) | 2 CUPS CRANBERRIES, FRESH OR FROZEN (THAWED), COARSELY CHOPPED |
| 5 TABLESPOONS ALL-PURPOSE FLOUR, DIVIDED USE | ⅓ CUP ROASTED SHELLED PISTACHIOS, CHOPPED |
| PINCH OF SALT | 1 OUNCE BITTERSWEET CHOCOLATE, FINELY CHOPPED |

Position rack in center of oven; preheat to 350°F. Spray an 8-inch-square baking pan with nonstick cooking spray.

For the crust, beat the butter, brown sugar, and 2 tablespoons sugar in a medium bowl with an electric mixer on medium until creamy. Stir in whole wheat pastry flour, cocoa powder, 3 tablespoons all-purpose flour, and salt until well combined (mixture will still be crumbly). Using a large square of wax paper, evenly press mixture into the bottom of the prepared pan.

Bake crust 11 minutes. Keep oven on.

In a medium bowl combine the remaining ¾ cup sugar, remaining 2 tablespoons all-purpose flour, and baking powder. Add the egg, egg white, orange zest, and orange juice, stirring until blended and smooth.

Sprinkle the cranberries over the baked crust. Pour the orange mixture over the cranberries and sprinkle with pistachios and chocolate.

Bake 40–45 minutes until golden and set. Transfer pan to wire rack. Cool completely. Chill before cutting into 16 squares. **Makes 16 squares.**

NUTRITION PER SERVING (1 BAR):
CALORIES 123; FAT 3.5G (POLY .18G, MONO 1.3G, SAT 1.7G);
PROTEIN 2G; CHOLESTEROL 19.3MG; CARBOHYDRATE 22G.

# CHOCOLATE-CHERRY
## *Streusel Bars*

*Forgo the fussiness (along with the high fat): these homey bar cookies are a pleasure to prepare. Apricot and raspberry preserves are equally delicious choices for the filling.*

| | |
|---|---|
| 1 CUP QUICK-COOKING OATS | ¼ TEASPOON SALT |
| ¾ CUP PLUS 2 TABLESPOONS WHOLE WHEAT PASTRY FLOUR (OR ALL-PURPOSE FLOUR) | ¼ TEASPOON BAKING SODA |
| | ¼ CUP CANOLA OIL |
| 3 TABLESPOONS UNSWEETENED COCOA POWDER (NOT DUTCH PROCESS) | 3 TABLESPOONS APPLE JUICE |
| | 1 10-OUNCE JAR CHERRY PRESERVES (1 SCANT CUP) |
| ⅔ CUP PACKED LIGHT BROWN SUGAR | |

Preheat oven to 325°F. Spray an 8-inch square baking pan with nonstick cooking spray.

In a large bowl combine the oats, flour, cocoa powder, brown sugar, salt, and baking soda with fingertips until no lumps of brown sugar remain. Drizzle the oil and apple juice over the mixture and mix in with fingertips until evenly moistened and crumbly.

Set aside ½ cup of the oats mixture for the topping. Using a square of wax paper, press the remaining oats mixture evenly in the bottom of the prepared pan. Spread cherry preserves over the top. Sprinkle with the reserved oats mixture.

Bake for 32-37 minute or until streusel is set. Transfer pan to wire rack. Cool completely. Cut into 15 bars. Store at room temperature in an airtight container. **Makes 15 bars.**

NUTRITION PER SERVING (1 BAR):
CALORIES 167; FAT 4.3G (POLY 1.2G, MONO 2.3G, SAT .41G);
PROTEIN 2G; CHOLESTEROL 0MG; CARBOHYDRATE 32G.

# BITTERSWEET CHOCOLATE-STUDDED

# *Blondies*

*Granted, I love chocolate, but brown sugar-y treats, like these easy blondies, rank a very high second on my list of favorite flavors. These freeze well, too, so I typically wrap up half of the batch for future treats and company (as well as to keep myself from eating them all).*

| | |
|---|---|
| 1 CUP ALL-PURPOSE FLOUR | 10 TABLESPOONS (1¼ STICKS) UNSALTED BUTTER, MELTED |
| 1 CUP WHOLE WHEAT PASTRY FLOUR (OR ALL-PURPOSE FLOUR) | ¾ CUP EGG SUBSTITUTE |
| 2½ CUPS PACKED LIGHT BROWN SUGAR | 1 TEASPOON VANILLA EXTRACT |
| 2 TEASPOONS BAKING POWDER | 4 OUNCES BITTERSWEET CHOCOLATE, CHOPPED INTO CHUNKS |
| ½ TEASPOON SALT | |

Preheat oven to 350°F. Spray a 13 x 9-inch baking pan with nonstick cooking spray.

In a large bowl whisk the flours, brown sugar, baking powder, and salt.

In a small bowl whisk the butter, egg substitute, and vanilla. Pour butter mixture over flour mixture and stir until just blended. Stir in chocolate. Spread batter into prepared pan, smoothing top.

Bake 25–30 minutes or until a wooden pick inserted in the center comes out clean. Transfer pan to wire rack and cool completely. Cut into 36 squares. **Makes 36 squares.**

NUTRITION PER SERVING (1 BLONDIE):
CALORIES 132; FAT 4.4G (POLY .18G, MONO 1.7G, SAT 2.3G);
PROTEIN 1.5G; CHOLESTEROL 8.9MG; CARBOHYDRATE 23G.

# Bars

*I know it's an overly simplistic dichotomy, but two groups of "food people" do seem to exist when it comes to raisins: those who love them and those who hate them. I am of the former category, so I can easily gobble up two or three of these chewy bars without blinking. For the latter group: substitute 1 cup of another dried fruit—dried cranberries, tart cherries, snipped apricots—and you'll love the bars, too.*

| | |
|---|---|
| 2 LARGE EGGS | 2 CUPS REDUCED-FAT VANILLA WAFER |
| 1 LARGE EGG WHITE | CRUMBS (ABOUT 40 WAFERS) |
| ¾ CUP SUGAR | 1 CUP SEEDLESS RAISINS |
| 2 TEASPOONS VANILLA EXTRACT | 1½ OUNCES BITTERSWEET CHOCOLATE, |
| ¼ TEASPOON SALT | CHOPPED |
| ¼ CUP UNSWEETENED COCOA POWDER (NOT DUTCH PROCESS) | |

Preheat oven to 325°F. Spray an 8 x 12-inch or 7 x 11-inch baking pan with nonstick cooking spray.

In a large bowl beat the eggs, egg white, sugar, vanilla, and salt with an electric mixer set on high speed 2 minutes or until the eggs are thick and pale. Beat in the cocoa powder, beating 30 seconds.

Using a large rubber spatula, fold in the vanilla wafer crumbs and raisins until just combined. Spread mixture evenly in prepared pan, smoothing the top. Sprinkle with chocolate.

Bake 30–35 minutes until a toothpick inserted near the center comes out clean. Transfer pan to wire rack. Cool completely. Cut into 15 pieces. **Makes 15 bars.**

NUTRITION PER SERVING (1 BAR):
CALORIES 143; FAT 3.5G (POLY .55G, MONO 1.4G, SAT 1.3G);
PROTEIN 2.5G; CHOLESTEROL 33.6MG; CARBOHYDRATE 28G.

# CHOCOLATE-COCONUT

# *Macaroon Bars*

*Much richer than the average cookie, these treats start with a chocolate crust, which gets topped with a crisp-chewy chocolate-coconut meringue mixture.*

---

5    TABLESPOONS BUTTER, SOFTENED

1½ TABLESPOONS FAT-FREE MILK

½   TEASPOON VANILLA EXTRACT

1    CUP PLUS 6 TABLESPOONS SUGAR, DI-
     VIDED USE

⅔   CUP ALL-PURPOSE FLOUR

⅔   CUP WHOLE WHEAT PASTRY FLOUR (OR
     ALL-PURPOSE FLOUR)

3    TABLESPOONS UNSWEETENED COCOA POW-
     DER (NOT DUTCH PROCESS)

4    LARGE EGG WHITES (AT ROOM
     TEMPERATURE)

½   TEASPOON CREAM OF TARTAR

½   TEASPOON ALMOND EXTRACT

¼   TEASPOON SALT

1    CUP SWEETENED FLAKE COCONUT

1    OUNCE BITTERSWEET CHOCOLATE, FINELY
     CHOPPED

---

Preheat oven to 350°F. Spray a 13 x 9-inch baking pan with nonstick cooking spray.

To prepare crust, place the butter, milk, vanilla, and 6 tablespoons sugar in a large bowl. Beat with an electric mixer at medium speed until well blended. Add the flours and cocoa powder to sugar mixture, beating until mixture resembles coarse meal. Using a large square of wax paper, press mixture into bottom of prepared pan.

Bake crust 12 minutes or until lightly browned; cool on a wire rack. Set aside. Lower oven temperature to 325°F.

To prepare topping, combine the egg whites, cream of tartar, almond extract, and salt in a large bowl. Beat with an electric mixer at high speed until soft peaks form. Gradually add the remaining 1 cup sugar, 1 tablespoon at a time, beating until stiff peaks form. Fold in the coconut and chocolate; spread evenly over prepared crust.

Bake 38–40 minutes or until top is dry and lightly browned. Transfer pan to wire rack. Cool completely. Cut into 32 bars. **Makes 32 bars.**

NUTRITION PER SERVING (1 BAR):
CALORIES 93; FAT 3.4G (POLY .11G, MONO .96G, SAT 2.1G);
PROTEIN 2G; CHOLESTEROL 5.1MG; CARBOHYDRATE 15G.

# Raspberry—Chocolate Chip Squares

*If there is a way to build on the old-fashioned, homey goodness of oatmeal cookies, it's by turning them into bars, studding them with bittersweet chocolate, and sandwiching them with raspberry jam.*

| | |
|---|---|
| 1 CUP WHOLE WHEAT PASTRY FLOUR (OR ALL-PURPOSE FLOUR) | ¾ CUP PACKED LIGHT BROWN SUGAR |
| 1 CUP QUICK-COOKING OATS | 5 TABLESPOONS BUTTER, SOFTENED |
| ½ TEASPOON BAKING SODA | ½ CUP BITTERSWEET CHOCOLATE CHIPS |
| ½ TEASPOON SALT | 1 10-OUNCE JAR SEEDLESS RASPBERRY JAM |

Preheat oven to 375°F. Line an 8-inch square baking pan with aluminum foil; spray foil with nonstick cooking spray.

In a small bowl whisk the flour, oats, baking soda, and salt. Set aside.

In a medium bowl beat the brown sugar and butter with an electric mixer set at medium speed until smooth. Using a wooden spoon, stir the flour mixture into butter mixture until well blended (mixture will be crumbly).

Remove ¾ cup of dough; toss with chocolate chips. Set aside. Press the remaining dough into prepared pan. Spread evenly with jam. Sprinkle with reserved chocolate chip mixture.

Bake 28–30 minutes or until golden brown. Transfer pan to wire rack. Cool 10 minutes. Lift bars from pan using foil. Cut into 24 small squares while still warm. **Makes 24 squares.**

NUTRITION PER SERVING (1 SQUARE):
CALORIES 138; FAT 4.1G (POLY .31G, MONO 1.2G, SAT 2.3G);
PROTEIN 2G; CHOLESTEROL 6.4MG; CARBOHYDRATE 25G.

# Very Best Brownies

These have all the qualities you want in a brownie: dense, chewy, and rich with chocolate flavor. Applesauce is the surprise ingredient that keeps them moist and fudgy.

4   OUNCES UNSWEETENED CHOCOLATE, COARSELY CHOPPED

2   TABLESPOONS (¼ STICK) UNSALTED BUTTER

1   CUP WHOLE WHEAT PASTRY FLOUR (OR ALL-PURPOSE FLOUR)

¼   CUP UNSWEETENED COCOA POWDER (NOT DUTCH PROCESS)

¼   TEASPOON SALT

4   LARGE EGG WHITES

3   LARGE EGGS

1⅓ CUPS PACKED LIGHT BROWN SUGAR

¾   CUP UNSWEETENED APPLESAUCE

2   TABLESPOONS CANOLA OIL

1   TEASPOON VANILLA EXTRACT

3   OUNCES BITTERSWEET CHOCOLATE, CHOPPED

OPTIONAL: ⅓ CUP CHOPPED WALNUTS OR PECANS

Preheat oven to 350°F. Spray the bottom only of a 13 x 9-inch baking pan with nonstick cooking spray.

Melt the unsweetened chocolate and butter in a double boiler over barely simmering water. Remove from heat.

In a medium bowl whisk the flour, cocoa powder, and salt.

In a large bowl whisk the egg whites, eggs, and brown sugar with until smooth. Whisk in the applesauce, oil, and vanilla until blended. Add the chocolate-butter mixture, whisking until blended. Add the flour mixture with a wooden spoon, stirring just until moistened. Stir in the chocolate.

Spread the batter evenly into the prepared baking dish. Sprinkle with nuts, if desired.

Bake 20–25 minutes or until the top of the brownies springs back when touched lightly. Transfer to a wire rack. Cool completely. Cut into 24 squares. **Makes 24 brownies.**

NUTRITION PER SERVING (1 BROWNIE):
CALORIES 146; FAT 6.7G (POLY .60G, MONO 2.6G, SAT 3.1G);
PROTEIN 3G; CHOLESTEROL 29.1MG; CARBOHYDRATE 21G.

# Espresso-Fudge Brownies

*Chocolate and espresso yield a symphony of flavor, and these intense brownies—which taste anything but low-fat—warrant a standing ovation.*

| | |
|---|---|
| 2 OUNCES BITTERSWEET CHOCOLATE, CHOPPED, DIVIDED USE | 1 LARGE EGG |
| 4 TABLESPOONS (½ STICK) UNSALTED BUTTER, DIVIDED USE | 2 TABLESPOONS PLUS 1 TEASPOON COFFEE-FLAVORED LIQUEUR (E.G., KAHLUA), DIVIDED USE |
| 1 CUP PACKED LIGHT BROWN SUGAR | ¾ CUP ALL-PURPOSE FLOUR |
| ½ CUP UNSWEETENED COCOA POWDER (NOT DUTCH PROCESS) | ¼ TEASPOON BAKING POWDER |
| 1 TABLESPOON INSTANT ESPRESSO POWDER | ¼ TEASPOON BAKING SODA |
| 2 TEASPOONS VANILLA EXTRACT | ¼ TEASPOON SALT |
| 1 LARGE EGG WHITE | 2 TABLESPOONS SUGAR |
| | 1 TABLESPOON WATER |
| | 1 TABLESPOON DARK CORN SYRUP |

Preheat oven to 350°F. Spray bottom only of an 8-inch square baking pan with nonstick cooking spray.

In a microwave-safe bowl combine 1 ounce chocolate and 3 tablespoons butter. Cover and microwave on HIGH 1 minute or until chocolate almost melts. Stir until completely melted. Stir in brown sugar, cocoa powder, espresso powder, vanilla, egg white, egg, and 2 tablespoons coffee liqueur.

In a large bowl whisk the flour, baking powder, baking soda, and salt. Add the chocolate mixture, stirring just until moistened. Spread into prepared pan.

Bake 21–23 minutes or until a wooden pick inserted in the center comes out almost clean (be careful not to overbake; brownies will continue to set as they cool). Cool in pan on a wire rack.

To prepare glaze, combine the sugar, water, corn syrup, and remaining 1 tablespoon butter in a small microwave-safe bowl. Microwave on HIGH 40 seconds or until sugar dissolves, stirring once. Add remaining 1 ounce chocolate and 1 teaspoon coffee liqueur, stirring until chocolate melts.

Spread warm glaze over brownies. Cool 20 minutes or until glaze is set. Cut into 16 squares. **Makes 16 brownies.**

NUTRITION PER SERVING (1 BROWNIE):
CALORIES 154; FAT 4.8G (POLY .21G, MONO 1.2G, SAT 2.2G);
PROTEIN 2G; CHOLESTEROL 21.0MG; CARBOHYDRATE 26G.

# Raspberry—Cream Cheese Brownies

*Raspberries, cheesecake, and chocolate? Nirvana. To make cutting these brownies simpler, coat a sharp knife with cooking spray. Wipe the knife clean after each cut and re-coat with the cooking spray.*

| | |
|---|---|
| ½ OF AN 8-OUNCE PACKAGE REDUCED-FAT CREAM CHEESE (NEUFCHATEL), SOFTENED | ¼ TEASPOON BAKING POWDER |
| | ¼ TEASPOON BAKING SODA |
| 2 TEASPOONS ALL-PURPOSE FLOUR | ⅛ TEASPOON SALT |
| 1¼ CUPS SUGAR, DIVIDED USE | ⅔ CUP UNSWEETENED COCOA POWDER (NOT DUTCH PROCESS) |
| 1½ TEASPOONS VANILLA EXTRACT, DIVIDED USE | |
| | ¼ CUP (½ STICK) UNSALTED BUTTER, MELTED |
| 3 LARGE EGG WHITES, DIVIDED USE | 1 TABLESPOON WATER |
| ¾ CUP WHOLE WHEAT PASTRY FLOUR (OR ALL-PURPOSE FLOUR) | 1 LARGE EGG |
| | ¼ CUP SEEDLESS RASPBERRY PRESERVES |

Preheat oven to 350°. Spray the bottom only of an 8-inch baking pan with nonstick cooking spray.

In a medium bowl beat the cream cheese, all-purpose flour, ¼ cup sugar, ½ teaspoon vanilla, and 1 egg white with an electric mixer set at medium speed until blended and smooth; set filling aside.

In a medium bowl whisk the whole wheat pastry flour, baking powder, baking soda, and salt. In another medium bowl whisk the cocoa powder, melted butter, water, egg, remaining 1 teaspoon vanilla, remaining 2 egg whites, and remaining 1 cup sugar until well blended. Add to the flour mixture, stirring just until moistened.

Spread two-thirds of batter in bottom of prepared pan. Pour cream cheese filling over batter, spreading evenly. Carefully drop the remaining batter and preserves by spoonfuls over filling; swirl together using the tip of a knife to marble.

Bake 38–40 minutes or until a wooden pick inserted in the center comes out almost clean (be careful not to overbake; brownies will continue to set as they cool). Transfer pan to wire rack. Cool completely. Cut into 16 squares. **Makes 16 brownies.**

NUTRITION PER SERVING (1 BROWNIE):
CALORIES 155; FAT 5.2G (POLY .26G, MONO 1.9G, SAT 2.7G);
PROTEIN 4G; CHOLESTEROL 25MG; CARBOHYDRATE 26G.

# Mint Julep Brownies

*These lush brownies, inspired by the Kentucky Derby drink of choice, will delight your palate with rich chocolate, cool mint, and sassy bourbon.*

| | |
|---|---|
| 1 CUP ALL-PURPOSE FLOUR | ¼ CUP (½ STICK) UNSALTED BUTTER |
| ½ CUP UNSWEETENED COCOA POWDER (NOT DUTCH PROCESS) | 1 CUP SUGAR |
| ¼ TEASPOON BAKING SODA | ½ CUP EGG SUBSTITUTE |
| ¼ TEASPOON SALT | ¼ CUP BOURBON OR WHISKEY |
| 2 OUNCES BITTERSWEET CHOCOLATE, CHOPPED | ¾ TEASPOON PURE PEPPERMINT EXTRACT |

Preheat oven to 350°F. Spray the bottom only of a 9-inch square baking pan with nonstick cooking spray.

In a small bowl whisk the flour, cocoa powder, baking soda, and salt; set aside.

Place the chocolate and butter in a large microwave-safe bowl. Microwave on HIGH 1½ minutes or until the chocolate and butter melt, stirring every 30 seconds. Cool slightly. Whisk in the sugar, egg substitute, bourbon, and peppermint extract until well blended and smooth.

Microwave chocolate mixture on HIGH 1 minute or until sugar dissolves, stirring every 30 seconds. Fold in the flour mixture, stirring just until moistened. Spread batter in a thin layer in prepared pan.

Bake 19–21 minutes or until a wooden pick inserted in the center comes out almost clean (be careful not to overbake; brownies will continue to set as they cool). Transfer pan to wire rack. Cool completely. Cut into 16 squares. **Makes 16 brownies.**

NUTRITION PER SERVING (1 BROWNIE):
CALORIES 149; FAT 4.6G (POLY .31G, MONO 1.3G, SAT 2.7G);
PROTEIN 2.5G; CHOLESTEROL 7.7MG; CARBOHYDRATE 22G.

## Variations

**Grand Marnier Brownies:** Prepare as directed above, but substitute Grand Marnier or another orange liqueur for the bourbon and 1 teaspoon vanilla extract for the peppermint extract. Also add 1½ teaspoons fresh grated orange zest to the batter.

**Irish Cream Brownies:** Prepare as directed above, but substitute Irish Cream liqueur for the bourbon and 1 teaspoon vanilla extract for the peppermint extract.

# Peanut Butter-Swirled Brownies

*Love for the combination of chocolate & peanut butter must be part of my genetic make-up: my father and grandfather were nuts for it, too. If you follow suit, you'll want to whip these up ASAP.*

½ OF AN 8-OUNCE PACKAGE FAT-FREE CREAM CHEESE, SOFTENED

1½ CUPS PACKED LIGHT BROWN SUGAR, DIVIDED USE

3 TABLESPOONS CREAMY REDUCED-FAT PEANUT BUTTER

1 TABLESPOON ALL-PURPOSE FLOUR

1½ TEASPOONS VANILLA EXTRACT, DIVIDED USE

2 LARGE EGGS, DIVIDED USE

⅔ CUP WHOLE WHEAT PASTRY FLOUR (OR ALL-PURPOSE FLOUR)

½ CUP UNSWEETENED COCOA POWDER (NOT DUTCH PROCESS)

¼ TEASPOON SALT

2 LARGE EGG WHITES

¼ CUP CANOLA OIL

¼ CUP WATER

Preheat oven to 350° F. Spray the bottom only of an 11 x 7-inch baking pan with non-stick cooking spray.

In a small mixing bowl beat the cream cheese and ¼ cup brown sugar with an electric mixer set on medium speed until smooth and creamy. Add the peanut butter, all-purpose flour, ½ teaspoon vanilla, and 1 egg, beating until well blended. Set aside.

In a small bowl whisk the whole wheat pastry flour, cocoa powder, and salt. In a large bowl beat the egg whites, remaining 1 egg, and remaining 1¼ cups brown sugar with an electric mixer set on medium speed until smooth. Add the oil, water, and remaining 1 teaspoon vanilla; beat until well blended. Stir in the flour-cocoa mixture with a wooden spoon until just blended.

Spread about half of the brownie batter into the prepared pan. Slowly pour the peanut butter mixture evenly on top. Drop the remaining brownie batter in large dollops over the topping. Draw the tip of a sharp knife or skewer through the two batters to create a swirled effect.

Bake 18–20 minutes until the top is just firm to the touch (do not overbake). Transfer to a wire rack. Cool completely in the pan on a wire rack. Cut into 20 squares. **Makes 20 brownies.**

NUTRITION PER SERVING (1 BROWNIE):
CALORIES 132; FAT 3.4G (POLY 1.2G, MONO 2.2G, SAT .77G);
PROTEIN 3G; CHOLESTEROL 21.6MG; CARBOHYDRATE 22G.

# Rocky Road Brownies

*Part brownie, part cake, and 100 percent irresistible, these treats are best cut and served warm. Use a sharp knife coated with nonstick cooking spray to keep them from sticking.*

| | |
|---|---|
| 1 CUP WHOLE WHEAT PASTRY FLOUR (OR ALL-PURPOSE FLOUR) | 1 CUP CUBED REDUCED-FAT FIRM TOFU (ABOUT 6 OUNCES) |
| ¾ CUP UNSWEETENED COCOA POWDER (NOT DUTCH PROCESS) | ½ CUP FAT-FREE MILK |
| ¾ TEASPOON BAKING POWDER | 1 TEASPOON VANILLA EXTRACT |
| ⅛ TEASPOON BAKING SODA | ¼ CUP (½ STICK) UNSALTED BUTTER, SOFTENED |
| ½ TEASPOON SALT | 1 CUP MINIATURE MARSHMALLOWS |
| 1¼ CUPS SUGAR | ⅓ CUP CHOPPED WALNUTS |

Preheat oven to 375°. Spray the bottom and sides of a 9-inch baking pan with nonstick cooking spray.

In a large bowl whisk the flour, cocoa powder, baking powder, baking soda, and salt.

Combine the sugar, tofu, milk, vanilla, and butter in a food processor or blender. Process until smooth. Add tofu mixture to flour mixture, stirring just until moist.

Spread batter into the prepared pan. Sprinkle with the walnuts.

Bake 15 minutes; sprinkle with marshmallows. Bake 8–10 minutes longer or until a wooden pick inserted in the center comes out clean. Cool in pan on a wire rack 5 minutes. Cut into 16 squares while still warm. **Makes 16 brownies.**

NUTRITION PER SERVING (1 BROWNIE):
CALORIES 156; FAT 5.2G (POLY .69G, MONO 1.9G, SAT 2.3G);
PROTEIN 3G; CHOLESTEROL 7.8MG; CARBOHYDRATE 27G.

# 3. LET THEM EAT

## *(Chocolate!) Cake*

CHOCOLATE-STRAWBERRY SHORTCAKES, PEANUT BUTTER & CHOCOLATE SWIRL CAKE, CHOCOLATE GINGERBREAD, VEGAN CHOCOLATE, CHERRY, & PECAN CAKE, BLACK-AND-TAN IRISH CREAM CAKE, BROWNIE BLISS CAKE, COCOA CABANA PUDDING CAKE, ONE-BOWL CHOCOLATE-BUTTERMILK CAKE, CHOCOLATE ESPRESSO BUNDT CAKE, ALMOND JOYFUL TUNNEL CAKE, CHOCOLATE PUMPKIN BUNDT CAKE, DOUBLE CHOCOLATE-HAZELNUT BUNDT CAKE, CHOCOLATE ZUCCHINI BUNDT CAKE, CHOCOLATE ANGEL FOOD CAKE WITH FRESH BERRY-HONEY COMPOTE, ZINFULLY CHOCOLATE MOUSSE CAKES, CHOCOLATE-ALMOND APRICOT CAKE, FLOURLESS CHOCOLATE TORTE, CHOCOLATE-RASPBERRY GANACHE CAKE, GLAZED CHOCOLATE RUM RAISIN CAKE, EXOTIC CHOCOLATE-DATE CAKE, ENGLISH MARMALADE CHOCOLATE CAKE, STRAWBERRIES & CREAM CHOCOLATE LAYER CAKE, BLACK & WHITE POUND CAKE, CHOCOLATE-GRAND MARNIER SOUFFLÉ CAKE, VERY CHOCOLATE CHEESECAKE, ITALIAN TRUFFLE CHEESECAKE, CHOCOLATE-SWIRLED PUMPKIN CHEESECAKE, COCO Y CACAO CHEESECAKE, TEXAS SHEET CAKE, CHOCOLATE-WHISKEY TRUFFLE CAKES, CHOCOLATE-CHILE LAVA CAKES WITH CASHEW CREMA, CHOCOLATE FUDGE-CINNAMON SNACK CAKE, FAVORITE DOUBLE-CHOCOLATE CUPCAKES, CHOCOLATE CUPCAKES WITH VANILLA FROSTING, MAPLE-CHOCOLATE CHIP CUPCAKES, BANANA-CHOCOLATE CHIP MINI-BUNDTS . . .

# CHOCOLATE-STRAWBERRY
# *Shortcakes*

*When summer strawberries are at their peak, I like to serve them without much fuss. Strawberry shortcake is one of my favorite options. Here I've made the all-American dessert even more inviting with chocolate biscuits and a lightened cream filling that's as easy as can be.*

| | |
|---|---|
| 1 CUP FAT-FREE FROZEN WHIPPED TOPPING, THAWED | ⅓ CUP UNSWEETENED COCOA POWDER (NOT DUTCH PROCESS) |
| ⅓ CUP REDUCED-FAT SOUR CREAM | 1 TEASPOON BAKING POWDER |
| 1½ TEASPOONS VANILLA EXTRACT, DIVIDED USE | ½ TEASPOON BAKING SODA |
| 1 PINT STRAWBERRIES, HULLED AND SLICED | ¼ TEASPOON SALT |
| ⅓ CUP PLUS 1 TABLESPOON SUGAR, DIVIDED USE | 1½ TABLESPOONS UNSALTED BUTTER |
| ⅔ CUP ALL-PURPOSE FLOUR | 1½ TABLESPOONS REDUCED-FAT CREAM CHEESE |
| | ½ CUP LOW-FAT BUTTERMILK |
| | 1 TABLESPOON POWDERED SUGAR |

To prepare the cream, whisk the whipped topping, sour cream, and ½ teaspoon vanilla in a small bowl until blended. Cover and chill.

In a medium bowl toss the strawberries with 1 tablespoon sugar. Let stand at room temperature about 30 minutes until they begin to give off their juice.

Preheat oven to 400°F. Lightly spray a cookie sheet with nonstick cooking spray.

In a medium bowl whisk the flour, cocoa powder, baking powder, baking soda, salt, and remaining ⅓ cup sugar. Using a pastry cutter or your fingertips, cut the butter and cream cheese into the flour mixture until it resembles fresh breadcrumbs. Make a well in the center of mixture; add the buttermilk and remaining 1 teaspoon vanilla to the well and mix with a fork until just blended (do not overmix).

Drop the dough in 4 equal mounds onto the prepared baking sheet, spacing about 2 inches apart. With moist fingers, gently press each mound into a 3-inch circle.

Bake 10–12 minutes or until tops spring back when touched. Transfer cake to a wire rack with a spatula and cool completely.

With a serrated knife, cut biscuits in half horizontally. Set the bottoms on dessert plates. Top with the berries and their juices and a dollop of the cream. Replace biscuit tops and sprinkle with powdered sugar. **Makes 4 servings.**

NUTRITION PER SERVING (1 ASSEMBLED SHORTCAKE): CALORIES 333; FAT 9.8G (POLY .53G, MONO 3.4G, SAT 5.4G); PROTEIN 6.5G; CHOLESTEROL 25.4MG; CARBOHYDRATE 59G.

# PEANUT BUTTER & CHOCOLATE SWIRL

*Cake*

*Tender chocolate cake, peanut butter, and 156 calories per serving . . . what better way to savor the PB-chocolate combo?*

NONSTICK BAKING SPRAY WITH FLOUR

6 TABLESPOONS (¾ STICK) UNSALTED BUTTER, SOFTENED

2 TABLESPOONS UNSWEETENED APPLESAUCE

1¼ CUPS FIRMLY PACKED LIGHT BROWN SUGAR

1 TEASPOON VANILLA EXTRACT

3 LARGE EGG WHITES

1 LARGE EGG

1 CUP ALL-PURPOSE FLOUR

½ CUP WHOLE WHEAT PASTRY FLOUR (OR ALL-PURPOSE FLOUR)

½ TEASPOON BAKING POWDER

⅛ TEASPOON SALT

¼ CUP UNSWEETENED COCOA POWDER (NOT DUTCH PROCESS)

¼ CUP REDUCED-FAT CREAMY PEANUT BUTTER

Preheat oven to 350°F. Spray a 9-inch square baking pan with nonstick baking spray with flour.

In a medium bowl place the butter, applesauce, and brown sugar and beat with an electric mixer at medium speed until light and fluffy. Add the vanilla, egg whites, and egg; mix until blended.

In a small bowl whisk the flours, baking powder, and salt. With mixer at low speed, add flour mixture to butter mixture until just blended. Reserve 1½ cups of batter. Pour the remaining batter into a bowl. Stir cocoa powder into the 1½ cups reserved batter; stir peanut butter into remaining batter.

Spoon cocoa batter alternately with peanut butter batter into prepared pan. Swirl together using the tip of a knife.

Bake 25–30 minutes or until a wooden pick inserted in the center comes out clean. Transfer to a wire rack and cool completely. **Makes 16 servings.**

NUTRITION PER SERVING (1 PIECE):
CALORIES 156; FAT 6.1G (POLY .62G, MONO 1.9G, SAT 3.2G);
PROTEIN 3G; CHOLESTEROL 25MG; CARBOHYDRATE 24G.

# CHOCOLATE

# *Gingerbread*

*I am a confessed ginger addict—I tend to double or triple the amounts in any given recipe, especially gingerbread. Together with a double dose of chocolate, this spicy cake is heaven (don't forget the tea, good book, and comfy chair).*

NONSTICK BAKING SPRAY WITH FLOUR

1 CUP CAKE FLOUR

¾ CUP WHOLE WHEAT PASTRY FLOUR

⅓ CUP UNSWEETENED COCOA POWDER (NOT DUTCH PROCESS)

½ CUP PACKED LIGHT BROWN SUGAR

1 TABLESPOON GROUND GINGER

1 TEASPOON CINNAMON

1½ TEASPOONS BAKING SODA

½ TEASPOON SALT

½ CUP DARK MOLASSES (NOT BLACKSTRAP)

½ CUP UNSWEETENED APPLESAUCE

6 TABLESPOONS CANOLA OIL

1 LARGE EGG, LIGHTLY BEATEN

½ CUP BOILING WATER

2 OUNCES BITTERSWEET CHOCOLATE, CHOPPED

1 TABLESPOON POWDERED SUGAR

Preheat oven to 350°F. Spray 10-inch Bundt pan (12-cup capacity) with nonstick baking spray with flour.

In a medium bowl whisk the flours, cocoa powder, brown sugar, ginger, cinnamon, baking soda, and salt. In a large bowl whisk the molasses, applesauce, oil, and egg until blended. Add dry ingredients and stir until well blended. Whisk in ½ cup boiling water until blended and smooth. Stir in chopped chocolate and immediately pour batter into prepared pan (batter will fill only half of pan).

Bake 30–35 minutes until cake begins to pull away from sides of pan and tester inserted near the center comes out clean, about 35 minutes. Transfer to a rack and cool in pan 30 minutes. Invert cake onto platter and cool to lukewarm, at least 15 minutes.

Sprinkle cake with powdered sugar. Cut into 12 wedges. Serve warm or at room temperature. **Makes 12 servings.**

NUTRITION PER SERVING ( 1 WEDGE):
CALORIES 246; FAT 9.3G (POLY 2.4G, MONO 4.3G, SAT .90G);
PROTEIN 3G; CHOLESTEROL 17.8MG; CARBOHYDRATE 40G.

# VEGAN CHOCOLATE, CHERRY, & PECAN

## *Cake*

*Dried cherries and toasted pecans highlight this impressive version of the one-bowl chocolate cake. Using a good-quality cocoa powder makes all the difference—it's worth the small splurge. An elegant dessert, it needs nothing more than a dusting of powdered sugar to finish it off.*

|   |   |
|---|---|
| NONSTICK BAKING SPRAY WITH FLOUR | ½ TEASPOON SALT |
| 1 CUP ALL-PURPOSE FLOUR | 1 CUP UNSWEETENED APPLESAUCE |
| ⅔ CUP WHOLE WHEAT PASTRY FLOUR (OR ALL-PURPOSE FLOUR) | ½ CUP PLAIN SOY MILK |
| | ¼ CUP CANOLA OIL |
| 1½ CUPS SUGAR | 1 CUP DRIED TART CHERRIES |
| ¾ CUP UNSWEETENED COCOA POWDER (NOT DUTCH PROCESS) | ½ CUP CHOPPED PECANS, TOASTED |
| | 1 TABLESPOON POWDERED SUGAR |
| 1 TEASPOON BAKING POWDER | |
| 1 TEASPOON BAKING SODA | |

Preheat oven to 350°F. Spray a 10-inch springform pan with nonstick baking spray with flour.

In a large bowl whisk the flours, sugar, cocoa powder, baking powder, baking soda, and salt. In a small bowl combine the applesauce, soy milk, and oil. Add applesauce mixture to flour mixture, stirring just until moist. Stir in cherries and pecans. Spread batter (it will be thick) into prepared pan.

Bake 40–45 minutes or until edges begin to pull away from sides of pan. Cool on a wire rack. Remove sides and bottom of pan. Place cake on serving plate and sprinkle with powdered sugar. **Makes 12 servings.**

NUTRITION PER SERVING (1 PIECE):
CALORIES 281; FAT 8.9G (POLY 2.6G, MONO 4.7G, SAT 1.1G);
PROTEIN 5.3G; CHOLESTEROL 1MG; CARBOHYDRATE 50G.

# Irish Cream Cake

*Saint Patrick would be oh-so-proud: part chocolate cake, part brown-sugary Irish Cream cake, this is the perfect dessert come March 17th. If it sounds too perfect, there is one drawback: it is destined to eclipse the corned beef and cabbage main course.*

|  |  |
|---|---|
| NONSTICK BAKING SPRAY WITH FLOUR | ½ TEASPOON SALT |
| 6 TABLESPOONS (¾ STICK) BUTTER, MELTED | ½ TEASPOON BAKING SODA |
| 1 CUP PACKED DARK BROWN SUGAR | 1½ CUPS ALL-PURPOSE FLOUR |
| 1½ TEASPOONS VANILLA EXTRACT | ½ CUP WHOLE WHEAT PASTRY FLOUR (OR |
| 4 LARGE EGG WHITES | ALL-PURPOSE FLOUR) |
| ⅔ CUP LOW-FAT BUTTERMILK | 3 TABLESPOONS UNSWEETENED COCOA |
| 2 TABLESPOONS IRISH CREAM LIQUEUR | POWDER (NOT DUTCH PROCESS) |
| (E.G., BAILEY'S) | |

Preheat oven to 350°F. Spray an 8-inch square baking pan with nonstick baking spray with flour.

Whisk the melted butter and brown sugar in a large bowl until blended. Mix in the vanilla and egg whites. Stir in the buttermilk, Irish cream liqueur, salt, and baking soda. Sift in the flours, mixing until just blended (do not overmix).

Spread half the batter into the prepared pan. Whisk the cocoa powder into the remaining batter until blended. Slowly pour the chocolate batter over batter in pan. Swirl batters with the tip of a knife. Bake 27–30 minutes or until a wooden pick inserted in the center comes out clean. Cool for 10 minutes in pan on a wire rack. Cut into 9 squares. **Makes 9 servings.**

NUTRITION PER SERVING (1 PIECE):
CALORIES 267; FAT 9.1G (POLY .44G, MONO 2.4G, SAT 5.6G);
PROTEIN 5G; CHOLESTEROL 23.8MG; CARBOHYDRATE 42G.

# Brownie Bliss Cake

*Rich, moist, and decadently chocolate, this is one my favorite cakes ever. Rich like a brownie, but delicate like a cake, it's delicious to the last crumb.*

| | |
|---|---|
| 2 OUNCES UNSWEETENED CHOCOLATE, CHOPPED | 1 TEASPOON BAKING POWDER |
| ⅔ CUP ALL PURPOSE FLOUR | ½ TEASPOON SALT |
| ⅓ CUP WHOLE WHEAT PASTRY FLOUR (OR ALL-PURPOSE FLOUR) | 2 LARGE EGGS |
| 1 CUP SUGAR | 2 LARGE EGG WHITES |
| ½ CUP UNSWEETENED COCOA POWDER (NOT DUTCH PROCESS) | ⅔ CUP UNSWEETENED APPLESAUCE |
| | ⅓ CUP CANOLA OIL |
| | 2 TEASPOONS VANILLA EXTRACT |
| | 1 TABLESPOON POWDERED SUGAR |

Preheat oven to 350°F. Spray a 9-inch springform pan with nonstick cooking spray.

Place the chocolate in top of a double boiler set over simmering water. Stir until melted. Cool 5 minutes.

In a medium bowl whisk the flours, sugar, cocoa powder, baking powder, and salt. In a large bowl whisk the eggs, egg whites, applesauce, oil, vanilla, and melted chocolate to blend. Sift flour mixture over the egg mixture. Whisk batter until smooth. Transfer to prepared pan and smooth top.

Bake 30–35 minutes until tester inserted into the center comes out with moist crumbs still attached (cake will be about halfway up sides of pan). Transfer pan to wire rack. Cool completely.

Release pan sides from cake. Place cake on plate and top with powdered sugar. **Makes 12 servings.**

NUTRITION PER SERVING (1 PIECE):
CALORIES 210; FAT 9.9G (POLY 2.2G, MONO 4.6G, SAT 2.6G);
PROTEIN 4G; CHOLESTEROL 35.3MG; CARBOHYDRATE 30G.

# Chocolate-Buttermilk Cake

*This old-fashioned chocolate cake makes my friends swoon. Not too sweet, it wins over those who contend they don't like dessert. The buttermilk in the batter draws out the chocolate flavor and delivers a delicate crumb texture. Come summertime, serve up slices with a big bowl of lightly sweetened strawberries.*

---

NONSTICK BAKING SPRAY WITH FLOUR

¾ CUP PLUS 2 TABLESPOONS WHOLE WHEAT PASTRY FLOUR (OR ALL-PURPOSE FLOUR)

1 CUP PACKED LIGHT BROWN SUGAR

⅓ CUP UNSWEETENED COCOA POWDER (NOT DUTCH PROCESS)

1 TEASPOON BAKING POWDER

1 TEASPOON BAKING SODA

¼ TEASPOON SALT

½ CUP LOW-FAT BUTTERMILK

1 LARGE EGG, LIGHTLY BEATEN

2 TABLESPOONS CANOLA OIL

1 TEASPOON VANILLA EXTRACT

½ CUP HOT STRONG-BREWED COFFEE

1 TABLESPOON POWDERED SUGAR

---

Preheat oven to 350°F. Spray a 9-inch round cake pan with nonstick baking spray with flour.

In a large bowl whisk the flour, brown sugar, cocoa powder, baking powder, baking soda, and salt. Add buttermilk, egg, oil, and vanilla. Beat with an electric mixer on medium speed 2 minutes. Add the hot coffee and beat to blend (the batter will be thin). Pour batter into the prepared pan.

Bake 30–35 minutes until a skewer inserted in the center comes out clean. Transfer pan to a wire rack and cool 10 minutes. Invert cake onto wire rack. Cool completely. Sprinkle the top with powdered sugar. **Makes 12 servings.**

NUTRITION PER SERVING (1 PIECE):
CALORIES 141; FAT 3.4G (POLY .82G, MONO 1.7G, SAT .63G);
PROTEIN 3G; CHOLESTEROL 18.4MG; CARBOHYDRATE 27G.

# *Pudding Cake*

*The beauty of this cake is that the fudge sauce is baked in the same pan with the batter. When scooped out into dessert dishes a few minutes after baking, it is bathed, miraculously, with fudge. Although this cake is best served warm, it is also delicious at room temperature.*

---

| | |
|---|---|
| 2 TABLESPOONS (¼ STICK) BUTTER, SOFTENED | 1½ TEASPOONS BAKING POWDER |
| ¾ CUP PACKED LIGHT BROWN SUGAR | ⅛ TEASPOON SALT |
| ⅓ CUP 1% LOW-FAT MILK | ½ CUP UNSWEETENED COCOA POWDER (NOT DUTCH PROCESS), DIVIDED USE |
| 2 TABLESPOONS DARK RUM | ⅔ CUP SUGAR |
| 1 TEASPOON COCONUT EXTRACT | 1¼ CUPS BOILING WATER |
| 1 CUP ALL-PURPOSE FLOUR | 2¼ CUPS LIGHT VANILLA ICE CREAM |

Preheat oven to 350°F. Spray an 8-inch square baking pan with nonstick cooking spray.

In a medium bowl beat the butter and brown sugar with an electric mixer at medium speed for 3 minutes. Add the milk, rum, and coconut extract; beat well.

Whisk flour, baking powder, salt, and ¼ cup cocoa powder in a small bowl; gradually add to sugar mixture, beating until just blended. Spoon batter into prepared pan.

In a small bowl combine the sugar and remaining ¼ cup cocoa powder; sprinkle over batter. Pour the boiling water over batter (do not stir).

Bake 28–30 minutes or until cake springs back when touched lightly in the center (cake will not test clean when a wooden pick is inserted in the center). Serve warm with vanilla ice cream. **Makes 9 servings.**

NUTRITION PER SERVING (1 PIECE):
CALORIES 258; FAT 4.2G (POLY .21G, MONO 1.1G, SAT 2.6G);
PROTEIN 4G; CHOLESTEROL 11.8MG; CARBOHYDRATE 53G.

**Variations**

**Mocha Fudge Pudding Cake:** Prepare as directed, but use coffee liqueur in place of the rum and vanilla extract in place of the coconut extract. Add 1 teaspoon instant espresso powder along with the vanilla extract.

**Butterscotch Fudge Pudding Cake:** Prepare as directed, but use butterscotch schnapps in place of the rum and vanilla extract in place of the coconut extract.

**Grand Marnier–Fudge Pudding Cake:** Prepare as directed, but use Grand Marnier or another orange-flavored liqueur in place of the rum and 1 teaspoon grated orange in place of the coconut extract.

# CHOCOLATE ESPRESSO

## *Bundt Cake*

*Coffee, meet your mate. This recipe creates enough batter for a 12-cup Bundt pan, but it can also be baked in smaller pans (though baking time will vary accordingly)—an especially nice option for eating some now, freezing some for later.*

| | |
|---|---|
| NONSTICK BAKING SPRAY WITH FLOUR | 1¼ CUPS LOW-FAT BUTTERMILK |
| 1¼ CUPS ALL-PURPOSE FLOUR | 1 CUP PACKED LIGHT BROWN SUGAR |
| ½ CUP WHOLE WHEAT PASTRY FLOUR (OR ALL-PURPOSE FLOUR) | 2 LARGE EGGS, LIGHTLY BEATEN |
| 1 CUP SUGAR | ¼ CUP CANOLA OIL |
| ¾ CUP UNSWEETENED COCOA POWDER (NOT DUTCH PROCESS) | 3 TEASPOONS VANILLA EXTRACT, DIVIDED USE |
| 1½ TEASPOONS BAKING SODA | 1 CUP BOILING WATER |
| 1½ TEASPOONS BAKING POWDER | 4 TEASPOONS INSTANT ESPRESSO OR COFFEE POWDER, DIVIDED USE |
| 1 TEASPOON SALT | 1¼ CUPS POWDERED SUGAR |
| | 1-2 TABLESPOONS LOW-FAT MILK |

Preheat oven to 350°F. Spray a 12-cup Bundt pan with nonstick baking spray with flour.

In a large bowl whisk the flours, sugar, cocoa powder, baking soda, baking powder, and salt. Add the buttermilk, brown sugar, eggs, oil, and 2 teaspoons vanilla. Beat with an electric mixer on medium speed for 2 minutes. In a small cup combine the boiling water and 3 teaspoons (1 tablespoon) espresso powder; beat into batter until completely incorporated (batter will be quite thin). Pour batter into the prepared pan.

Bake for 45–50 minutes, or until a cake tester inserted in the center comes out clean. Cool the cake in the pan on a wire rack for 10 minutes. Invert cake out of pan onto rack. Cool completely.

In a small bowl stir together the remaining 1 teaspoon vanilla and remaining 1 teaspoon espresso powder until dissolved. Add the powdered sugar and enough milk to make a thick but pourable icing. Set the cooled cake on a serving plate and drizzle the icing over the top. **Makes 16 servings.**

NUTRITION PER SERVING (1 PIECE):
CALORIES 242; FAT 4.9G (POLY 1.2G, MONO 2.5G, SAT .90G);
PROTEIN 4G; CHOLESTEROL 27.3MG; CARBOHYDRATE 49G.

# CHOCOLATE PUMPKIN
# *Bundt Cake*

*You can tell by its bright color that pumpkin is good for you. Loaded with vitamin A and anti-oxidant carotenoids, particularly alpha and beta-carotenes, it's a good source of vitamins C, K, and E, and lots of minerals, including magnesium, potassium, and iron. But here you'll pay more attention to how it enhances this easily assembled cake, adding moistness (without fat) and enhancing the deep chocolate flavor.*

| | | | |
|---|---|---|---|
| | NONSTICK BAKING SPRAY WITH FLOUR | 1 | CUP PLUS 1 TABLESPOON LOW-FAT |
| 1 | CUP ALL-PURPOSE FLOUR | | BUTTERMILK, DIVIDED USE |
| ¾ | CUP WHOLE WHEAT PASTRY FLOUR (OR | 1 | 15-OUNCE CAN UNSWEETENED SOLID-PACK |
| | ALL-PURPOSE FLOUR) | | PUMPKIN |
| 1 | CUP SUGAR | ¾ | CUP PACKED DARK BROWN SUGAR |
| ¾ | CUP UNSWEETENED COCOA POWDER (NOT | 1 | LARGE EGG, AT ROOM TEMPERATURE |
| | DUTCH-PROCESS) | 1 | LARGE EGG WHITE, AT ROOM TEMPERATURE |
| 1½ | TEASPOONS BAKING POWDER | ¼ | CUP CANOLA OIL |
| 1½ | TEASPOONS BAKING SODA | ¼ | CUP HONEY |
| 1 | TEASPOON PUMPKIN PIE SPICE | 2 | TEASPOONS VANILLA EXTRACT |
| ¾ | TEASPOON GROUND GINGER | 1 | CUP POWDERED SUGAR |
| ¼ | TEASPOON SALT | ½ | OUNCE BITTERSWEET CHOCOLATE, GRATED |

Preheat oven to 350°F. Spray a 12-cup Bundt pan with nonstick baking spray with flour.

In a medium bowl whisk the flours, sugar, cocoa powder, baking powder, baking soda, pumpkin pie spice, ginger, and salt.

In a large bowl blend 1 cup buttermilk, pumpkin, and brown sugar with an electric mixer on low speed. Beat in the egg and egg white. Stir in the oil, honey, and vanilla. Gradually add the dry ingredients, stirring until just combined. Transfer batter to the prepared pan.

Bake 1 hour and 10–15 minutes until a wooden skewer inserted in the center comes out with only a few moist crumbs attached. Transfer to a wire rack and cool 15 minutes. Invert cake onto rack. Cool completely.

In a small bowl combine the powdered sugar and remaining 1 tablespoon buttermilk, stirring until completely smooth. Place the cake on a serving plate and drizzle the glaze over the top. Garnish with grated chocolate while the glaze is still moist. **Makes 16 servings.**

NUTRITION PER SERVING (1 PIECE): CALORIES 245; FAT 5.0G (POLY 1.7G, MONO 2.4G, SAT .98G); PROTEIN 4G; CHOLESTEROL 13.9MG; CARBOHYDRATE 50G.

# CHOCOLATE ZUCCHINI
# *Bundt Cake*

*Both of my parents cooked and baked a lot when I was growing up, so I've had plenty of inspiration to draw on as a food writer and recipe developer. This cake reminds me of both parents: my mother, for her whole wheat zucchini bread (made with zucchini from her garden), and my dad, who loves a good, old-fashioned slice of cake—especially if it's chocolate.*

|  | NONSTICK BAKING SPRAY WITH FLOUR |
|---|---|
| ¾ | CUP SUGAR |
| ½ | CUP PACKED BROWN SUGAR |
| ½ | OF AN 8-OUNCE PACKAGE FAT-FREE CREAM CHEESE, SOFTENED |
| ⅓ | CUP CANOLA OIL |
| 2 | LARGE EGGS |
| 2 | LARGE EGG WHITES |
| 1½ | TEASPOONS VANILLA EXTRACT, DIVIDED USE |
| 1½ | CUPS ALL-PURPOSE FLOUR |
| 1 | CUP WHOLE WHEAT PASTRY FLOUR (OR ALL-PURPOSE FLOUR) |
| 2 | TEASPOONS BAKING POWDER |
| ½ | TEASPOON BAKING SODA |
| ½ | TEASPOON SALT |
| ½ | TEASPOON GROUND CINNAMON |
| ½ | CUP PLUS 3 TABLESPOONS UNSWEETENED COCOA POWDER (NOT DUTCH PROCESS), DIVIDED USE |
| ¾ | CUP LOW-FAT BUTTERMILK |
| 2 | CUPS SHREDDED ZUCCHINI (ABOUT 1 MEDIUM-LARGE ZUCCHINI) |
| 4 | OUNCES BITTERSWEET CHOCOLATE, CHOPPED, DIVIDED USE |
| ¾ | CUP POWDERED SUGAR |
| 2½ | TABLESPOONS FAT-FREE MILK |

Preheat oven to 350°F. Spray a 12-cup Bundt pan with nonstick baking spray with flour.

In a large bowl place the sugars, cream cheese, and oil. Beat 5 minutes with an electric mixer at medium speed until well blended. Add the eggs, egg whites, and 1 teaspoon of the vanilla. Beat 2 minutes until well blended.

In a medium bowl whisk the flours, baking powder, baking soda, salt, cinnamon, and ½ cup cocoa powder. Add the flour mixture and buttermilk alternately to sugar mixture, beginning and ending with flour mixture. Stir in zucchini and all but 2 tablespoons of the chopped chocolate. Pour batter into prepared pan.

Bake 55–60 minutes or until a wooden pick inserted in cake comes out clean. Cool in pan 10 minutes on a wire rack; remove from pan. Cool completely on wire rack.

For the glaze, combine the powdered sugar and remaining 3 tablespoons cocoa in a small bowl; stir with a whisk. In a glass measuring cup combine the milk, reserved 2 tablespoons chocolate, and remaining ½ teaspoon vanilla. Microwave at MEDIUM 45 seconds or until chocolate melts, stirring after 20 seconds. Whisk the powdered sugar mixture with chocolate mixture. Drizzle glaze over cake. **Makes 16 servings.**

NUTRITION PER SERVING (1 PIECE):
CALORIES 260; FAT 8.2G (POLY 1.6G, MONO 3.8G, SAT 2.2G);
PROTEIN 6G; CHOLESTEROL 27.5MG; CARBOHYDRATE 44G.

# DOUBLE CHOCOLATE-HAZELNUT
# Bundt Cake

*You'll feel utterly Continental after your first taste of this cake, made with the thoroughly Italian combination of chocolate and hazelnuts. The splash of hazelnut liqueur is just the thing to amp up the sophisticated flavors.*

| | |
|---|---|
| NONSTICK BAKING SPRAY WITH FLOUR | 2 LARGE EGGS, LIGHTLY BEATEN |
| 1½ CUPS ALL-PURPOSE FLOUR | ¼ CUP CANOLA OIL |
| 1 CUP SUGAR | 1 TEASPOON VANILLA EXTRACT |
| ¾ CUP UNSWEETENED COCOA POWDER (NOT DUTCH PROCESS) | ¼ CUP HOT WATER |
| | ¼ CUP HAZELNUT LIQUEUR (E.G., FRANGELICO) |
| ⅓ CUP FLAXSEED MEAL | |
| 1½ TEASPOONS BAKING POWDER | ½ CUP CANNED PRUNE PURÉE (E.G., SUNSWEET LIGHTER BAKE) |
| 1½ TEASPOONS BAKING SODA | |
| 1 TEASPOON SALT | 3 OUNCES BITTERSWEET CHOCOLATE, CHOPPED |
| 1¼ CUPS LOW-FAT BUTTERMILK | ½ CUP CHOPPED HAZELNUTS, TOASTED |
| 1 CUP PACKED DARK BROWN SUGAR | 1 TABLESPOON SIFTED POWDERED SUGAR |

Preheat oven to 350°F. Coat a 12-cup Bundt pan with nonstick baking spray with flour.

In a large mixing bowl whisk the flour, sugar, cocoa powder, flaxseed meal, baking powder, baking soda, and salt. Add the buttermilk, brown sugar, eggs, oil, and vanilla; beat with an electric mixer on medium speed until smooth. In a measuring cup mix the hot water, hazelnut liqueur, and prune purée; whisk into the batter. Fold in the chocolate and nuts with a rubber spatula. Spoon batter into the prepared pan, spreading evenly.

Bake 45–50 minutes until a tester inserted in the center comes out clean. Cool in the pan on a wire rack for 10 minutes. Invert the cake onto the rack. Cool completely. Sprinkle with powdered sugar. **Makes 16 servings.**

**Cook's Notes:** If flaxseed meal is unavailable, whole flax seeds may be ground in a clean coffee grinder. For homemade prune purée, combine 6 ounces (1 cup) pitted prunes with 6 tablespoons hot water in a food processor; process until smooth. Makes 1 cup.

NUTRITION PER SERVING (1 PIECE):
CALORIES 298; FAT 9.7G (POLY 2.2G, MONO 4.9G, SAT 2.1G);
PROTEIN 5G; CHOLESTEROL 27.2MG; CARBOHYDRATE 50G.

# ALMOND JOYFUL
# *Tunnel Cake*

*Here's an updated version of the tunnel cake—a dessert that swept the nation when Ella Rita Helfrich created her Tunnel of Fudge cake for the 1966 Pillsbury Bake-Off. The familiar tunnel is still part of the recipe, but it's coconut cake instead of fudge, making it easier to slice and sophisticated enough for company.*

---

NONSTICK BAKING SPRAY WITH FLOUR

1¼ CUPS SUGAR

6 TABLESPOONS CANOLA OIL

2 LARGE EGGS

3 CUPS ALL-PURPOSE FLOUR

1¼ TEASPOONS BAKING SODA

¼ TEASPOON SALT

1½ CUPS LOW-FAT BUTTERMILK

1 TEASPOON ALMOND EXTRACT

⅔ CUP FLAKED SWEETENED COCONUT

1½ TEASPOONS COCONUT EXTRACT, DIVIDED USE

½ CUP UNSWEETENED COCOA POWDER (NOT DUTCH PROCESS)

¾ CUP POWDERED SUGAR, SIFTED

1 TABLESPOON FAT-FREE MILK

---

Preheat oven to 350°F. Spray a 12-cup Bundt pan with nonstick baking spray with flour.

In a large bowl beat the sugar and oil with an electric mixer at medium speed until blended. Add eggs, 1 at a time, beating 30 seconds after each addition.

In a medium bowl whisk the flour, baking soda, and salt; add to sugar mixture alternately with buttermilk, beginning and ending with flour mixture. Mix after each addition. Stir in the almond extract.

In a small bowl combine 1 cup batter, coconut, and 1 teaspoon coconut extract; stir until well blended. Set aside. Add the cocoa powder to the remaining batter in the large bowl, stirring until well blended.

Reserve 1 cup chocolate batter and set aside. Pour remaining chocolate batter into prepared pan. Spoon coconut batter over center of batter to form a ring (be careful coconut mixture does not touch sides of pan). Top with reserved chocolate batter, spreading evenly to cover.

Bake 38–42 minutes or until a wooden pick inserted in center comes out clean. Transfer pan to wire rack and cool 10 minutes. Invert cake onto wire rack. Cool completely. Combine the powdered sugar, milk, and remaining ½ teaspoon coconut extract in a small bowl, stirring until well blended. Drizzle over cake. **Makes 16 servings.**

NUTRITION PER SERVING (1 PIECE): CALORIES 257; FAT 7.9G (POLY 1.8G, MONO 3.7G, SAT 2.0G); PROTEIN 5G; CHOLESTEROL 28.3MG; CARBOHYDRATE 43G.

# Chocolate Angel Food Cake

## WITH FRESH BERRY-HONEY COMPOTE

*Airy cakes, such as this angel food cake, are baked in ungreased pans. This gives them a surface to cling to in their rise to the top and it prevents their foamy egg batter from deflating, which would happen if it came into contact with grease.*

| | |
|---|---|
| 1 CUP ALL-PURPOSE FLOUR | 1 TEASPOON FRESH LEMON JUICE |
| ¼ CUP UNSWEETENED COCOA POWDER (NOT DUTCH PROCESS) | 1 TEASPOON VANILLA EXTRACT |
| ¼ TEASPOON SALT | 2 CUPS FRESH STRAWBERRIES, DIVIDED USE |
| 1½ CUPS SUGAR, DIVIDED USE | 2 CUPS FRESH RASPBERRIES, DIVIDED USE |
| 12 LARGE EGG WHITES (OR 1½ CUPS PREPACKAGED EGG WHITES) | 2 TABLESPOONS HONEY |

Position the oven rack to the lowest level. Preheat oven to 325°F.

Into a medium bowl sift the flour, cocoa powder, salt, and 1 cup sugar; set aside.

Using an electric mixer set at medium-high speed, beat the egg whites, lemon juice, and vanilla. In a medium bowl until peaks form. Set mixer to high speed and beat in remaining ½ cup sugar until semi-stiff peaks form (do not overbeat).

With a plastic spatula, slowly fold the flour mixture into egg whites, ¼ cup at a time, until flour mix disappears. Scoop batter into an ungreased 10-inch tube pan and spread evenly.

Bake 45–50 minutes until cake springs back when touched. Remove from oven, invert cake pan, and place upside down on a cooling rack.

Place 1 cup strawberries, 1 cup raspberries, and honey in a large bowl. Coarsely mash the berries with a fork. Add the remaining berries and toss to combine.

Remove cake gently from pan and cut into 8 slices. Serve each slice with the berry compote. **Makes 8 servings.**

NUTRITION PER SERVING (1 PIECE WITH ½ CUP COMPOTE):
CALORIES 282; FAT .8G (POLY .24G, MONO .05G, SAT .04G);
PROTEIN 8G; CHOLESTEROL 0MG; CARBOHYDRATE 62G.

# Mousse Cakes

*This is the chocolate (and wine!) lover's dream dessert: rich, creamy, and intensely flavored. The Zinfandel and chocolate combination is a match made in (baking) heaven.*

½ CUP UNSWEETENED COCOA POWDER (NOT DUTCH PROCESS)

2 TABLESPOONS ALL-PURPOSE FLOUR

⅛ TEASPOON SALT

1¼ CUPS SUGAR, DIVIDED USE

¾ CUP ZINFANDEL OR OTHER FRUITY RED WINE

5 OUNCES BITTERSWEET CHOCOLATE, FINELY CHOPPED

2 TEASPOONS VANILLA EXTRACT

2 LARGE EGGS

1 LARGE EGG WHITE

Preheat oven to 350°F. Spray ten 4-ounce ramekins with nonstick cooking spray. Place ramekins in a 13 x 9-inch baking pan; set aside.

In a small saucepan combine cocoa powder, flour, salt, and ¾ cup sugar. Add wine, whisking to combine. Bring mixture to a simmer over medium heat; cook 2 minutes, stirring constantly.

Place chopped chocolate in a large bowl. Pour hot cocoa mixture over chocolate; stir until chocolate melts. Stir in vanilla.

In a medium bowl place the eggs, egg white, and remaining ½ cup sugar; beat with a mixer at high speed for 6 minutes. Gently fold the egg mixture into chocolate mixture.

Divide batter evenly among prepared ramekins. Fill the pan holding the ramekins with hot water to a depth of 1 inch.

Bake mousse cakes 23–25 minutes or until puffy and set. Serve warm. **Makes 10 servings.**

NUTRITION PER SERVING (1 CAKE):
CALORIES 210; FAT 5.9G (POLY .30G, MONO 2.0G, SAT 3.2G);
PROTEIN 3G; CHOLESTEROL 42.3MG; CARBOHYDRATE 38G.

# CHOCOLATE-ALMOND APRICOT

## *Cake*

*Rich with cocoa, almonds, and apricot jam, this stately dessert strongly resembles the famous Austrian Sacher Torte.*

| | | | |
|---|---|---|---|
| | NONSTICK BAKING SPRAY WITH FLOUR | 1 | CUP SUGAR, DIVIDED USE |
| 6 | LARGE EGG WHITES, AT ROOM TEMPERATURE | ½ | CUP PACKED DARK BROWN SUGAR |
| 2 | LARGE EGGS | 1½ | CUPS TOASTED GROUND ALMONDS (ABOUT 2 CUPS WHOLE ALMONDS) |
| 2 | LARGE EGG YOLKS | | |
| 6 | TABLESPOONS ALL-PURPOSE FLOUR | 2 | TEASPOONS VANILLA EXTRACT |
| ⅓ | CUP UNSWEETENED COCOA POWDER (NOT DUTCH PROCESS), SIFTED | ½ | TEASPOON ALMOND EXTRACT |
| | | ¾ | CUP APRICOT JAM |
| ½ | TEASPOON SALT | 1 | TABLESPOON POWDERED SUGAR |
| ¼ | TEASPOON GROUND CINNAMON | | |

Preheat oven to 375°F. Spray a 9-inch springform pan with nonstick baking spray with flour.

Place the egg whites in a large bowl. In a separate large bowl place the whole eggs and egg yolks. In a small bowl whisk the flour, cocoa powder, salt, and cinnamon.

Beat the egg whites with an electric mixer at high speed until foamy. Add ⅓ cup sugar and continue beating until soft peaks form. Set aside.

Add the brown sugar and remaining ⅔ cup sugar to the whole egg bowl. Beat with mixer at medium speed until thick and light in color, about 3 minutes. Scrape down the sides of the bowl with a rubber spatula; beat in the toasted almonds, vanilla, and almond extract until combined. Beat in flour mixture just until combined, scraping down the sides as needed.

Fold in 1 cup of the beaten whites with a rubber spatula until smooth, then gently fold in the remaining whites, just until incorporated (some white streaks may still be visible). Gently pour batter into the prepared pan.

Place the pan in the oven and reduce heat to 325°F. Bake 40–45 minutes until cake is puffed and spongy, but firm. Transfer to a wire rack and let cool completely (the cake will shrink away from the sides of the pan as it cools).

Remove the pan's side ring. Release the cake from the pan's bottom using a long, thin, metal spatula and carefully transfer it to a serving plate. Slice the cake horizontally into two layers with a long, thin knife. Gently lift off the top. Spread the jam over the bottom layer and replace the top (do not press down). Sprinkle with the powdered sugar just before serving. **Makes 16 servings.**

NUTRITION PER SERVING (1 PIECE):
CALORIES 246; FAT 9.8G (POLY 2.3G, MONO 6.1G, SAT 1.2G);
PROTEIN 7G; CHOLESTEROL 52.7MG; CARBOHYDRATE 36G.

# Flourless Chocolate Torte

*This is the little black dress of chocolate cakes: rich and refined, yet adaptable for any occasion, any time of year.*

| | |
|---|---|
| ½  CUP MATZO MEAL | 2  TABLESPOONS UNSWEETENED COCOA |
| ⅓  CUP WALNUTS | POWDER (NOT DUTCH PROCESS) |
| 2  LARGE EGGS | 2  OUNCES BITTERSWEET CHOCOLATE, CHOPPED |
| 1¼ CUPS SUGAR, DIVIDED USE | 8  LARGE EGG WHITES, ROOM TEMPERATURE |
| 2  TEASPOONS VANILLA EXTRACT | ½  TEASPOON SALT |
| 1  CUP GRATED PEELED TART APPLE | 1  TABLESPOON POWDERED SUGAR |

Preheat oven to 350°F.

Combine the matzo meal and walnuts in a food processor; process until nuts are finely chopped. Spread on a baking sheet and toast until fragrant, 5–10 minutes. Let cool.

In a large bowl whisk the eggs, ¾ cup sugar, and vanilla until blended. Stir in the matzo mixture, apple, cocoa powder, and chocolate.

Beat egg whites and salt in large, clean bowl, with an electric mixer on medium speed until frothy. Increase speed to high and beat until soft peaks form. Add remaining ½ cup sugar, 1 tablespoon at a time, beating until glossy, stiff peaks form.

Stir one-fourth of the beaten whites into the batter. Gently fold in remaining whites with a rubber spatula. Scrape the batter into an ungreased 9-inch springform pan, spreading evenly. Tap pan lightly on counter to release air bubbles.

Bake 40–45 minutes until the top springs back when touched lightly and a skewer inserted in the center comes out clean. Transfer pan to a wire rack and immediately run a knife around the edges of the pan to loosen. Let torte cool in pan (it will sink in the center).

Remove the pan sides and place torte on a serving platter. Dust with the powdered sugar and serve. **Makes 8 servings.**

NUTRITION PER SERVING (1 PIECE):
CALORIES 260; FAT 6.4G (POLY 2.2G, MONO 1.6G, SAT 2.0G);
PROTEIN 7G; CHOLESTEROL 52.9MG; CARBOHYDRATE 46G.

# BLACK & WHITE

# *Pound Cake*

*Inspired by the oversized black & white cookies that are practically an institution in delis all over the country, this pound cake recipe simplifies all by creating the dark and light contrasts inside the cake (part chocolate batter, part vanilla batter) rather than as an icing.*

| | | | |
|---|---|---|---|
| | NONSTICK BAKING SPRAY WITH FLOUR | 3 | LARGE EGGS |
| 3 | CUPS ALL-PURPOSE FLOUR | 1 | CUP 1% LOW-FAT MILK |
| 1 | TEASPOON BAKING POWDER | ½ | CUP WATER |
| ¼ | TEASPOON SALT | 3 | TABLESPOONS LIGHT CORN SYRUP |
| ¾ | CUP (1½ STICKS) UNSALTED BUTTER, SOFTENED | ¼ | TEASPOON BAKING SODA |
| 2 | CUPS SUGAR | ⅓ | CUP PLUS 1 TABLESPOON COCOA POWDER (NOT DUTCH PROCESS), DIVIDED USE |
| 2 | TEASPOONS VANILLA EXTRACT | | |

Preheat oven to 350°F. Spray a 10-inch tube pan with nonstick baking spray with flour.

Whisk the flour, baking powder, and salt in a medium bowl.

In a large bowl beat the butter with an electric mixer at medium speed until light and fluffy. Gradually add the sugar and vanilla, beating until well blended. Add the eggs, one at a time, beating well after each addition.

Add the flour mixture to sugar mixture alternately with the milk, beating at low speed, beginning and ending with the flour mixture.

Spoon two-thirds of batter (about 4 cups) into prepared pan. Add the water, corn syrup, baking soda, and ⅓ cup cocoa powder to remaining batter in bowl, stirring just until blended; spoon on top of vanilla batter.

Bake 1 hour and 15 minutes or until cake pulls away from sides of pan. Cool in pan 10 minutes on a wire rack; remove from pan. Cool completely on wire rack. Sift remaining cocoa over top of cake. **Makes 18 servings.**

NUTRITION PER SERVING (1 PIECE):
CALORIES 262; FAT 9.1G (POLY .50G, MONO 2.5G, SAT 5.4G);
PROTEIN 4.1G; CHOLESTEROL 56MG; CARBOHYDRATE 43G.

# CHOCOLATE-RASPBERRY

# *Ganache Cake*

*This over-the-top cake has impressive looks and moistness. "Ganache" is a French term referring to a smooth mixture of chopped chocolate and heavy cream. Here I've lightened the fat without sacrificing the flavor by using fat-free evaporated milk in place of the heavy cream, and substituting cocoa powder for part of the chocolate. It is still divine!*

¾ CUP UNSWEETENED DUTCH PROCESS COCOA POWDER, DIVIDED USE

½ CUP BOILING WATER

1⅓ CUPS PACKED LIGHT BROWN SUGAR

10 TABLESPOONS (1¼ STICKS) BUTTER, SOFTENED

1 8-OUNCE CARTON EGG SUBSTITUTE

2 CUPS CAKE FLOUR

1 TEASPOON BAKING SODA

¼ TEASPOON PLUS PINCH OF SALT, DIVIDED USE

1 8-OUNCE CARTON FAT-FREE SOUR CREAM

2½ TEASPOONS VANILLA EXTRACT, DIVIDED USE

½ CUP SEEDLESS RASPBERRY JAM

½ CUP SUGAR

⅓ CUP CANNED EVAPORATED FAT-FREE MILK

3 OUNCES BITTERSWEET CHOCOLATE, CHOPPED

1 PINT FRESH RASPBERRIES

GARNISH: FRESH MINT LEAVES

Preheat oven to 350°F. Spray a 13 x 9-inch baking pan with nonstick cooking spray. Line the bottom of the pan with wax paper. Spray wax paper with nonstick cooking spray; set aside.

Place ½ cup cocoa powder in a small bowl; pour the boiling water over cocoa, stirring to dissolve. Cool.

In a large bowl place the brown sugar and butter; beat with an electric mixer at medium speed 5 minutes or until well blended. Add the cocoa mixture and egg substitute, beating until well blended.

In a medium bowl whisk the flour, baking soda, and ¼ teaspoon salt. Add the flour mixture and sour cream alternately to cocoa mixture, beginning and ending with flour mixture; mix after each addition. Beat in 2 teaspoons vanilla. Pour batter into prepared pan. Tap pan on counter to remove air bubbles.

Bake 25–30 minutes or until a wooden pick inserted in the center comes out clean. Cool in pan 10 minutes on a wire rack; remove from pan. Carefully peel off wax paper. Cool completely on wire rack. Spread the raspberry jam over top of cake.

For the ganache, combine the sugar, evaporated milk, and remaining ¼ cup cocoa powder in a medium saucepan over medium heat. Bring to a boil, stirring frequently. Cook 1 minute, stirring constantly. Remove from heat and add the remaining ½ teaspoon vanilla, chopped chocolate, and pinch of salt, stirring until smooth. Spread warm ganache evenly over top of cake, allowing ganache to run down the sides. Let cake stand for 20 minutes or until set. Garnish with raspberries and mint leaves. **Makes 20 servings.**

NUTRITION PER SERVING (1 PIECE):
CALORIES 260; FAT 8.3G (POLY .68G, MONO 2.3G, SAT 4.8G);
PROTEIN 5G; CHOLESTEROL 16.6MG; CARBOHYDRATE 44G.

# Rum Raisin Cake

*I love the combination of chocolate and raisins—Raisinets are one of my favorite movie treats. This cake takes my favorite one step further, with a hearty dose of dark rum in the mix.*

| | | | |
|---|---|---|---|
| ⅓ | CUP PACKED LIGHT BROWN SUGAR | ¼ | CUP BOILING WATER |
| 3 | TABLESPOONS HOT WATER | 2 | TABLESPOONS DARK RUM |
| 1⅓ | CUPS UNSWEETENED COCOA POWDER (NOT DUTCH PROCESS), DIVIDED USE | 1 | TEASPOON VANILLA EXTRACT |
| 1 | CUP WATER | 5 | 1-OUNCE SQUARES UNSWEETENED BAKING CHOCOLATE, MELTED |
| 1 | CUP SEEDLESS RAISINS | 2 | LARGE EGG YOLKS |
| 1 | TABLESPOON BUTTER | 1 | TEASPOON CREAM OF TARTAR |
| ½ | CUP ALL-PURPOSE FLOUR | 10 | LARGE EGG WHITES |
| 1¾ | CUPS SUGAR, DIVIDED USE | | |

To make the chocolate glaze, whisk the brown sugar, hot water, and ⅓ cup cocoa powder in a small bowl until blended and smooth; set aside.

Preheat oven to 350°F. Spray the bottoms of two 9-inch round cake pans with nonstick cooking spray. Line bottoms of pans with wax paper. Spray wax paper with nonstick cooking spray; set aside.

In a small saucepan combine the 1 cup water, raisins, and butter. Bring to a boil; and cook 5 minutes. Remove from heat.

In a large bowl whisk the flour, 1½ cups sugar, and remaining 1 cup cocoa powder. Add the raisin mixture and boiling water; stir until well blended. Stir in the rum, vanilla, melted chocolate, and egg yolks until well blended. Set batter aside.

Beat the cream of tartar and egg whites with an electric mixer at high speed until foamy. Gradually add the remaining ¼ cup sugar, 1 tablespoon at a time, beating until stiff peaks form. Gently stir one-fourth of egg white mixture into batter; gently fold in remaining egg white mixture. Pour batter into prepared pans.

Bake 30–35 minutes or until cakes spring back when touched lightly in center. Let cool in pans 10 minutes on a wire rack; remove from pans. Peel off wax paper. Cool completely.

Place 1 cake layer on a serving plate. Spread with half of chocolate glaze, and top with other cake layer. Spread remaining glaze over top of cake. **Makes 16 servings.**

NUTRITION PER SERVING (1 PIECE):
CALORIES 215; FAT 7.1G (POLY .32G, MONO 2.2G, SAT 4.2G);
PROTEIN 6G; CHOLESTEROL 28.1MG; CARBOHYDRATE 39G.

# Cake

*Velvety and sophisticated, this cake intoxicates through its remarkably sensual, intense flavors of chocolate, walnuts and spices. Dates lend it an unbelievably unctuous texture.*

---

NONSTICK BAKING SPRAY WITH FLOUR

½ CUP CHOPPED PITTED DATES

½ CUP BOILING WATER

2 TEASPOONS INSTANT ESPRESSO POWDER, DIVIDED USE

½ CUP PLUS 6 TABLESPOONS UNSWEETENED COCOA POWDER (NOT DUTCH PROCESS), DIVIDED USE

½ CUP WALNUT HALVES, TOASTED, DIVIDED USE

⅓ CUP ALL-PURPOSE FLOUR

1 TEASPOON GROUND CARDAMOM

¼ TEASPOON GROUND CORIANDER

¼ TEASPOON GROUND GINGER

¼ TEASPOON SALT

½ CUP FRESH BREADCRUMBS

2 TABLESPOONS CANOLA OIL

1½ TEASPOONS VANILLA EXTRACT, DIVIDED USE

1 LARGE EGG

⅔ CUP SUGAR, DIVIDED USE

3 LARGE EGG WHITES

2 OUNCES BITTERSWEET CHOCOLATE, CHOPPED

¼ CUP BOILING WATER

1 TABLESPOON DARK CORN SYRUP

1 CUP POWDERED SUGAR

---

Preheat oven to 350°F. Spray a 9-inch round cake pan with nonstick baking spray with flour. Line bottom of pan with wax paper. Coat wax paper with cooking spray; set pan aside.

In a small bowl combine the dates, ½ cup boiling water, 1 teaspoon espresso powder, and ½ cup cocoa powder. Let stand 20 minutes.

Reserve 5 walnut halves for garnish. Combine the remaining walnuts, flour, cardamom, coriander, ginger, and salt in food processor. Process until finely ground. Place walnut mixture and breadcrumbs in a large bowl.

Place the date mixture, oil, 1 teaspoon vanilla, egg, and ⅓ cup sugar in food processor. Process until smooth, scraping the sides of bowl as needed. Add date mixture to breadcrumb mixture, stirring well.

Beat egg whites with an electric mixer at high speed until soft peaks form. Gradually add remaining ⅓ cup sugar, 1 tablespoon at a time, beating until stiff peaks form. Gently stir one-fourth of the egg white mixture into batter; gently fold in the remaining egg white mixture. Spread batter into prepared pan.

Bake 22–25 minutes or until cake springs back when lightly touched. Cool in pan for 10 minutes on a wire rack, and remove from pan. Remove the wax paper. Cool completely on wire rack.

For the glaze, combine the chocolate, boiling water, corn syrup, remaining 6 tablespoons cocoa powder, and remaining teaspoon instant espresso powder, stirring until smooth. Stir in remaining ½ teaspoon vanilla. Cover and chill for 1 hour. Gradually add the powdered sugar to the cocoa mixture, beating with a mixer at medium speed until smooth and thick.

Place the cake on a serving plate. Spread the glaze evenly over top and sides of cake. Arrange reserved walnut halves on top. **Makes 12 servings.**

NUTRITION PER SERVING (1 PIECE):
CALORIES 239; FAT 8.7G (POLY 3.3G, MONO 2.8G, SAT 2.1G);
PROTEIN 5G; CHOLESTEROL 17.7MG; CARBOHYDRATE 41G.

# ENGLISH MARMALADE
# *Chocolate Cake*

*This rich, old-fashioned cake is just the recipe for a formal afternoon tea or bridal shower. Decorate it with candied orange zest or a few edible flowers (rose petals are especially pretty). Raspberry or apricot preserves can stand in for the marmalade.*

¾ CUPS ALL-PURPOSE FLOUR

½ CUP WHOLE WHEAT PASTRY FLOUR (OR ALL-PURPOSE FLOUR)

⅓ CUP UNSWEETENED COCOA POWDER (NOT DUTCH PROCESS)

¾ CUP SUGAR

1 TEASPOON BAKING POWDER

1 TEASPOON BAKING SODA

PINCH OF SALT

½ CUP LOW-FAT BUTTERMILK

1 4-OUNCE JAR BABY FOOD CARROT PURÉE

1 4-OUNCE JAR BABY FOOD PRUNE PURÉE

3 TABLESPOONS WATER

1 TABLESPOON VANILLA EXTRACT

1 TABLESPOON GRATED ORANGE ZEST

2 TEASPOONS INSTANT ESPRESSO POWDER

1 LARGE EGG

1 LARGE EGG WHITE

1 OUNCE UNSWEETENED BAKING CHOCOLATE, FINELY CHOPPED

1½ OUNCES BITTERSWEET CHOCOLATE, FINELY CHOPPED

½ CUP ORANGE MARMALADE

¼ CUP JARRED FAT-FREE CHOCOLATE FUDGE ICE CREAM TOPPING

Preheat oven to 350°F. Lightly coat a 9-inch cake pan with nonstick cooking spray.

In a large bowl whisk the flours, cocoa powder, sugar, baking powder, baking soda, and salt.

In a medium bowl whisk the buttermilk, carrot purée, prune purée, water, vanilla, orange zest, espresso powder, egg, and egg white until blended. Using an electric mixer set on low speed, mix the wet ingredients into the dry ingredients.

Place the unsweetened chocolate in a small cup. Microwave 45 seconds. Stir until melted and smooth, then add to batter. Beat on medium speed until blended and smooth. Fold in the bittersweet chocolate. Pour into prepared cake pan.

Bake for 25–30 minutes or until a toothpick inserted in the center comes out clean. Place on rack and cool.

Invert the cake onto a cake platter and slice in half horizontally. Spread orange marmalade on bottom layer. Replace top. Warm the chocolate fudge sauce in the microwave for 15 seconds, then spread or decoratively drizzle over top of cake. **Makes 16 servings.**

NUTRITION PER SERVING (1 PIECE):
CALORIES 150; FAT 2.7G (POLY .17G, MONO .85G, SAT 1.5G);
PROTEIN 3G; CHOLESTEROL 13.8MG; CARBOHYDRATE 31G.

# CHOCOLATE–GRAND MARNIER

## Soufflé Cake

*When elegance is in order, put this dramatic, liqueur-rich cake on the menu. Have no fear of the word* soufflé: *this really is quite simple to make. Do be sure to use cake flour: it is a fine-textured, soft wheat flour with a high starch content, and usually comes in a box rather than a bag. It can be found with the other flours at the supermarket.*

| | |
|---|---|
| ⅓ CUP PACKED DARK BROWN SUGAR | 2 TABLESPOONS GRAND MARNIER OR OTHER ORANGE-FLAVORED LIQUEUR |
| ¾ CUP WATER | 3 LARGE EGG YOLKS |
| 1 CUP SUGAR, DIVIDED USE | 2 TEASPOONS GRATED ORANGE ZEST |
| ⅔ CUP UNSWEETENED COCOA POWDER (NOT DUTCH PROCESS) | ⅓ CUP CAKE FLOUR, SIFTED |
| ¼ TEASPOON SALT | 6 LARGE EGG WHITES, AT ROOM TEMPERATURE |
| 2 OUNCES BITTERSWEET CHOCOLATE, CHOPPED | ¼ TEASPOON CREAM OF TARTAR |
| 2 OUNCES UNSWEETENED CHOCOLATE, CHOPPED | 1 TABLESPOON POWDERED SUGAR |
| | OPTIONAL: ½ CUP FRESH RASPBERRIES |

Combine the brown sugar, water, and ⅔ cup sugar in a large saucepan set over high heat; stir well and bring to a boil. Remove from heat. Whisk in the cocoa powder, salt, and chocolates, whisking until chocolate melts. Stir in liqueur, egg yolks, and orange zest. Stir in flour. Cool to room temperature. Set aside.

Preheat oven to 300°F. Spray the bottom of a 9-inch springform pan with nonstick cooking spray. Set aside.

In a large bowl beat the egg whites and cream of tartar with an electric mixer at high speed until foamy. Add the remaining ⅓ cup sugar, 1 tablespoon at a time, beating until stiff peaks form. Gently fold one-fourth of egg white mixture into chocolate mixture; repeat procedure with remaining egg white mixture, one-fourth at a time. Spoon into prepared pan.

Bake 55–60 minutes or until a wooden pick inserted in the center comes out almost clean. Cool completely on wire rack. Remove sides from pan. Sift powdered sugar over cake. Garnish with raspberries, if desired. **Makes 12 servings.**

NUTRITION PER SERVING (1 PIECE): CALORIES 193; FAT 5.8G (POLY .34G, MONO 2.0G, SAT 3.2G); PROTEIN 5G; CHOLESTEROL 52MG; CARBOHYDRATE 35G.

# VERY CHOCOLATE

## Cheesecake

*Cheesecake may have been at the height of fashion a few decades ago, but it never went out of fashion in my kitchen. The simple ingredients in this rich version let good-quality cocoa powder and bittersweet chocolate shine.*

| | |
|---|---|
| 32 THIN CHOCOLATE WAFER COOKIES, FINELY CRUSHED | 1⅓ CUPS SUGAR |
| 2 TABLESPOONS BUTTER, MELTED | ¾ CUP UNSWEETENED COCOA POWDER (NOT DUTCH PROCESS) |
| 1 LARGE EGG WHITE | ¼ CUP REDUCED-FAT SOUR CREAM |
| 4 8-OUNCE PACKAGES FAT-FREE CREAM CHEESE, SOFTENED | 3 OUNCES UNSWEETENED CHOCOLATE, MELTED |
| 1 8-OUNCE PACKAGE REDUCED-FAT CREAM CHEESE, SOFTENED | 2 TEASPOONS VANILLA EXTRACT |
| | 4 LARGE EGGS |

Preheat oven to 325°F. Spray a 9-inch springform pan with nonstick cooking spray.

In a medium bowl combine the cookie crumbs, butter, and egg white, tossing with a fork until moist. Firmly press the mixture into the bottom of the prepared pan.

To prepare the filling, beat the cream cheeses with an electric mixer at high speed until smooth. Add the sugar, cocoa powder, sour cream, melted chocolate, and vanilla; beat well. Add eggs, one at a time, beating well after each addition. Pour cheese mixture into prepared crust in pan.

Bake cheesecake 1 hour and 10 minutes or until almost set. Cheesecake is done when the center barely moves when pan is touched. Remove cheesecake from oven; run a knife around outside edge. Cool to room temperature. Chill at least 8 hours. **Makes 20 servings.**

NUTRITION PER SERVING ( 1 PIECE):
CALORIES 213; FAT 8.6G (POLY .5G, MONO 2.9G, SAT 4.7G);
PROTEIN 11G; CHOLESTEROL 54.2MG; CARBOHYDRATE 26G.

# ITALIAN TRUFFLE
## *Cheesecake*

*An intensely chocolate filling, a chocolate-cookie crust, and a hint of hazelnut liqueur add up to an incredible cheesecake with a pronounced Italian accent. Begin making the cheesecake one day before serving to allow the flavors to meld.*

¼ CUP SLICED ALMONDS, TOASTED

1 CUP PLUS 1 TABLESPOON PACKED LIGHT BROWN SUGAR, DIVIDED USE

15 THIN CHOCOLATE WAFER COOKIES

1 TABLESPOON BUTTER, SOFTENED

1 TABLESPOON INSTANT ESPRESSO OR COFFEE POWDER

1 TABLESPOON HAZELNUT OR COFFEE-FLAVORED LIQUEUR

1 16-OUNCE CONTAINER (2 CUPS) FAT-FREE COTTAGE CHEESE

1 8-OUNCE PACKAGE REDUCED-FAT CREAM CHEESE (NEUFCHATEL), SOFTENED

¾ CUP PLUS 1 TABLESPOON UNSWEETENED COCOA POWDER (NOT DUTCH PROCESS), DIVIDED USE

½ CUP CHOCOLATE-HAZELNUT SPREAD (E.G., NUTELLA)

2 TABLESPOONS CORNSTARCH

1 TEASPOON ALMOND EXTRACT

¼ TEASPOON SALT

3 LARGE EGGS

Preheat oven to 325°F.

Place the almonds, 1 tablespoon brown sugar, and chocolate wafers in a food processor. Process until finely ground. Add the butter and process until crumbs are moist. Using a large square of wax paper, firmly press crumb mixture into bottom of a 9-inch springform pan coated with nonstick cooking spray. Wrap outside of pan with a double layer of aluminum foil.

Combine espresso powder and liqueur in a small bowl. Place cottage cheese and cream cheese in bowl of a large food processor and process until smooth. Add espresso mixture, ¾ cup cocoa powder, chocolate-hazelnut spread, cornstarch, salt, and remaining cup brown sugar. Process until well blended. Add eggs, one at a time, processing each until just incorporated and smooth. Pour mixture into prepared crust.

Place pan in a large baking pan. Add hot water to baking pan to a depth of 1 inch. Bake cheesecake 1 hour or until the center barely moves when pan is touched.

Remove cheesecake from oven and run a knife around outside edge. Cool to room temperature. Chill at least 8 hours. Remove cheesecake from springform pan and dust with remaining 1 tablespoon cocoa powder. **Makes 16 servings.**

NUTRITION PER SERVING (1 PIECE): CALORIES 291; FAT 9.0G (POLY 1.2G, MONO 3.5G, SAT 3.7G) PROTEIN 24G; CHOLESTEROL 58MG; CARBOHYDRATE 29G.

# CHOCOLATE-SWIRLED

# *Pumpkin Cheesecake*

*Move over pumpkin pie—this cheesecake will make everyone give thanks for a new reason come Turkey Day. Rich and luscious, I guarantee no one will suspect it's a light dessert. Have fun delivering the good news.*

| | |
|---|---|
| 32 THIN CHOCOLATE WAFER COOKIES, FINELY CRUSHED | 1¾ CUPS PACKED LIGHT BROWN SUGAR |
| 2 TABLESPOONS BUTTER, MELTED | ⅓ CUP ALL-PURPOSE FLOUR |
| 1 LARGE EGG WHITE | 1 15-OUNCE CAN SOLID PACK PUMPKIN |
| 4 OUNCES BITTERSWEET CHOCOLATE, CHOPPED | 1½ TABLESPOONS GROUND GINGER |
| 1 8-OUNCE CONTAINER (1 CUP) LOW-FAT COTTAGE CHEESE | 1 TABLESPOON GROUND CINNAMON |
| | ¾ TEASPOON GROUND NUTMEG |
| 1 8-OUNCE CONTAINER (1 CUP) FAT-FREE COTTAGE CHEESE | ½ TEASPOON GROUND CARDAMOM |
| | 2 TEASPOONS VANILLA EXTRACT |
| 2 8-OUNCE PACKAGES REDUCED-FAT CREAM CHEESE, SOFTENED | 3 LARGE EGGS |

Preheat oven to 350°F. Spray a 9-inch springform pan with nonstick cooking spray.

In a medium bowl combine the cookie crumbs, melted butter, and egg white, tossing with a fork until moist. Firmly press the mixture into the bottom of the prepared pan.

Place chocolate in a small microwave-safe bowl. Microwave on MEDIUM, stirring every 30 seconds until melted. Set aside.

Purée the cottage cheeses in a large food processor for 3 minutes. Add the cream cheese, brown sugar, and flour, and process until smooth. Add pumpkin, ginger, cinnamon, nutmeg, cardamom, and vanilla. Process 1 minute, or until smooth. Add eggs, one at a time, processing each time until eggs are just blended.

Whisk 1 cup cream cheese batter into bowl of melted chocolate. Pour remaining batter into crust. Spoon dollops of chocolate mixture onto batter, and swirl with knife to create a marbled effect.

Bake cheesecake 1 hour and 20 minutes or until almost set. Cheesecake is done when the center barely moves when pan is touched. Remove cheesecake from oven; run a knife around outside edge. Cool to room temperature. Chill at least 8 hours. **Makes 20 servings.**

NUTRITION PER SERVING (1 PIECE): CALORIES 228; FAT 9.1G (POLY .52G, MONO 3.0G, SAT 4.9G); PROTEIN 8G; CHOLESTEROL 49MG; CARBOHYDRATE 29.7G.

# Coco y Cacao Cheesecake

*Chocolate cheesecake goes tropical while lightening up. Chocoholics, take note: in addition to the cocoa powder and bits of bittersweet chocolate in the filling, there's a buttery chocolate crust.*

| | | | |
|---|---|---|---|
| 1 | TABLESPOON BUTTER, SOFTENED | 1 | 8-OUNCE PACKAGE REDUCED-FAT CREAM CHEESE (NEUFCHATEL), SOFTENED |
| 1 | LARGE EGG WHITE | ½ | CUP UNSWEETENED COCOA POWDER (NOT DUTCH PROCESS) |
| ¼ | CUP SUGAR | | |
| 1½ | CUPS CHOCOLATE GRAHAM CRACKER CRUMBS (ABOUT 17 CRACKERS) | 1½ | CUPS PACKED LIGHT BROWN SUGAR |
| 3 | TABLESPOONS DARK RUM | 3 | TABLESPOONS ALL-PURPOSE FLOUR |
| 3 | OUNCES BITTERSWEET CHOCOLATE | 2 | TEASPOONS COCONUT EXTRACT |
| ¼ | CUP SWEETENED CREAM OF COCONUT | 4 | LARGE EGGS |
| 4 | 8-OUNCE PACKAGE FAT-FREE CREAM CHEESE, SOFTENED | 3 | TABLESPOONS SWEETENED COCONUT, TOASTED |

Preheat oven to 325°F. Spray an 8-inch springform pan with nonstick cooking spray.

Place the butter, egg white, and sugar in a medium bowl. Beat with an electric mixer set on medium speed until blended. Add crumbs, stirring well to combine. Firmly press mixture into bottom and 1 inch up sides of prepared pan. Bake 10 minutes; let cool on a wire rack.

Combine rum and chocolate in the top of a double boiler. Cook over simmering water 2 minutes or until chocolate melts, stirring frequently. Remove from heat and add cream of coconut, stirring until smooth.

Place cream cheeses in a large bowl, then beat with an electric mixer set at medium speed until smooth. Beat in the cocoa powder, brown sugar, flour, and coconut extract until well blended. Beat in the chocolate mixture until well blended. Add eggs, one at a time, beating well after each addition. Pour filling into prepared crust.

Bake 1 hour and 10 minutes or until almost set. Cheesecake is done when the center barely moves when the pan is touched. Remove cheesecake from oven; run a knife around outside edge. Cool to room temperature. Chill at least 8 hours before serving. Sprinkle with toasted coconut. **Makes 16 servings.**

NUTRITION PER SERVING (1 PIECE): CALORIES 288; FAT 8.9G (POLY .69G, MONO 2.5G, SAT 5.1G); PROTEIN 13G; CHOLESTEROL 67MG; CARBOHYDRATE 39G.

# Texas Sheet Cake

*I have only been a Texan for two years, but the adage is true: things are bigger and better here. Case in point, Texas sheet cake, a one-bowl buttermilk cake embellished with a buttery chocolate glaze and a smattering of pecans. My enlightened version of the cake preserves all of the great, big goodness while slashing the fat and calories found in traditional recipes.*

NONSTICK BAKING SPRAY WITH FLOUR

2 CUPS ALL-PURPOSE FLOUR

2 CUPS SUGAR

1 TEASPOON BAKING SODA

1 TEASPOON GROUND CINNAMON

¼ TEASPOON SALT

¾ CUP WATER

½ CUP PLUS 6 TABLESPOONS (1¾ STICKS) BUTTER, DIVIDED USE

½ CUP UNSWEETENED COCOA POWDER (NOT DUTCH PROCESS), DIVIDED USE

½ CUP LOW-FAT BUTTERMILK

3 TEASPOONS VANILLA EXTRACT, DIVIDED USE

2 LARGE EGGS

⅓ CUP FAT-FREE MILK

3 CUPS POWDERED SUGAR

¼ CUP CHOPPED PECANS, TOASTED

Preheat oven to 375°F. Spray a 15 x 10-inch jelly roll pan with nonstick baking spray with flour.

For the cake, whisk the flour, sugar, baking soda, cinnamon, and salt in a large bowl.

Combine the water, ½ cup butter, and ¼ cup cocoa powder in a small saucepan; bring to a boil, stirring frequently. Remove from heat and pour into flour mixture. Beat at medium speed with an electric mixer until well blended. Add the buttermilk, 1 teaspoon vanilla, and eggs, beating well. Pour batter into prepared pan.

Bake 16–18 minutes or until a wooden pick inserted in center comes out clean. Transfer pan to a wire rack.

To prepare the icing, combine the milk, remaining 6 tablespoons butter, and remaining ¼ cup cocoa powder in a medium saucepan; bring to a boil, stirring constantly. Remove from heat, and gradually stir in powdered sugar, pecans, and remaining 2 teaspoons vanilla. Spread over hot cake. Cool completely on wire rack. **Makes 20 servings.**

**Cook's Note:** The cake may also be made in a 13 x 9-inch baking pan. Bake for 20–22 minutes.

NUTRITION PER SERVING (1 PIECE):
CALORIES 290; FAT 9.9G (POLY .74G, MONO 3.0G, SAT 5.6G); PROTEIN 3G; CHOLESTEROL 42.9MG; CARBOHYDRATE 49G.

# CHOCOLATE-WHISKEY
## Truffle Cakes

*In this show-stopping dessert, deep chocolate cakes are intensified with a dose of whiskey. Just as enticing: the preparation is a breeze.*

| | |
|---|---|
| 2 TABLESPOONS ALL-PURPOSE FLOUR | 5 OUNCES BITTERSWEET CHOCOLATE, FINELY CHOPPED |
| ⅛ TEASPOON SALT | |
| ½ CUP PLUS 1 TABLESPOON UNSWEETENED COCOA POWDER (NOT DUTCH PROCESS), DIVIDED USE | 2 TABLESPOONS WHISKEY |
| | 1 TEASPOON VANILLA EXTRACT |
| | 2 LARGE EGGS |
| 1¼ CUPS SUGAR, DIVIDED USE | 1 LARGE EGG WHITE |
| ⅔ CUP WATER | |

Preheat oven to 350°F. Spray 10 4-ounce ramekins with nonstick cooking spray.

In a small saucepan combine the flour, salt, ½ cup cocoa powder, and ¾ cup sugar. Add water; stir well with a whisk. Bring to a simmer over medium heat; cook 2 minutes, stirring constantly.

Place chopped chocolate in a large bowl. Pour hot cocoa mixture over chocolate; stir until chocolate melts. Stir in the whiskey and vanilla.

Place the eggs, egg white, and remaining ½ cup sugar in a bowl; beat with a mixer at high speed for 6 minutes. Gently fold the egg mixture into chocolate mixture.

Divide chocolate mixture evenly among prepared ramekins. Place ramekins in a 13x9-inch baking pan. Add hot water to pan to a depth of 1 inch.

Bake 22–25 minutes or until cakes are puffy and set. Serve warm, sifting the reserved 1 tablespoon cocoa powder over the tops. **Makes 10 servings.**

NUTRITION PER SERVING (1 CAKE):
CALORIES 205; FAT 6.0G (POLY .30G, MONO 2.0G, SAT 3.2G);
PROTEIN 3G; CHOLESTEROL 42.3MG; CARBOHYDRATE 38G.

# Chocolate-Chile Lava Cakes

## WITH CASHEW CREMA

*It's all about the interplay between cake, cashews, and spice in this sophisticated dessert. Be careful not to overbake the cakes: the center should be slightly gooey, which will cause the centers to sink in.*

| | |
|---|---|
| 1 CUP ROASTED, LIGHTLY SALTED CASHEWS | 1¾ CUPS PACKED LIGHT BROWN SUGAR, DIVIDED USE |
| ¼ CUP UNSWEETENED COCOA POWDER (NOT DUTCH PROCESS) | 2 OUNCES BITTERSWEET CHOCOLATE, COARSELY CHOPPED |
| ½ TEASPOON ANCHO CHILE POWDER | ½ TEASPOON BAKING POWDER |
| ⅛ TEASPOON CINNAMON | ½ TEASPOON VANILLA EXTRACT |
| PINCH OF GROUND CLOVES | 1 CUP 2% LOW-FAT MILK |
| 2 LARGE EGGS | PINCH OF SALT |
| 5 LARGE EGG WHITES | 1 TABLESPOON POWDERED SUGAR |

Spray the cups of a standard-size 12-muffin pan with nonstick cooking spray.

Process the cashews in a food processor for 3–4 minutes until a crumbly paste forms, scraping sides of bowl as needed (will yield about ½ cup paste).

In the top of a double boiler whisk the cocoa powder, chile powder, cinnamon, cloves, eggs, egg whites, ¼ cup of the cashew paste, and 1¼ cups of the brown sugar until blended. Add the chocolate to the double boiler. Cook over simmering water until chocolate melts and sugar dissolves, about 2–3 minutes.

Remove double boiler from heat. Whisk in the baking powder and vanilla until smooth. Spoon batter into prepared muffin cups. Chill 2 hours.

Process the remaining ¼ cup cashew paste and remaining ½ cup brown sugar in food processor until combined. Add the milk and salt; process until smooth. Strain mixture through a fine-mesh sieve into a small saucepan, discarding solids. Bring to a boil. Reduce heat and simmer 4 minutes until thickened. Remove from heat. Pour into a bowl. Cover and chill.

Preheat oven to 450°F. Bake cakes 8–10 minutes or until almost set (centers will not be firm). Let cool in pan 5 minutes. Invert each cake onto a dessert plate. Dust tops of cakes with powdered sugar and drizzle with the crema. **Makes 12 servings.**

NUTRITION PER SERVING (1 CAKE WITH ABOUT 1½ TABLESPOONS CREMA): CALORIES 247; FAT 8.2G (POLY 1.1G, MONO 4.0G, SAT 2.5G); PROTEIN 5.7G; CHOLESTEROL 37MG; CARBOHYDRATE 41G.

# CHOCOLATE FUDGE—CINNAMON

## Snack Cake

*A wonderfully homey cake that's equally good with a cold glass of skim milk, hot afternoon tea, or for a midafternoon break with a cup of strong-roast coffee.*

NONSTICK BAKING SPRAY WITH FLOUR

½ CUP ALL-PURPOSE FLOUR

½ CUP WHOLE WHEAT PASTRY FLOUR (OR ALL-PURPOSE FLOUR)

½ CUP UNSWEETENED COCOA POWDER (NOT DUTCH PROCESS)

¾ TEASPOON CINNAMON

½ TEASPOON BAKING SODA

¼ TEASPOON SALT

5 TABLESPOONS BUTTER, SOFTENED

1 TEASPOON VANILLA EXTRACT

1¼ CUPS PACKED LIGHT BROWN SUGAR

2 LARGE EGGS

⅔ CUP LOW-FAT BUTTERMILK

1 TABLESPOON POWDERED SUGAR

Preheat oven to 350°F. Spray an 8-inch square baking pan with nonstick baking spray with flour.

In a small bowl whisk the flours, cocoa powder, cinnamon, baking soda, and salt. Place the butter in a large bowl and beat with an electric mixer at medium speed until smooth. Add the vanilla and brown sugar. Beat 3 minutes at medium-high speed. Add the eggs, one at a time, beating well after each addition.

Beating at low speed, add the flour mixture and buttermilk alternately to the butter mixture, beginning and ending with flour mixture. Beat just until smooth. Pour batter into prepared pan.

Bake 30–35 minutes or until a wooden pick inserted in the center comes out clean. Transfer pan to wire rack and cool 10 minutes. Invert cake from pan onto wire rack. Cool completely. Sift powdered sugar over top of cake. **Makes 9 servings.**

NUTRITION PER SERVING (1 PIECE):
CALORIES 258; FAT 8.5G (POLY .50G, MONO 2.4G, SAT 4.9G);
PROTEIN 5G; CHOLESTEROL 64.7MG; CARBOHYDRATE 44G.

# *Cupcakes*

*Extremely fudgy, these exceptionally delicious, very chocolate mouthfuls have an almost ganache-like texture. Extras can be frozen and quickly defrosted for easy additions to the daily lunchbag.*

---

⅔ CUP WATER

⅓ CUP PITTED DATES, COARSELY CHOPPED

⅓ CUP SEEDLESS RAISINS

½ CUP UNSWEETENED COCOA POWDER (NOT DUTCH PROCESS)

2 OUNCES BITTERSWEET CHOCOLATE, COARSELY CHOPPED

6 TABLESPOONS PACKED LIGHT BROWN SUGAR

2 LARGE EGGS

1 TEASPOON VANILLA EXTRACT

½ TEASPOON BAKING SODA

PINCH OF SALT

¼ CUP WHOLE WHEAT PASTRY FLOUR (OR ALL-PURPOSE FLOUR)

1 TABLESPOON POWDERED SUGAR

Preheat oven to 325°F. Spray the 24 cups of a mini muffin pan with nonstick cooking spray (or line with paper liners).

Place the water, dates, and raisins in a medium, heavy-bottomed saucepan. Bring mixture to a boil over medium-high heat.

Transfer mixture (do not drain) to a blender or food processor; add the cocoa powder and chocolate, and pulse to combine. Cool 2 minutes, then add the brown sugar, eggs, vanilla, baking soda, and a pinch of salt to the blender or food processor; purée until smooth. Add flour and pulse just until combined. Divide batter evenly into prepared cups.

Bake 18–22 minutes in middle of oven until a wooden pick or skewer comes out clean. Transfer pan to wire rack and cool 10 minutes, then turn out onto rack. Cool completely, right side up. Just before serving, sprinkle tops lightly with powdered sugar. **Makes 2 dozen mini cupcakes.**

NUTRITION PER SERVING (1 MINI CUPCAKE):
CALORIES 54; FAT 1.4G (POLY .09G, MONO .47G, SAT .69G);
PROTEIN 1.2G; CHOLESTEROL 17.6MG; CARBOHYDRATE 11G.

# FAVORITE DOUBLE-CHOCOLATE

## *Cupcakes*

*These petite cakes are favorites in my kitchen—I almost always have all of the ingredients on hand and I can whip them up in no time. The lack of eggs isn't a misprint; the yogurt and milk do all of the moistening. And because these are not frosted, they make ideal travelers, wonderful for picnics and lunchboxes.*

| | | | |
|---|---|---|---|
| ¾ | CUP ALL-PURPOSE FLOUR | ½ | TEASPOON SALT |
| ¾ | CUP WHOLE WHEAT PASTRY FLOUR (OR ALL-PURPOSE FLOUR) | ¾ | CUP FAT-FREE PLAIN YOGURT |
| ¾ | CUP SUGAR | ⅔ | CUP FAT-FREE MILK |
| ⅓ | CUP UNSWEETENED COCOA POWDER (NOT DUTCH PROCESS) | 1 | TEASPOON VANILLA EXTRACT |
| | | ½ | TEASPOON ALMOND EXTRACT |
| 2 | TEASPOONS BAKING POWDER | 3 | OUNCES BITTERSWEET CHOCOLATE, CHOPPED |
| 1 | TEASPOON BAKING SODA | | OPTIONAL: POWDERED SUGAR |

Preheat oven to 400°F. Place 12 paper muffin cup liners in the cups of a standard-size 12-muffin pan.

In a large bowl whisk the flours, sugar, cocoa powder, baking powder, baking soda, and salt. In a small bowl whisk the yogurt, milk, vanilla, and almond extract until blended. Stir yogurt mixture and chocolate into flour mixture until moistened (do not overmix or cupcakes will be tough).

Fill each of the prepared muffin cups two-thirds full.

Bake 15–20 minutes or until a toothpick comes out clean. Transfer to wire rack and cool 5 minutes. Remove cupcakes from pan and cool completely. If desired, sprinkle tops with powdered sugar. **Makes 1 dozen cupcakes.**

NUTRITION PER SERVING (1 CUPCAKE):
CALORIES 156; FAT 2.7G (POLY .16G, MONO .84G, SAT 1.5G);
PROTEIN 4G; CHOLESTEROL .58MG; CARBOHYDRATE 32G.

# Chocolate Cupcakes

## WITH VANILLA FROSTING

*For kids of all ages, this dessert is oh-so-chocolaty, and comes in a cute package. These cupcakes are likewise a sweet and sophisticated finale—don't forget the espresso—for a dinner party.*

| | |
|---|---|
| 1 CUP SUGAR | 1 TEASPOON BAKING SODA |
| ½ CUP EGG SUBSTITUTE | ½ TEASPOON BAKING POWDER |
| ⅓ CUP CANOLA OIL | ¼ TEASPOON SALT PLUS PINCH OF SALT, DIVIDED USE |
| 1½ TEASPOONS VANILLA EXTRACT, DIVIDED USE | |
| 1 CUP ALL-PURPOSE FLOUR (OR ALL-PURPOSE FLOUR) | 1 CUP LOW-FAT BUTTERMILK |
| | 1 CUP POWDERED SUGAR |
| ½ CUP WHOLE WHEAT PASTRY FLOUR | PINCH OF SALT |
| ⅔ CUP UNSWEETENED DUTCH PROCESS COCOA POWDER | 1 8-OUNCE PACKAGE REDUCED-FAT CREAM CHEESE (NEUFCHATEL), SOFTENED |

Preheat oven to 350°F. Place 16 paper muffin cup liners in the cups of two standard-size 12-muffin pans.

In a large bowl place the sugar, egg substitute, oil, and 1 teaspoon vanilla. Beat 2 minutes with an electric mixer at medium speed until well blended.

In a medium bowl whisk the flours, cocoa powder, baking soda, baking powder, and salt. Stir flour mixture into sugar mixture alternately with buttermilk, beginning and ending with flour mixture. Mix after each addition until just blended. Spoon about 2½ tablespoons batter into each prepared cup.

Bake 17–19 minutes or until a wooden pick inserted in center of a cupcake comes out with moist crumbs attached (do not overbake). Transfer pan to wire rack and cool 5 minutes. Remove cupcakes from pan to wire rack. Cool completely.

To prepare frosting, in a medium bowl combine the powdered sugar, pinch of salt, cream cheese, and remaining ½ teaspoon vanilla. Beat with an electric mixer at medium speed until combined. Increase speed to medium-high, and beat until smooth. Spread about 1 tablespoon frosting on top of each cupcake. **Makes 16 cupcakes.**

NUTRITION PER SERVING (1 CUPCAKE):
CALORIES 214; FAT 8.2G (POLY 1.6G, MONO 3.7G, SAT 2.4G);
PROTEIN 5G; CHOLESTEROL 9.1MG; CARBOHYDRATE 32G.

# *Cupcakes*

*Maple syrup isn't exclusive to New England; Michigan, northern Minnesota, and Wisconsin produce it, too, not to mention Canada. For a more pronounced flavor, choose grade B maple syrup over the more subtle Grade A. No matter which variety used, though, you'll find that the sweet syrup and bittersweet chocolate team up deliciously.*

½ CUP PACKED LIGHT BROWN SUGAR

7 TABLESPOONS BUTTER, SOFTENED, DIVIDED USE

2 TEASPOONS VANILLA EXTRACT, DIVIDED USE

2 TEASPOONS MAPLE EXTRACT, DIVIDED USE

2 LARGE EGGS

1¼ CUPS ALL-PURPOSE FLOUR

1¼ TEASPOONS BAKING POWDER

¼ TEASPOON PLUS PINCH OF SALT, DIVIDED USE

¼ CUP FAT-FREE MILK

7 TABLESPOONS MAPLE SYRUP, DIVIDED USE

2 OUNCES BITTERSWEET CHOCOLATE, FINELY CHOPPED

1½ CUPS POWDERED SUGAR

2 TABLESPOONS UNSWEETENED COCOA POWDER (NOT DUTCH PROCESS)

Preheat oven to 350°F. Place 12 paper muffin cup liners in the cups of a standard-size 12-muffin pan.

In a medium bowl place the brown sugar, 5 tablespoons butter, 1 teaspoon vanilla, and 1 teaspoon maple extract. Beat with an electric mixer at medium speed until well blended, about 4–5 minutes. Add the eggs, one at a time, beating well after each addition.

In a small bowl whisk the flour, baking powder, and ¼ teaspoon salt. In another small bowl combine the milk and 4 tablespoons maple syrup. Add the flour mixture to the sugar mixture alternately with milk mixture, beginning and ending with flour mixture, mixing after each addition. Stir in chopped chocolate. Spoon batter into prepared cups.

Bake 19–22 minutes or until a wooden pick inserted in center comes out clean. Transfer pan to wire rack and cool 5 minutes. Remove cupcakes from pan to wire rack. Cool completely.

For the frosting, beat the remaining 3 tablespoons maple syrup, remaining 2 tablespoons butter, remaining 1 teaspoon vanilla, remaining 1 teaspoon maple extract, and a pinch of salt with an electric mixer at medium speed for 1 minute. Gradually sift in the powdered sugar and cocoa powder, beating just until blended. Spread the frosting over the cooled cupcakes. **Makes 12 cupcakes.**

NUTRITION PER SERVING (1 CUPCAKE):
CALORIES 269; FAT 9.3G (POLY .49G, MONO 2.6G, SAT 5.5G);
PROTEIN 3G; CHOLESTEROL 53.2MG; CARBOHYDRATE 45G.

# BANANA—CHOCOLATE CHIP

## *Mini Bundts*

*These little gems stir up sweet childhood memories of chocolate-coated bananas. I bake the cakes in decorative mini-Bundt pans to make them more like little individual cakes. If you choose, regular muffin cups work just fine, too.*

NONSTICK BAKING SPRAY WITH FLOUR

1½ CUPS WHOLE WHEAT PASTRY FLOUR (OR
    ALL-PURPOSE FLOUR)

1  CUP ALL-PURPOSE FLOUR

1½ TEASPOONS BAKING POWDER

1  TEASPOON GROUND CINNAMON

½  TEASPOON BAKING SODA

¼  TEASPOON SALT

¼  TEASPOON GROUND NUTMEG

1  LARGE EGG

2  LARGE EGG WHITES

1  CUP LOW-FAT BUTTERMILK

⅔  CUP PACKED LIGHT BROWN SUGAR

2  TABLESPOONS (¼ STICK) BUTTER, MELTED

2  TABLESPOONS CANOLA OIL

1  TEASPOON VANILLA EXTRACT

2  CUPS DICED BANANA

3  OUNCES BITTERSWEET CHOCOLATE,
    CHOPPED

Preheat oven to 400°F. Spray twelve ½-cup mini Bundt cake molds with nonstick baking spray with flour.

In a large bowl whisk the flours, baking powder, cinnamon, baking soda, salt, and nutmeg.

Whisk the egg, egg whites, buttermilk, brown sugar, butter, oil, and vanilla in a medium bowl until well combined.

Make a well in the center of the dry ingredients; pour in the wet ingredients and stir until just combined. Add the banana and chocolate. Stir until just combined (do not overmix). Transfer batter to the prepared molds.

Bake 11–13 minutes until a wooden skewer inserted into the center comes out clean.

Transfer molds to wire rack and cool 10 minutes. Turn out cakes onto the wire rack. Cool completely or serve warm. **Makes 12 mini-Bundt cakes.**

NUTRITION PER SERVING (1 CAKE):
CALORIES 250; FAT 7.7G (POLY 1.1G, MONO 2.9G, SAT 3.1G);
PROTEIN 5G; CHOLESTEROL 24MG; CARBOHYDRATE 42G.

# 4. *Chocolate*

## DESSERT DECADENCE

Dark Chocolate Panini, Rich, Old-Fashioned Chocolate Pudding, Chocolate, Caramel, & Rum Flan, Bittersweet Chocolate Mousse, Chocolate Bread Pudding, Cuban Chocolate Natillas, Chocolate Panna Cotta, Tapioca Brulee with Chocolate & Raspberries, Chocolate-Cardamom Pots de Crème, Irish-Chocolate Crème Caramel, Chocolate-Hazelnut Rice Pudding, Chocolate Framboise Milk Shake, Zuppe Inglese Parfaits, Chocolate Soufflés with Raspberry Sauce, Milk Chocolate Crème Brûlée, Cherry-Berry Chocolate Crumbles, Baked Apples with Chocolate, Dried Fruit, & Pecan Stuffing, Chocolate Fudge Ice Cream, Espresso Chip Gelato, Dairy-Free Chocolate Ice Cream, Dark Chocolate Sorbet, Chocolate Earl Grey Sorbet, Chocolate Granita, Bittersweet Chocolate-Mint Sorbet, Grand Marnier-Chocolate Fondue, Poached Pears with Chocolate-Riesling Sauce, Chocolate-Whiskey Fudge Pie, Chocolate Cream Pie with Cinnamon Meringue, French Chocolate Truffle Tart, Café Con Leche & Chocolate Pie, Blueberry-Raspberry Chocolate Schaum Torte, Chocolate Baklava with Honey & Spice, Chocolate Fudge Sauce, Cabernet-Chocolate Fudge Sauce, Chocolate Syrup, Chocolate-Raspberry Sauce, Chocolate-Coconut Sauce, Chocolate-Orange Sauce . . .

# *Panini*

*A chocolate sandwich? Oh yes. Try it once and you'll be instantly—and forever—converted. The bread makes all the difference here, so be picky: choose a fresh, crusty peasant loaf for the best results.*

---

3　TABLESPOONS CANNED FAT-FREE EVAPO-
　RATED MILK

5　BITTERSWEET CHOCOLATE, FINELY
　CHOPPED, DIVIDED USE

1　TABLESPOON LIQUEUR OF CHOICE (E.G.,
　GRAND MARNIER, IRISH CREAM,
　FRANGELICO, OR AMARETTO)

1½ TABLESPOONS EXTRA-VIRGIN OLIVE OIL

8　THIN SLICES CRUSTY PEASANT BREAD

OPTIONAL: PINCH OF FLEUR DE SEL FLAKES
　(SEA SALT FLAKES)

In a small saucepan, heat evaporated milk just until boiling. Add 3 ounces of the chopped chocolate. Let stand for 1 minute. Add the liqueur to the pan and whisk until smooth. Let cool slightly.

Brush olive oil on one side of each slice of bread. Divide the chocolate mixture on the unoiled side of 4 slices, leaving a slight border. Sprinkle with remaining chopped chocolate and a sprinkle of Fleur de Sel. Cover with the remaining slices of bread, oiled-side up, and press lightly.

Cook the sandwiches in a large nonstick skillet over medium-high heat for 1-2 minutes. Turn over, press with a spatula, and cook until nicely browned and the chocolate is barely melted, 30 seconds to 1 minute. Cut sandwiches in half and serve immediately, while still warm. **Makes 8 servings.**

NUTRITION PER SERVING (½ SANDWICH):
CALORIES 154; FAT 9.07G (POLY .55G, MONO 4.1G, SAT 4.1G);
PROTEIN 2G; CHOLESTEROL 0MG; CARBOHYDRATE 18G.

# Chocolate Pudding

*Rich, smooth, and decadent: there's a reason why chocolate pudding is always in fashion.*

| | |
|---|---|
| ½  CUP SUGAR | 2⅓ CUPS 1% LOW-FAT MILK |
| ⅔  CUP UNSWEETENED COCOA POWDER (NOT DUTCH PROCESS) | 1  OUNCE BITTERSWEET CHOCOLATE, CHOPPED |
| 3  TABLESPOONS CORNSTARCH | 1  TEASPOON VANILLA EXTRACT |
| PINCH OF SALT | ⅛  TEASPOON ALMOND EXTRACT |

In a medium, heavy-bottomed saucepan mix the sugar, cocoa powder, cornstarch, and salt. Add 1 cup milk and whisk to dissolve cornstarch. Whisk in remaining milk.

Whisk mixture over medium heat until thickened and beginning to simmer, about 5 minutes. Simmer 1 minute, stirring constantly. Remove from heat. Stir in chocolate, vanilla, and almond extract until chocolate is melted and mixture is smooth.

Divide pudding among 4 custard cups. Cover with plastic wrap, pressing against pudding surface. Chill until cold, about 2 hours. **Makes 4 servings.**

**Cook's Note:** Pudding can be made 1 day ahead. Cover with plastic wrap and keep chilled.

NUTRITION PER SERVING (1 CUSTARD CUP OF PUDDING): CALORIES 247; FAT 5.5G (POLY .18G, MONO 1.8G, SAT 3.3G); PROTEIN 8G; CHOLESTEROL 7.1MG; CARBOHYDRATE 50G.

# CHOCOLATE, CARAMEL, & RUM

## *Flan*

*This delicious last course has the flavor of the islands thanks to a splash of dark rum. It's a great make-ahead dessert for summer barbecues.*

½ CUP SUGAR

1⅓ CUPS 1% LOW-FAT MILK

3½ TABLESPOONS UNSWEETENED COCOA POW-
DER (NOT DUTCH PROCESS)

2 TABLESPOONS DARK RUM

1 TEASPOON VANILLA EXTRACT

2 LARGE EGGS

1 14-OUNCE CAN FAT-FREE SWEETENED
CONDENSED MILK

Preheat oven to 300°F.

Place sugar in a medium, heavy skillet over medium heat; cook until sugar dissolves. Continue cooking an additional 1–2 minutes or until golden. Immediately pour into a 9-inch quiche dish coated with nonstick cooking spray, tipping quickly until caramelized sugar coats bottom of dish.

In a food processor combine the low-fat milk, cocoa powder, rum, vanilla, eggs, and sweetened condensed milk; process mixture until smooth. Pour milk mixture over caramelized syrup in dish. Place dish in a shallow roasting pan, and add hot water to pan to a depth of 1 inch.

Bake 50–55 minutes or until a knife inserted in the center of the flan comes out clean. Remove dish from roasting pan, and cool 30 minutes on a wire rack. Cover flan, and chill at least 3 hours. Place a serving plate upside down on top of dish, and invert flan onto plate. Drizzle any remaining caramelized syrup over the flan. Cut into 9 wedges. **Makes 9 servings.**

NUTRITION PER SERVING (1 WEDGE):
CALORIES 209; FAT 1.7G (POLY .17G, MONO .61G, SAT .73G);
PROTEIN 5G; CHOLESTEROL 49.9MG; CARBOHYDRATE 14G.

# BITTERSWEET
# Chocolate Mousse

*This mousse is so simple to prepare and so delicious—no one ever guesses that tofu is one of the primary ingredients. Experiment and use any favorite liqueur or spirit in place of the crème de cacao: Grand Marnier, Irish Cream, Frangelico, Crème de Menthe, brandy, and whiskey are just a few of the sumptuous options.*

½  CUP SUGAR

7  TABLESPOONS UNSWEETENED COCOA
   POWDER (NOT DUTCH PROCESS)

2  TABLESPOONS CRÈME DE CACAO (CHOCO-
   LATE-FLAVORED LIQUEUR)

1  TEASPOON VANILLA EXTRACT

PINCH OF SALT

2  12.3-OUNCE PACKAGES REDUCED-FAT
   SILKEN TOFU, DRAINED

3  OUNCES BITTERSWEET CHOCOLATE,
   CHOPPED

In a blender or food processor combine the sugar, cocoa powder, crème de cacao, vanilla, salt, and tofu. Process mixture until perfectly smooth.

Place chocolate in a small microwave-safe bowl. Microwave on HIGH 1 minute or until almost melted; remove from microwave and stir until smooth. Add chocolate to tofu mixture in blender or processor and process until smooth.

Divide mousse evenly among six 6-ounce ramekins. Cover and chill at least 1 hour. **Makes 6 servings.**

NUTRITION PER SERVING (1 RAMEKIN OF MOUSSE):
CALORIES 209; FAT 6G (POLY .69G, MONO 1.9G, SAT 3.2G);
PROTEIN 9G; CHOLESTEROL 0MG; CARBOHYDRATE 33G.

# CHOCOLATE
# *Bread Pudding*

*Even if you don't typically eat white bread, use it here. It readily absorbs the cocoa-custard, resulting in a light, tender, and very chocolate pudding.*

⅔ CUP PACKED LIGHT BROWN SUGAR

¾ CUP EGG SUBSTITUTE

2½ CUPS 1% LOW-FAT MILK

½ CUP UNSWEETENED COCOA POWDER (NOT DUTCH PROCESS)

2 OUNCES SEMISWEET CHOCOLATE, FINELY CHOPPED

2 TEASPOONS VANILLA EXTRACT

12 OUNCES (1-INCH) CUBED FRENCH BREAD (ABOUT 10 CUPS)

2 TABLESPOONS SUGAR

OPTIONAL: LIGHT CHOCOLATE OR VANILLA ICE CREAM

In a large bowl whisk the brown sugar and egg substitute. Heat milk over medium-high heat in a small, heavy saucepan until tiny bubbles form around edge (do not boil). Remove from heat and add cocoa powder and chocolate, stirring with a whisk until cocoa dissolves and chocolate melts.

Gradually add hot milk mixture to brown sugar mixture, stirring constantly with a whisk. Whisk in vanilla. Add bread, tossing to coat. Let mixture stand for 30 minutes, tossing occasionally.

Preheat oven to 350°F.

Spoon bread mixture into an 8-inch square baking dish coated with nonstick cooking spray; sprinkle the sugar evenly over bread mixture.

Bake 38–40 minutes or until just set. Cool 10 minutes. Serve warm or cool to room temperature and serve with ice cream, if desired. **Makes 8 servings.**

NUTRITION PER SERVING (⅛ OF BREAD PUDDING):
CALORIES 297; FAT 5.7G (POLY .79G, MONO 1.9G, SAT 2.6G);
PROTEIN 11G; CHOLESTEROL 4.1MG; CARBOHYDRATE 55G.

**Variations**

**Spiked Chocolate Bread Pudding:** Reduce milk to 2¼ cups. Add ¼ cup liqueur or other spirit (e.g., Grand Marnier, Irish Cream, Frangelico, crème de menthe, crème de cacao, brandy, framboise, bourbon, or whiskey) along with the cocoa powder and chocolate.

**Cinnamon-Chocolate Bread Pudding:** Add 1 teaspoon ground cinnamon along with the cocoa powder and chocolate. Also, add ¼ teaspoon cinnamon to the 2 tablespoons sugar before sprinkling over pudding.

# CUBAN CHOCOLATE

# *Natillas*

*Natilla is the Cuban answer to a French pot de crème. This is a great make-ahead dessert, because the puddings need to chill overnight.*

| | |
|---|---|
| 2 LARGE EGGS | ½ TEASPOON CINNAMON |
| 2 LARGE EGG WHITES | ⅛ TEASPOON CAYENNE PEPPER |
| 2¼ CUPS FAT-FREE MILK | ⅛ TEASPOON SALT |
| 1 CUP CANNED FAT-FREE SWEETENED CONDENSED MILK (FROM A 14-OUNCE CAN) | 2.5 OUNCES BITTERSWEET CHOCOLATE, CHOPPED |
| ½ CUP UNSWEETENED COCOA POWDER (NOT DUTCH PROCESS) | 1 TEASPOON VANILLA EXTRACT |

Preheat oven to 350°F. Place eight 4-ounce ramekins in a 13 x 9-inch baking pan.

Whisk the eggs and egg whites in a medium bowl until lightly beaten.

In a medium saucepan combine milk, sweetened condensed milk, cocoa powder, cinnamon, cayenne, and salt. Cook over medium heat for 3 minutes, stirring occasionally. Add chocolate and vanilla, stirring until chocolate melts.

Gradually add ¼ cup hot milk mixture to eggs, stirring constantly with a whisk. Add egg mixture to milk mixture in pan, stirring with a whisk to combine. Pour mixture into the ramekins. Add hot water to the pan to a depth of 1 inch.

Bake for 30–35 minutes or until a knife inserted in the center comes out clean. Remove ramekins from pan; cool completely on a wire rack. Chill 8 hours or overnight. **Makes 8 servings.**

NUTRITION PER SERVING (1 NATILLA):
CALORIES 214; FAT 5.1G (POLY .3G, MONO 1.8G, SAT 2.7G);
PROTEIN 8.9G; CHOLESTEROL 55MG; CARBOHYDRATE 12G.

# Tapioca Brulee

## WITH CHOCOLATE & RASPBERRIES

*In this exquisite little pudding with hidden treasures of melted chocolate and fresh raspberries, tapioca may have its finest hour.*

2   CUPS 1% LOW-FAT MILK

3   TABLESPOONS SUGAR

2   TABLESPOONS INSTANT TAPIOCA

1   LARGE EGG

½   TEASPOON VANILLA EXTRACT

1   CUP RASPBERRIES

2   OUNCES BITTERSWEET CHOCOLATE, CHOPPED

4   TEASPOONS BROWN SUGAR

Combine the milk, sugar, and tapioca in small, heavy-bottomed saucepan. Let stand 5 minutes. Whisk in egg and vanilla. Stir over medium heat until mixture thickens and comes to boil. Cool.

Divide raspberries and chocolate among four 4-ounce ramekins. Spoon tapioca over berries and chocolate; smooth tops. Loosely cover and chill overnight.

Preheat broiler. Sprinkle 1 teaspoon brown sugar over each pudding. Broil until brown sugar melts and bubbles. Refrigerate until sugar hardens, at least 15 minutes. Serve. **Makes 4 servings.**

NUTRITION PER SERVING (1 RAMEKIN OF CUSTARD):
CALORIES 206; FAT 5.6G (POLY .3G, MONO 1.8G, SAT 3.3G);
PROTEIN 5G; CHOLESTEROL 6.1MG; CARBOHYDRATE 37G.

# Chocolate Panna Cotta

## WITH TART CHERRY SAUCE

*I am something of a panna cotta apostle: I attempt to convince one and all to make it. Why? Because it is one of the simplest desserts to prepare, yet it has a tremendous "wow" factor. A delicate slip of a custard traditionally made with cream, gelatin, and sugar, it is lightened here with reduced-fat milk products and intensified with unsweetened cocoa powder. The tart cherry sauce is an elegant match. Chocolate Fudge Sauce (see page 206) is a decadent substitute for the cherry sauce.*

| | |
|---|---|
| ¼ CUP WATER | ½ CUP SUGAR |
| 2 TEASPOONS UNFLAVORED GELATIN | 1 CUP REDUCED-FAT (NOT FAT-FREE) SOUR |
| 2¼ CUPS CANNED EVAPORATED FAT-FREE MILK | CREAM |
| (FROM 2 12-OUNCE CANS) | ½ TEASPOON VANILLA EXTRACT |
| ½ CUP UNSWEETENED COCOA POWDER (NOT | 1 RECIPE TART CHERRY SAUCE (SEE NEXT |
| DUTCH PROCESS) | PAGE) |

Place water in a small bowl. Sprinkle gelatin over water. Let stand 5 minutes to soften gelatin.

In a medium, heavy-bottomed saucepan place the evaporated milk, cocoa powder, and sugar. Bring to a simmer over medium-high heat, stirring until sugar is dissolved; remove from heat. Whisk in gelatin mixture until blended and gelatin is dissolved. Whisk in sour cream and vanilla until blended.

Ladle or pour mixture into eight ¾-cup custard cups, ramekins, or small molds. Loosely cover with plastic wrap and chill 4 hours or up to overnight.

Cut around edges of each panna cotta to loosen. Set each cup in shallow bowl of hot water for 10 seconds. Immediately invert each onto a plate. Serve each with 2½ tablespoons Tart Cherry Sauce. **Makes 8 servings.**

# TART CHERRY SAUCE

| | |
|---|---|
| 1 | CUP DRIED TART CHERRIES |
| 1½ | CUPS PLUS 1 TABLESPOON WATER, DIVIDED USE |
| 2 | TABLESPOONS SUGAR |
| 1 | TEASPOON CORNSTARCH |
| ½ | TEASPOON VANILLA EXTRACT |
| ¼ | TEASPOON ALMOND EXTRACT |

Combine the cherries and 1½ cups water in a medium saucepan; bring to a boil. Reduce heat, and simmer 20 minutes. Stir in sugar and simmer 5 minutes. Combine remaining 1 tablespoon water and cornstarch in a small bowl until combined. Add mixture to saucepan; bring to a boil. Cook 1 minute or until slightly thick, stirring constantly.

Remove from heat and stir in vanilla and almond extract. Cool completely.

NUTRITION PER SERVING (1 PANNA COTTA WITH 2½ TABLESPOONS SAUCE):
CALORIES 183; FAT 4.0G (POLY .18G, MONO .19G, SAT 2.4G);
PROTEIN 8G; CHOLESTEROL 12.9MG; CARBOHYDRATE 33G.

# CHOCOLATE-CARDAMOM

# *Pots de Crème*

*I have developed a lot of recipes over the years, but the ones I make over and over are the ones I like best—which means the easy-to-make ones, like these refined pots de crème. Pots de crème are creamy custards served in tiny cups. This one is best served chilled, so plan on making the night before serving.*

---

| | |
|---|---|
| 2 LARGE EGGS | ¾ TEASPOON GROUND CARDAMOM |
| 2½ CUPS FAT-FREE MILK | ⅛ TEASPOON SALT |
| ⅔ CUP SUGAR | 1 TEASPOON VANILLA EXTRACT |
| 5 TABLESPOONS UNSWEETENED COCOA POWDER (NOT DUTCH PROCESS) | 3 OUNCES BITTERSWEET CHOCOLATE, CHOPPED |

Preheat oven to 350°F.

In a medium bowl, whisk the eggs until lightly beaten.

In a medium saucepan combine the milk, sugar, cocoa powder, cardamom, and salt. Cook over medium heat until sugar dissolves, stirring occasionally (about 3 minutes). Stir in the vanilla and chocolate, stirring until chocolate melts.

Gradually add ¼ cup hot milk mixture to eggs, stirring constantly with a whisk. Add egg mixture to milk mixture in pan, stirring with a whisk to combine. Pour into eight 4-ounce ramekins. Place ramekins in a 13 x 9-inch baking pan. Add hot water to pan to a depth of 1 inch.

Bake 32–35 minutes or until a knife inserted in the center comes out clean. Remove ramekins from pan; cool completely on a wire rack. Chill 8 hours or overnight. **Makes 8 servings.**

NUTRITION PER SERVING ( 1 CUSTARD):
CALORIES 278; FAT 5.2G (POLY .3G, MONO 1.8G, SAT 2.7G);
PROTEIN 16G; CHOLESTEROL 60.4MG; CARBOHYDRATE 45G.

# Crème Caramel

*France and Ireland come together in delicious harmony in this crème caramel. Also known in France as crème renversée, crème caramel is a custard baked in a caramel-coated mold. Once chilled, the custard is turned out onto a serving plate, caramel sauce and all. The additions of chocolate and Irish cream liqueur increase the "ooh-la-la".*

½ CUP SUGAR

4 LARGE EGGS

1 TEASPOON VANILLA EXTRACT

2 TABLESPOONS IRISH CREAM LIQUEUR
(E.G., BAILEY'S)

½ CUP UNSWEETENED COCOA POWDER (NOT
DUTCH PROCESS)

1 14-OUNCE CAN FAT-FREE SWEETENED
CONDENSED MILK

1 12-OUNCE CAN FAT-FREE EVAPORATED
MILK

Preheat oven to 350°F.

Pour sugar into a 9-inch round metal cake pan. Place cake pan over medium heat. Cook 6 minutes or until sugar is dissolved and golden, shaking cake pan occasionally with tongs. Immediately remove from heat; set aside.

Place eggs in a medium bowl; stir with a whisk until foamy. Whisk in the vanilla, Irish cream liqueur, cocoa powder, condensed milk, and evaporated milk until blended and smooth

Pour milk mixture into prepared cake pan. Cover with foil and place in a large shallow roasting pan. Place roasting pan in oven; add water to a depth of 1 inch.

Bake 50–55 minutes or until a knife inserted in the center comes out clean.

Remove cake pan from water and transfer to a wire rack. Remove foil. Let custard cool in cake pan 30 minutes. Loosen edges with a knife or rubber spatula. Place a serving plate upside down on top of cake pan and invert custard onto plate, allowing syrup to drizzle over custard. Cut into 9 wedges. **Makes 9 servings.**

NUTRITION PER SERVING (1 WEDGE):
CALORIES 253; FAT 3.4G (POLY .35G, MONO 1.2G, SAT 1.4G);
PROTEIN 7G; CHOLESTEROL 97.1MG; CARBOHYDRATE 16G.

# CHOCOLATE-HAZELNUT

## *Rice Pudding*

*This refined rice pudding has the flavors of Gianduia, a classic Italian combination of chocolate and hazelnuts. The recipe calls for Arborio rice, the traditional rice for risotto, which releases starch as it cooks, yielding a creamy rice pudding—without the cream. Rich, chocolate-y, and laced with hazelnut liqueur, it is Italian through and through.*

3½ CUPS 1% LOW-FAT MILK

½ CUP UNCOOKED ARBORIO RICE

6 TABLESPOONS PACKED LIGHT BROWN SUGAR

⅓ CUP UNSWEETENED COCOA POWDER (NOT DUTCH PROCESS)

¼ TEASPOON SALT

1 LARGE EGG

2 TABLESPOONS HAZELNUT-FLAVORED LIQUEUR (E.G., FRANGELICO)

1 TABLESPOON UNSALTED BUTTER

2 OUNCES BITTERSWEET CHOCOLATE, FINELY CHOPPED

1 TEASPOON VANILLA EXTRACT

OPTIONAL: 3 TABLESPOONS CHOPPED HAZELNUTS, TOASTED

In a medium saucepan combine the milk, Arborio rice, brown sugar, cocoa powder, and salt; bring to a boil, stirring frequently. Reduce heat and simmer, uncovered, for 20 minutes, stirring occasionally.

Place egg in a medium bowl and lightly beat with fork until slightly frothy. Gradually stir about one-fourth of hot rice mixture into egg mixture. Return egg-rice mixture to pan, stirring constantly. Simmer, uncovered, 20 minutes or until mixture is thick and rice is tender, stirring occasionally. Remove from heat; add liqueur, butter, chocolate, and vanilla, stirring until butter and chocolate are melted.

Spoon pudding into six ¾-cup ramekins and sprinkle each with 1½ teaspoons hazelnuts, if desired. Serve warm or cool to room temperature. **Makes 6 servings.**

NUTRITION PER SERVING (1 RAMEKIN OF PUDDING):
CALORIES 276; FAT 7.7G (POLY .38G, MONO 2.4G, SAT 4.5G);
PROTEIN 8G; CHOLESTEROL 47.5MG; CARBOHYDRATE 45G.

# CHOCOLATE FRAMBOISE
# *Milk Shake*

*Easygoing, elegant, and fun, this milkshake has everything going for it.*

2   CUPS VANILLA LOW-FAT ICE CREAM

¾   CUP FROZEN UNSWEETENED RASPBERRIES
    (DO NOT THAW)

½   CUP 1% LOW-FAT MILK

2   TABLESPOONS RASPBERRY LIQUEUR

2   TABLESPOONS UNSWEETENED COCOA POW-
    DER (NOT DUTCH PROCESS)

Place all ingredients in a blender and process on high speed until smooth. Pour into two chilled glasses and serve immediately. **Makes 2 servings.**

NUTRITION PER SERVING (1 GLASS):
CALORIES 241; FAT 4.6G (POLY .35G, MONO 1.1G, SAT 2.7G);
PROTEIN 8G; CHOLESTEROL 21.3MG; CARBOHYDRATE 39G.

## ZUPPE INGLESE

# Parfaits

The origin of this extravagant dessert, which resembles an English trifle (the name translates as "English soup"), is most likely with the homesick Victorians who fled the cold English climate for the warmth of Italy. In this enlightened version, the custard "soup" is chocolate and packaged ladyfingers take the place of homemade sponge cake.

| | |
|---|---|
| ½ CUP SUGAR | ½ TEASPOON ALMOND EXTRACT |
| ⅓ CUP UNSWEETENED COCOA POWDER (NOT DUTCH PROCESS) | 1½ CUPS FROZEN REDUCED-CALORIE WHIPPED TOPPING, THAWED, DIVIDED USE |
| 3 TABLESPOONS CORNSTARCH | 20 PACKAGED SOFT LADYFINGERS |
| 1 LARGE EGG | 3 TABLESPOONS CHERRY PRESERVES |
| 2½ CUPS FAT-FREE MILK | 8 FRESH MINT LEAVES, FOR GARNISH |
| 2 TABLESPOONS UNSALTED BUTTER | |

In a medium bowl whisk the sugar, cocoa powder, cornstarch, and egg until well blended; set aside.

Heat milk over medium-high heat in a medium, heavy-bottomed saucepan to 180°F or until tiny bubbles form around edge (do not boil). Remove from heat. Gradually add ¼ of hot milk to sugar mixture, stirring constantly with whisk; return to pan of remaining milk. Add butter, and cook over medium heat 5 minutes or until thickened and bubbly, stirring constantly. Reduce heat to low and cook an additional 2 minutes, stirring constantly.

Remove from heat and stir in almond extract. Pour into a medium bowl. Cover surface with plastic wrap, and let cool completely. Uncover and gently fold in 1 cup whipped topping; cover and chill at least 2 hours.

Split ladyfingers in half lengthwise. Line each of 8 dessert compotes with 5 ladyfinger halves, standing upright. Spoon ½ cup custard into center of each compote. Melt preserves, and drizzle over custard. Top each serving with 1 tablespoon of the remaining whipped topping. Garnish with mint leaves. **Makes 8 servings.**

NUTRITION PER SERVING (1 PARFAIT):CALORIES 279; FAT 8.4G (POLY .69G, MONO 2.4G, SAT 4.9G); PROTEIN 7.3G; CHOLESTEROL 136.3MG; CARBOHYDRATE 45G.

# MILK CHOCOLATE

## *Crème Brûlée*

*A small amount of cocoa powder lends these custards a delicate, milk chocolate flavor. To give the custards their caramelized-sugar shells, I recommend using a small kitchen torch. Make the custards one to two days before serving—the well-chilled custard will hold up especially well to the heat of the torch.*

| | |
|---|---|
| 2 CUPS 2% LOW-FAT MILK | 2 TABLESPOONS UNSWEETENED COCOA |
| ¾ CUP DRY NONFAT MILK POWDER | POWDER (NOT DUTCH PROCESS) |
| 4 TABLESPOONS PACKED LIGHT BROWN | PINCH OF SALT |
| SUGAR, DIVIDED USE | 4 LARGE EGG YOLKS |
| 1 TEASPOON VANILLA EXTRACT | 4 TABLESPOONS SUGAR |

Combine the milk, dry milk, and 3 tablespoons brown sugar in a medium saucepan. Heat mixture over medium heat to 180°F or until tiny bubbles form around edge (do not boil), stirring occasionally. Remove milk mixture from heat. Cool 20 minutes, then whisk in vanilla.

Preheat oven to 300°F.

In a medium bowl combine remaining 1 tablespoon brown sugar, cocoa powder, salt, and egg yolks, stirring well with a whisk.

Gradually whisk milk mixture into egg mixture, whisking constantly. Divide the mixture evenly among four 4-ounce ramekins, custard cups, or shallow baking dishes. Place ramekins in a 13 x 9-inch baking pan, and add hot water to pan to a depth of ½ inch.

Bake 22–25 minutes or until center barely moves when ramekin is touched. Remove ramekins from pan; cool completely on a wire rack. Cover and chill at least 4 hours or overnight.

Sift 1 tablespoon sugar evenly over each custard. Holding a kitchen torch about 2 inches from the top of each custard, heat the sugar, moving the torch back and forth, until sugar is completely melted and caramelized (about 1 minute). Serve immediately or within 1 hour. **Makes 4 servings.**

NUTRITION PER SERVING (1 CUSTARD):
CALORIES 312; FAT 7.5G (POLY .74G, MONO 2.2G, SAT 3.5G);
PROTEIN 16G; CHOLESTEROL 224.1MG; CARBOHYDRATE 47G.

# Chocolate Soufflés

## WITH RASPBERRY SAUCE

*To relieve any stress of delivering the soufflés from oven to dining room table, have everyone gather in the kitchen; they'll ooh and ahh when the desserts emerge with their glorious poufs. And to make things even simpler on yourself, make the soufflé batter in advance: you can spoon it into the ramekins and refrigerate it for up to 24 hours before baking.*

| | |
|---|---|
| 2 CUPS FRESH RASPBERRIES OR FROZEN (THAWED) UNSWEETENED RASPBERRIES | ½ CUP COLD WATER |
| 2 TABLESPOONS HONEY | 4 LARGE EGG WHITES, ROOM TEMPERATURE |
| ½ TEASPOON FRESH LEMON JUICE | OPTIONAL: ¼ TEASPOON GROUND CARDAMOM |
| 1 CUP POWDERED SUGAR | ⅛ TEASPOON CREAM OF TARTAR |
| ½ CUP UNSWEETENED COCOA POWDER (NOT DUTCH PROCESS) | 4 TEASPOONS SUGAR |
| 2 TABLESPOONS ALL-PURPOSE FLOUR | 3 LARGE EGG YOLKS, ROOM TEMPERATURE |
| ½ CUP 2% LOW-FAT MILK | ½ TEASPOON ALMOND EXTRACT |

To make the raspberry sauce, blend the raspberries, honey, and lemon juice in a food processor or blender. If desired, strain through a mesh sieve to remove seeds. Cover and chill until ready to use.

Preheat oven to 350°F. Spray the bottoms of eight 10-ounce straight-sided ramekins with nonstick cooking spray.

Whisk the powdered sugar, cocoa powder and flour in the top of a double boiler. Whisk the milk and cold water into the pan until blended and smooth. Continue to gently whisk the mixture without stopping for about 8–10 minutes or until it begins to thicken. Remove the pan from the heat and set aside.

Beat the egg whites, cardamom, if desired, and cream of tartar in a large bowl with an electric mixer on high until peaks begin to form. Gradually add the sugar, beating until stiff peaks form.

Whisk the egg yolks and almond extract into the cocoa mixture. Fold in half the egg-white mixture, then fold in the rest. Spoon the batter into the prepared ramekins, leaving about a ½-inch space from the top. Place the ramekins on a baking sheet.

Bake the soufflés 16–18 minutes or until puffy but still slightly jiggly at the center.

Spoon the raspberry sauce over each soufflé and serve. **Makes 8 servings.**

NUTRITION PER SERVING (1 SOUFFLÉ AND 3 TABLESPOONS SAUCE):
CALORIES 158; FAT 3.1G (POLY .42G, MONO 1.1G, SAT 1.1G);
PROTEIN 5G; CHOLESTEROL 80.5MG; CARBOHYDRATE 31G.

# *Chocolate Crumbles*

*A delicious and colorful crumble, warm from the oven, is priceless in the chilly months of the year. You can't do much better than this tart-sweet cherry-berry filling topped with a buttery chocolate topping.*

¾ CUP WATER

½ CUP SUGAR

1 12-OUNCE BAG FRESH OR FROZEN CRAN-
   BERRIES, THAWED

⅓ CUP CHERRY PRESERVES

2 OUNCES BITTERSWEET CHOCOLATE, FINELY
   CHOPPED

⅓ CUP WHOLE WHEAT PASTRY FLOUR (OR
   ALL-PURPOSE FLOUR)

⅓ CUP OLD-FASHIONED OATS

2 TABLESPOONS UNSWEETENED COCOA
   POWDER (NOT DUTCH PROCESS)

¼ CUP FIRMLY PACKED LIGHT BROWN SUGAR

3 TABLESPOONS BUTTER, MELTED

Preheat oven to 350°F. Place six 6-ounce custard cups on a baking sheet. Spray the cups with nonstick cooking spray.

Combine the water, sugar, and cranberries in a medium saucepan; bring to a boil. Reduce heat, and simmer for 10 minutes, stirring occasionally. Remove from heat; stir in the preserves. Divide mixture evenly among the prepared custard cups. Sprinkle with chocolate chips.

In a small bowl combine flour, oats, cocoa powder, brown sugar, and melted butter; toss well. Sprinkle oat mixture evenly over cranberry mixture.

Bake for 18–21 minutes or until bubbly. Cool at least 15 minutes. Serve warm or at room temperature. **Makes 6 servings.**

NUTRITION PER SERVING (1 CUSTARD CUP OF CRUMBLE):
CALORIES 321; FAT 9.6G (POLY .58G, MONO 2.7G, SAT 5.6);
PROTEIN 3G; CHOLESTEROL 15.3MG; CARBOHYDRATE 59G.

# Baked Apples

## WITH CHOCOLATE, DRIED FRUIT, & PECAN STUFFING

*Equally delicious for breakfast as for dessert, this new take on baked apples is enlivened with chocolate and the flavors of fall.*

| | | | |
|---|---|---|---|
| 4 | 6-OUNCE RED APPLES SUCH AS GALA OR ROME BEAUTY | 1 | TABLESPOON UNSWEETENED COCOA POWDER (NOT DUTCH PROCESS) |
| 1 | TABLESPOON FRESH LEMON JUICE | ¼ | TEASPOON CINNAMON |
| 3 | TABLESPOONS FINELY CHOPPED DRIED APRICOTS | ⅛ | TEASPOON GROUND NUTMEG |
| 1 | OUNCE BITTERSWEET CHOCOLATE, CHOPPED | 1 | TABLESPOON UNSALTED BUTTER (½ TABLESPOON SOFTENED AND ½ TABLESPOON CUT INTO 4 PIECES) |
| 2 | TABLESPOONS DRIED CRANBERRIES OR RAISINS | ½ | CUP APPLE CIDER |
| 2 | TABLESPOONS CHOPPED PECANS, TOASTED | ¼ | TEASPOON VANILLA EXTRACT |
| 2 | TABLESPOONS PACKED DARK BROWN SUGAR | ½ | CUP LOW-FAT VANILLA YOGURT |

Preheat oven to 350°F.

Core apples with an apple corer. Stand apples up and make 4 evenly spaced vertical cuts starting from top of each apple and stopping halfway from bottom to keep apple intact. Brush inside of apples with lemon juice and stand apples in a 9-inch ceramic or glass pie plate.

In a small bowl combine the apricots, chocolate, cranberries, pecans, brown sugar, cocoa powder, cinnamon, and nutmeg. Rub ½ tablespoon of the softened butter into dried-fruit mixture with fingers until combined well. Pack the centers of each apple with mixture. Put a piece of remaining butter on top of each apple. Mix the cider and vanilla in a small cup and pour around apples. Cover pie plate tightly with foil.

Bake in middle of oven 40–45 minutes, basting once, until apples are just tender when pierced with a fork. Remove foil and continue to bake until apples are very tender but not falling apart, 20–25 minutes more.

Transfer apples to serving dishes and spoon sauce over and around apples. Serve with dollops of yogurt. **Makes 4 servings.**

NUTRITION PER SERVING (1 APPLE, SAUCE, AND 2 TABLESPOONS YOGURT): CALORIES 255; FAT 3G (POLY 1G, MONO 3G, SAT 3.7G); PROTEIN 3G; CHOLESTEROL 9.2MG; CARBOHYDRATE 47G.

## CHOCOLATE FUDGE

# *Ice Cream*

*I tweaked a traditional chocolate fudge ice cream recipe with cocoa powder in place of melted unsweetened chocolate and fat-free sweetened condensed milk in place of the full-fat variety, and the amazing result knocked me out.*

2   CUPS WHOLE MILK, DIVIDED USE

½   CUP PLUS 1 TABLESPOON UNSWEETENED COCOA POWDER (NOT DUTCH PROCESS)

1   CUP CANNED FAT-FREE SWEETENED CONDENSED MILK (FROM 1 14-OUNCE CAN)

2   TEASPOONS VANILLA EXTRACT

1   12-OUNCE CAN EVAPORATED LOW-FAT MILK

PINCH OF SALT

Heat 1 cup milk in a heavy saucepan over medium-high heat to 180° or until tiny bubbles form around edge (do not boil). Remove from heat and whisk in the cocoa powder until dissolved. Cool to room temperature.

Process the sweetened condensed milk, vanilla, evaporated milk, salt, and remaining cup whole milk in a blender until smooth. Add cocoa mixture and pulse to blend.

Pour mixture into the freezer can of an ice cream freezer; freeze according to manufacturer's instructions. **Makes 10 servings**.

NUTRITION PER SERVING (½ CUP):
CALORIES 161; FAT 2.8G (POLY .12G, MONO .6G, SAT 1.7G);
PROTEIN 5G; CHOLESTEROL 7.2MG; CARBOHYDRATE 6G.

# ESPRESSO CHIP

## Gelato

*Gelato gets a wake-up call with a dose of instant espresso powder and the uber-flavor of premium bittersweet chocolate.*

| | |
|---|---|
| ½ CUP 1% LOW-FAT MILK | 2½ TEASPOONS INSTANT ESPRESSO POWDER |
| 2 TABLESPOONS CORNSTARCH | 1 TEASPOON VANILLA EXTRACT |
| ⅓ CUP PACKED LIGHT BROWN SUGAR | PINCH OF SALT |
| 1 TABLESPOON UNSWEETENED COCOA POWDER (NOT DUTCH PROCESS) | 2 OUNCES BITTERSWEET CHOCOLATE, FINELY CHOPPED, DIVIDED USE |
| 1 12-OUNCE CAN FAT-FREE EVAPORATED MILK | |

In a small bowl stir together the low-fat milk and cornstarch until blended and smooth.

In a small, heavy-bottomed saucepan set over medium heat whisk the brown sugar, cocoa powder, and evaporated milk, stirring until mixture comes to a boil. Whisk in the espresso powder. Stir cornstarch mixture again and whisk into espresso mixture. Return to a boil, whisking, then remove from heat.

Add vanilla, a pinch of salt, and 1 ounce chocolate to saucepan, stirring. Set saucepan in a large bowl of ice water to cool, whisking frequently.

Freeze chocolate mixture in ice cream maker. When nearly frozen, add remaining chocolate and churn until blended. **Makes 4 servings.**

NUTRITION PER SERVING (½ CUP):
CALORIES 242; FAT 4.9G (POLY .16G, MONO 1.6G, SAT 2.9G);
PROTEIN 9G; CHOLESTEROL 5.4MG; CARBOHYDRATE 43G.

# Chocolate Ice Cream

*I've used this recipe to convert many to tofu—perhaps because you would never know that it's in there. All that you taste is rich, chocolate fudge, but with a fraction of the fat of regular ice cream. You can vary the flavor quite easily, too—a teaspoon of espresso powder, a bit of spice, or peppermint extract in place of vanilla. Use your imagination to create your own unique blend.*

16 OUNCES SILKEN TOFU, DRAINED

1 CUP PACKED LIGHT BROWN SUGAR

1 CUP PLAIN, UNSWEETENED SOY MILK

½ CUP UNSWEETENED COCOA POWDER (NOT DUTCH PROCESS)

1 TABLESPOON VANILLA EXTRACT

PINCH OF SALT

In blender, purée all ingredients in 2 equal batches until very smooth.

Pour mixture into the freezer can of an ice cream freezer; freeze according to manufacturer's instructions. **Makes 10 servings.**

NUTRITION PER SERVING (½ CUP):
CALORIES 161; FAT 2.8G (POLY .12G, MONO .6G, SAT 1.7G);
PROTEIN 5G; CHOLESTEROL 7.2MG; CARBOHYDRATE 6G.

# ORANGE & CHOCOLATE BUTTERMILK

# *Sherbet*

*Inspired by the bright orange sherbet of my youth, this deeply flavored chocolate interpretation proves how delicious a low-fat dessert can be.*

2 CUPS LOW-FAT BUTTERMILK

¾ CUP LIGHT CORN SYRUP

1 TABLESPOON FINELY GRATED ORANGE ZEST

⅓ CUP UNSWEETENED COCOA POWDER (NOT DUTCH PROCESS)

¼ CUP FRESHLY SQUEEZED ORANGE JUICE

¼ CUP SUGAR

Blend all ingredients in a blender or food processor until sugar is dissolved. Refrigerate, covered, until cold, at least 2 hours.

Freeze mixture in ice cream maker according to manufacturer's directions. Transfer to an airtight container and freeze until hardened. **Makes 8 servings.**

**Cook's Note:** The buttermilk mixture can be refrigerated for up to 24 hours; the sherbet can be made up to 1 week ahead.

NUTRITION PER SERVING (½ CUP):
CALORIES 150; FAT 1.1G (POLY .04G, MONO .32G, SAT .62G);
PROTEIN 3G; CHOLESTEROL 2.5MG; CARBOHYDRATE 36G.

# DARK CHOCOLATE

## *Sorbet*

*Combining five basic ingredients with wonderfully chocolate depth, this sorbet is sure to become one of your standbys. Not only is it easy to prepare, but you've likely got all the ingredients in your pantry.*

2   CUPS WATER

¾   CUP SUGAR

½   CUP UNSWEETENED COCOA POWDER (NOT
     DUTCH PROCESS)

1½ TEASPOONS INSTANT ESPRESSO POWDER

1   TEASPOON VANILLA EXTRACT

Whisk the water, sugar, and cocoa powder in a medium, heavy-bottomed saucepan over medium-high heat until sugar dissolves and mixture comes to a boil. Stir in espresso powder and vanilla. Remove from heat and transfer to a bowl. Cover and chill until cold.

Transfer mixture to ice cream maker and process according to manufacturer's instructions. Transfer sorbet to a container and freeze until firm. **Makes 4 servings.**

**Cook's Notes:** The sorbet can be prepared 3 days ahead. Transfer to a covered container and keep frozen. For a denser, more solid consistency to the sorbet, transfer the prepared sorbet to a covered container and freeze 30 minutes before serving.

NUTRITION PER SERVING (½ CUP):
CALORIES 170; FAT 1.5G (POLY .05G, MONO.49G, SAT .87G);
PROTEIN 2.1G; CHOLESTEROL 0MG; CARBOHYDRATE 43G.

# CHOCOLATE

# *Earl Grey Sorbet*

*Loose tea leaves tend to be of higher quality than tea in bags, giving the sorbet a distinct, aromatic flavor—with sophisticated notes of bergamot—that marries beautifully with the chocolate.*

4   CUPS WATER

1   CUP SUGAR

2   TABLESPOONS LOOSE EARL GRAY TEA
    LEAVES

1   CUP UNSWEETENED COCOA POWDER (NOT
    DUTCH PROCESS)

1   OUNCE BITTERSWEET CHOCOLATE, FINELY
    CHOPPED

Bring water and sugar to a boil in a large saucepan. Add the tea leaves and remove from the heat. Cover the pan and steep for 15 minutes.

Strain tea and discard the leaves. Return tea to pan. Place pan over medium-high heat and slowly add cocoa powder, whisking until smooth. Bring to a boil, reduce heat to low and simmer until the mixture thickens slightly, about 20 minutes.

Remove pan from heat. Add chocolate and stir until completely melted and smooth. Pass through a strainer into a medium bowl. Cover and refrigerate until thoroughly chilled, at least 2 hours.

Transfer the mixture to an ice cream maker and freeze according to manufacturer's directions. **Makes 6 servings.**

**Cook's Notes:** The sorbet can be prepared 3 days ahead. Transfer to a covered container and keep frozen. For a denser, more solid consistency to the sorbet, transfer the prepared sorbet to a covered container and freeze 30 minutes before serving.

NUTRITION PER SERVING (½ CUP):
CALORIES 185; FAT 3.4G (POLY .11G, MONO 1.1G, SAT 2.1G);
PROTEIN 3G; CHOLESTEROL 0MG; CARBOHYDRATE 44G.

# Chocolate Granita

*This method is faster than traditional methods of making granita, which involve freezing and scraping the cocoa mixture every 30 minutes. I actually find the texture of this version preferable: less icy and more slushy than the traditional.*

4   CUPS WATER

⅔   CUP SUGAR

1   CUP UNSWEETENED COCOA POWDER (NOT DUTCH PROCESS)

In a medium saucepan, combine the water, sugar, and cocoa powder. Cook over medium-low heat just until mixture starts to bubble at edges. Cook, whisking, until slightly thickened, about 1 minute. Cool.

Pour the granita mixture into ice trays, cover with plastic wrap, and allow to freeze solid.

Just before serving, place the cubes in a food processor. Process until almost smooth. Spoon into serving dishes and serve immediately. **Makes 6 servings.**

NUTRITION PER SERVING (½ CUP):
CALORIES 119; FAT 2G (POLY .06G, MONO .66G, SAT 1.2G);
PROTEIN 3G; CHOLESTEROL 0MG; CARBOHYDRATE 30G.

# BITTERSWEET
# *Chocolate-Mint Sorbet*

*The symphony of chocolate and peppermint in this sublime sorbet is worthy of a standing ovation.*

2½ CUPS WATER

1¼ CUPS SUGAR

½ CUP UNSWEETENED COCOA POWDER (NOT DUTCH PROCESS)

3 OUNCES BITTERSWEET CHOCOLATE, FINELY CHOPPED

1 TEASPOON VANILLA EXTRACT

¾ TEASPOON PURE PEPPERMINT EXTRACT

Bring water to a boil in a medium saucepan set over high heat. Stir in sugar and cocoa powder; reduce heat and simmer 5 minutes, stirring frequently. Remove from heat and add the chocolate, vanilla, and peppermint extract, stirring until chocolate melts. Cover and chill completely.

Transfer the mixture to an ice cream maker and freeze according to manufacturer's directions. **Makes 6 servings.**

**Cook's Notes:** The sorbet can be prepared 3 days ahead. Transfer to a covered container and keep frozen. For a denser, more solid consistency to the sorbet, transfer the prepared sorbet to a covered container and freeze 30 minutes before serving.

NUTRITION PER SERVING (½ CUP):
CALORIES 246; FAT 5.2G (POLY 1.7G, MONO 1.7G, SAT 3.1G);
PROTEIN 2G; CHOLESTEROL 0MG; CARBOHYDRATE 55G.

# *Fondue*

*Quite possibly the perfect date dessert, fondue is fun, festive, and interactive: bananas, straw-berries and angel food cake stand up deliciously to this silky dark-chocolate interpretation spiked with a double shot of Grand Marnier.*

⅔ CUP FAT-FREE EVAPORATED MILK (FROM A
    12-OUNCE CAN)

6 OUNCES BITTERSWEET CHOCOLATE,
    CHOPPED

1⅓ CUPS POWDERED SUGAR, SIFTED

3 TABLESPOONS UNSWEETENED COCOA POW-
    DER (NOT DUTCH PROCESS)

¼ CUP ORANGE LIQUEUR (E.G., GRAND
    MARNIER)

2 TABLESPOONS DARK CORN SYRUP

2 TEASPOONS GRATED ORANGE ZEST

4 CUPS (1-INCH) CUBED PURCHASED ANGEL
    FOOD CAKE

2 CUPS SLICED BANANA

2 CUPS QUARTERED STRAWBERRIES

Combine the evaporated milk and chocolate in a medium saucepan. Cook over medium-low heat for 5 minutes or until smooth, stirring constantly. Stir in the powdered sugar, cocoa powder, orange liqueur, corn syrup, and orange zest until blended.

Cook for 10 minutes or until the mixture is smooth, stirring constantly. Pour into a fondue pot. Keep warm over low flame. Serve with cake, banana, and strawberries. **Makes 10 servings.**

NUTRITION PER SERVING (ABOUT 3 TABLESPOONS FONDUE, ⅓ CUP CAKE, AND ⅓ CUP FRUIT):
CALORIES 298; FAT 5.8G (POLY .35G, MONO 1.8G, SAT 3.3G);
PROTEIN 4G; CHOLESTEROL .69MG; CARBOHYDRATE 60G.

# Poached Pears

## WITH CHOCOLATE-RIESLING SAUCE

*Pears poached in wine and honey are appealing by themselves, but the chocolate-Riesling sauce, made with ease from the poaching liquid and the addition of chopped bittersweet chocolate, makes this dessert a showstopper.*

| | |
|---|---|
| 1 CUP PEAR NECTAR | 4 SLIGHTLY UNDERRIPE BOSC PEARS, |
| 1 CUP RIESLING OR OTHER SWEET WHITE | PEELED, HALVED, CORED |
| DESSERT WINE | 3 OUNCES BITTERSWEET CHOCOLATE, |
| ⅓ CUP HONEY | CHOPPED |
| ⅛ TEASPOON GROUND NUTMEG | 1 PINT LIGHT VANILLA ICE CREAM |

Stir pear nectar, wine, honey, and nutmeg in large, heavy-bottomed saucepan over medium-high heat until mixture comes to a boil. Add the pears to the pan. Cover pan, reduce heat to medium-low, and simmer until pears are tender, about 8 minutes.

Using a slotted spoon, transfer pears to a plate. Increase heat to medium-high and boil poaching liquid until reduced to ⅔ cup, about 8 minutes. Remove pan from heat. Add chocolate; whisk until chocolate melts and sauce is smooth.

Place 1 warm pear half, cut side up, on each plate. Top with light vanilla ice cream, then drizzle with warm chocolate sauce. **Makes 8 servings.**

**Cook's Note:** The pears and chocolate sauce may be made ahead of time and stored, separately, and chilled for up to 2 days. Serve pears cold with ice cream and sauce, re-warming sauce, if desired.

NUTRITION PER SERVING (1 PEAR HALF, 1½ TABLESPOONS SAUCE, AND ½ CUP ICE CREAM):
CALORIES 208; FAT 3.3G (POLY .13G, MONO 1.1G, SAT 1.9G);
PROTEIN 1G; CHOLESTEROL 0MG; CARBOHYDRATE 40G.

# CHOCOLATE-WHISKEY

# *Fudge Pie*

*Yes, this spirited chocolate pie really is light in fat and calories, but you would never know it from the tasting. Try serving it alongside the traditional pumpkin and pecan pies at Thanksgiving—it will fly out of the pie plate.*

1   CRUST OF REFRIGERATED PIE DOUGH

1   CUP PACKED BROWN SUGAR

½   CUP UNSWEETENED COCOA POWDER (NOT DUTCH PROCESS)

1   TABLESPOON ALL-PURPOSE FLOUR

⅔   CUP 2% LOW-FAT MILK

2   TABLESPOONS WHISKEY OR BOURBON

⅓   CUP LIGHT-COLORED CORN SYRUP

1   TABLESPOON UNSALTED BUTTER, MELTED

2   LARGE EGGS

2   LARGE EGG WHITES

1½   TEASPOONS VANILLA EXTRACT, DIVIDED USE

1   CUP FROZEN REDUCED-FAT WHIPPED TOPPING, THAWED

¼   CUP REDUCED-FAT SOUR CREAM

Preheat oven to 350°F.

Unroll pie dough and fit into a 9-inch pie plate. Fold edges under and decoratively flute. Place pie plate in freezer until ready to use.

In a large bowl whisk the brown sugar, cocoa powder, and flour. In a medium bowl whisk the milk, whiskey, corn syrup, melted butter, eggs, egg whites, and 1 teaspoon vanilla until well blended. Whisk milk mixture into brown sugar mixture until well blended. Pour mixture into crust.

Bake 38–42 minutes or until just set. Cool on a wire rack to room temperature. Loosely cover and chill at least 4 hours. Just before serving, whisk the whipped topping, sour cream, and remaining ½ teaspoon vanilla in a small bowl until blended. Spread mixture evenly over filling. Cut into 10 wedges. **Makes 10 servings.**

NUTRITION PER SERVING (1 WEDGE):
CALORIES 236; FAT 8.8G (POLY 1.8G, MONO 3.2G, SAT 3.3G);
PROTEIN 5G; CHOLESTEROL 49.2MG; CARBOHYDRATE 35G.

# Chocolate Cream Pie

## WITH CINNAMON MERINGUE

*In a word, this pie is fabulous. It boasts a stunning appearance (thanks to the sky-high meringue) and is sure to please each and every time.*

| | | | |
|---|---|---|---|
| ⅔ | CUP PACKED LIGHT BROWN SUGAR | 1 | TEASPOON VANILLA EXTRACT |
| ½ | CUP UNSWEETENED COCOA POWDER (NOT DUTCH PROCESS) | 1 | 6-OUNCE REDUCED-FAT GRAHAM CRACKER CRUST |
| 3 | TABLESPOONS CORNSTARCH | 1 | CUP SUGAR |
| ⅛ | TEASPOON SALT | ½ | CUP WATER |
| 1 | LARGE EGG | 8 | LARGE EGG WHITES |
| 2 | CUPS FAT-FREE MILK, DIVIDED USE | 2 | TEASPOONS CINNAMON |
| 2 | OUNCES BITTERSWEET CHOCOLATE, CHOPPED | 1 | TEASPOON CREAM OF TARTAR |

In a large bowl whisk the brown sugar, cocoa powder, cornstarch, salt, egg, and ½ cup of the milk until well blended.

Heat remaining 1½ cups milk in a heavy-bottomed saucepan over medium-high heat until tiny bubbles form around edge (do not boil). Remove from heat. Gradually whisk the hot milk into the brown sugar–cocoa mixture, constantly whisking.

Return milk mixture along with the chopped chocolate to the pan. Cook 4–5 minutes over medium heat until thick and bubbly, whisking constantly. Reduce heat to low. Cook 2 minutes, whisking constantly. Remove from heat and stir in vanilla. Pour into crust. Cover surface of filling with plastic wrap. Chill 3 hours or until cold.

Preheat oven to 350°F.

To prepare meringue, combine 1 cup sugar and water in a saucepan; bring to a boil. Cook, without stirring, until candy thermometer registers 240°F. In a bowl beat the egg whites, cinnamon, and cream of tartar with a mixer on high speed until foamy. Pour hot sugar syrup in a thin stream over egg white mixture, beating at high speed until stiff peaks form. Remove wrap from filling. Spread meringue evenly over filling; seal to edge of crust.

Bake 12–15 minutes or until lightly browned. Transfer to a wire rack and cool completely. Chill until set. Cut into 10 wedges. **Makes 10 servings.**

NUTRITION PER SERVING (1 WEDGE): CALORIES 297; FAT 5.2G (POLY 1.1G, MONO 1.7G, SAT 2.4G); PROTEIN 7G; CHOLESTEROL 23MG; CARBOHYDRATE 56G.

# BLUEBERRY-RASPBERRY CHOCOLATE

# *Schaum Torte*

*Everybody loves a showstopper dessert. With that in mind, I created this double chocolate Schaum torte, which is traditionally a combination of a meringue (or layers of meringue), whipped cream, and fruit. It is absolutely gorgeous topped with blueberries, raspberries, and melted chocolate. Perhaps even more beautiful, it has a mere 214 calories per serving.*

| | |
|---|---|
| ⅓ CUP UNSWEETENED COCOA POWDER (NOT DUTCH PROCESS) | 1⅓ CUPS REDUCED-FAT FROZEN NON-DAIRY WHIPPED TOPPING, THAWED |
| PINCH OF SALT | 3 TABLESPOONS REDUCED-FAT SOUR CREAM |
| ¾ CUP SUGAR, DIVIDED USE | 3 OUNCES BITTERSWEET CHOCOLATE, CHOPPED |
| 4 LARGE EGG WHITES | 2 CUPS FRESH BLUEBERRIES |
| ½ TEASPOON CREAM OF TARTAR | 2 CUPS FRESH RASPBERRIES |
| 1 TEASPOON VANILLA EXTRACT, DIVIDED USE | OPTIONAL: FRESH MINT SPRIGS |

Preheat oven to 200°F.

For the meringue, cover a cookie sheet with parchment paper. Trace a 9-inch circle on paper. Turn paper over and secure with masking tape.

In a small bowl sift the cocoa powder, salt, and ¼ cup sugar. In large bowl beat the egg whites and cream of tartar with an electric mixer set at high speed until soft peaks begin to form. Add remaining ½ cup sugar, 1 tablespoon at a time, and beat until medium-firm peaks form. Add ½ teaspoon vanilla, then the cocoa mixture, 1 tablespoon at a time, and beat until meringue is stiff and glossy.

Spoon the egg white mixture into the 9-inch circle on prepared baking sheet. Shape meringue into a nest with 1-inch sides using the back of a spoon.

Bake 1 hour. Turn oven off and cool the meringue in closed oven for 30 minutes. Carefully remove meringue from paper. Cool completely.

In a small bowl whisk the whipped topping, sour cream, and remaining ½ teaspoon vanilla until blended. Place chocolate in a small microwave-safe bowl. Microwave on HIGH 1 minute or until chocolate melts, stirring every 20 seconds.

Spread whipped topping mixture over the meringue. Arrange berries on top of topping and drizzle with chocolate. Garnish with mint sprigs, if desired. **Makes 8 servings.**

NUTRITION PER SERVING (⅛ OF TORTE): CALORIES 214; FAT 6.4G (POLY .35, MONO 1.6G, SAT 4.1G); PROTEIN 4G; CHOLESTEROL 2.2MG; CARBOHYDRATE 40G.

# FRENCH CHOCOLATE
## Truffle Tart

*A rich chocolate filling encased in a chocolate crust and topped with more chocolate makes this tart simple and elegant—very French. The lavender honey adds a subtle layer of sophistication and flavor.*

---

| | |
|---|---|
| 32 CHOCOLATE WAFER COOKIES, FINELY CRUSHED | ½ OF AN 8-OUNCE PACKAGE REDUCED-FAT CREAM CHEESE, SOFTENED |
| 2 TABLESPOONS BUTTER, MELTED | 3 TABLESPOONS LAVENDER HONEY (OR OTHER HONEY) |
| 1 LARGE EGG WHITE | 1 TEASPOON VANILLA EXTRACT |
| ½ CUP UNSWEETENED COCOA POWDER (NOT DUTCH PROCESS) | 2 LARGE EGGS |
| 1 14-OUNCE CAN FAT-FREE SWEETENED CONDENSED MILK | 2 OUNCES BITTERSWEET CHOCOLATE |

Preheat oven to 350°F.

In a medium bowl combine the cookie crumbs, melted butter, and egg white, tossing with a fork until moist. Firmly press the mixture into the bottom of a 9-inch springform pan.

To prepare filling, beat the cocoa powder and condensed milk with an electric mixer set at medium speed until blended. Add cream cheese; beat well. Add the honey, vanilla, and eggs, beating just until smooth. Pour mixture into prepared crust.

Bake 32–35 minutes or until set (do not overbake). Transfer to a wire rack and cool completely. Loosely cover and chill 4 hours.

To prepare topping, shave long edge of chocolate using a vegetable peeler. Sprinkle tart with shaved chocolate. Cut into 10 wedges. **Makes 10 servings.**

NUTRITION PER SERVING ( 1 WEDGE ):
CALORIES 248; FAT 8.4G (POLY .44G, MONO 3G, SAT 4.5G);
PROTEIN 7G; CHOLESTEROL 56.4MG; CARBOHYDRATE 14G.

# CAFÉ CON LECHE &
# *Chocolate Pie*

*Food snobs, turn the page, for this dessert features not one, but (gasp!) two store-bought mixes. Everyone else will want to dog-ear the page because this is one very easy, very yummy pie. Unsweetened cocoa powder deepens the flavor of the brownie mix and also gets stirred into instant vanilla pudding, transforming it into a rich chocolate custard filling.*

⅓ CUP HOT WATER

4 TEASPOONS INSTANT ESPRESSO POWDER, DIVIDED USE

½ OF A 20.5-OUNCE BOX LIGHT FUDGE BROWNIE MIX (ABOUT 2 CUPS)

2 LARGE EGG WHITES

3 TABLESPOONS UNSWEETENED COCOA POWDER (NOT DUTCH PROCESS), DIVIDED USE

2 TEASPOONS VANILLA EXTRACT, DIVIDED USE

¾ CUP 1% LOW-FAT MILK

3 TABLESPOONS COFFEE-FLAVORED LIQUEUR, DIVIDED USE

1 3.9-OUNCE PACKAGE VANILLA INSTANT PUDDING MIX

3 CUPS FROZEN REDUCED-CALORIE FROZEN WHIPPED TOPPING, THAWED, DIVIDED USE

OPTIONAL: BITTERSWEET CHOCOLATE CURLS

Preheat oven to 325°F. Spray a 9-inch pie plate with nonstick cooking spray.

In a medium bowl combine the hot water and 2 teaspoons espresso powder, stirring until dissolved. Add the 2 cups brownie mix, egg whites, 1 tablespoon cocoa powder, and 1 teaspoon vanilla; stir until well blended. Spread mixture into prepared pie plate. Bake 22 minutes. Transfer to a wire rack and cool completely.

In a medium bowl combine the milk, 2 tablespoons coffee liqueur, pudding mix, 1 of the remaining teaspoons espresso powder, and remaining 1 teaspoon vanilla. Beat at medium speed using an electric mixer 1 minute. Sprinkle in remaining 2 tablespoons cocoa powder; beat 30 seconds longer. Gently fold in 1½ cups of the whipped topping. Spread mixture evenly into brownie crust.

In a medium bowl combine remaining 1 tablespoon coffee liqueur and remaining 1 teaspoon espresso powder until dissolved. Gently fold in remaining 1½ cups whipped topping. Spread whipped topping mixture evenly over pudding mixture. If desired, garnish with chocolate curls. Serve immediately or store loosely covered in refrigerator. Cut into 8 wedges. **Makes 8 servings.**

**Cook's Note:** There will be enough brownie mix in one box to make two pies. Store the remaining brownie mix in a heavy-duty, ziplock plastic bag in refrigerator until ready to use. It will keep for approximately 2 months.

# Chocolate Baklava

## WITH HONEY & SPICE

*For best results, chop the walnuts and almonds by hand—chopping them in a food processor makes them release more oil, resulting in a heavier baklava. This is one of those desserts that magically improves as it sits—yes, it's darn good on day one, but it's smashing on days two and three as the syrup seeps in and deepens the flavors.*

| | |
|---|---|
| 1½ CUPS HONEY | 3 TABLESPOONS UNSWEETENED COCOA POW- |
| ½ CUP WATER | DER (NOT DUTCH PROCESS) |
| 1 TABLESPOON FRESH LEMON JUICE | 1 OUNCE BITTERSWEET CHOCOLATE, FINELY |
| 3 WHOLE CLOVES | CHOPPED OR GRATED |
| 1 3-INCH CINNAMON STICK | ¾ TEASPOON GROUND CINNAMON |
| 1 CUP WALNUTS, FINELY CHOPPED | ¼ TEASPOON GROUND CARDAMOM |
| ½ CUP BLANCHED UNSALTED ALMONDS, | ⅛ TEASPOON SALT |
| FINELY CHOPPED | 24 (14 X 9-INCH) SHEETS FROZEN PHYLLO |
| ¼ CUP SUGAR | DOUGH, THAWED |
| | 1 TABLESPOON WATER |

In a medium saucepan over low heat combine the honey, ½ cup water, lemon juice, cloves, and cinnamon stick; stir until honey is completely dissolved, about 2 minutes. Increase heat to medium and cook, without stirring, 8 minutes longer. Remove from heat. Remove and discard the cinnamon stick and cloves with a slotted spoon. Set syrup aside, keeping it warm.

Preheat oven to 350°F. Lightly spray a 13 x 9-inch baking dish with nonstick cooking spray.

In a medium bowl combine the walnuts, almonds, sugar, cocoa powder, chocolate, cinnamon, cardamom, and salt; set aside.

Working with 1 phyllo sheet at a time (cover remaining dough with a damp towel to prevent drying), place 1 phyllo sheet lengthwise in bottom of prepared pan, allowing end of sheet to extend over edges of dish, then lightly coat with nonstick cooking spray. Repeat procedure with 5 more phyllo sheets and cooking spray for a total of 6 layers.

Sprinkle phyllo evenly with one-third of nut mixture (about ⅔ cup).

Repeat procedure with phyllo, nonstick cooking spray, and nut mixture two more times. Top last layer of nut mixture with remaining 6 sheets phyllo, each one lightly coated with nonstick cooking spray. Lightly coat top phyllo sheet with nonstick cooking spray; press baklava gently into pan. Sprinkle baklava surface with 1 tablespoon water.

Make 3 even lengthwise cuts and 7 even crosswise cuts to form 32 diamonds using a sharp knife. Bake 30 minutes or until the phyllo is golden brown. Remove from oven. Drizzle honey mixture evenly over baklava. Cool in pan on a wire rack. Store covered at room temperature. **Makes 32 servings.**

NUTRITION PER SERVING (1 PIECE):
CALORIES 136; FAT 4.4G (POLY 2.1G, MONO 1.4G, SAT .7G);
PROTEIN 2G; CHOLESTEROL 0MG; CARBOHYDRATE 24G.

# Chocolate Fudge Sauce

*Espresso powder increases the chocolate intensity of this sauce. Don't be surprised if the sauce looks somewhat thin when hot; it will thicken as it cools.*

| | |
|---|---|
| 1 CUP PACKED LIGHT BROWN SUGAR | ⅔ CUP WATER |
| ⅔ CUP UNSWEETENED COCOA POWDER (NOT DUTCH PROCESS) | 2 TEASPOONS VANILLA EXTRACT |
| 2 TABLESPOONS CORNSTARCH | ½ TEASPOON INSTANT ESPRESSO POWDER |

Whisk the brown sugar, cocoa powder, and cornstarch in a medium saucepan. Whisk in the water.

Bring to a boil over medium heat; cook 1 minute. Remove from heat and stir in vanilla and espresso powder. Cool to room temperature. Transfer sauce to an airtight container and chill. **Makes about 18 servings.**

**Cook's Note:** Sauce will keep, tightly covered in the refrigerator, for up to 2 weeks.

NUTRITION PER SERVING (1½ TABLESPOONS):
CALORIES 57; FAT .44G (POLY .01G, MONO .15G, SAT .26G);
PROTEIN .5G; CHOLESTEROL 0MG; CARBOHYDRATE 14G.

## Variations

**Cinnamon-Chocolate Fudge Sauce:** Prepare as directed, but add ¾ teaspoon ground cinnamon.

**Peppermint-Chocolate Fudge Sauce:** Prepare as directed, but eliminate the espresso powder and replace the vanilla extract with ¾ teaspoon peppermint extract.

**Spiked Chocolate Fudge Sauce:** Prepare as directed, but replace the vanilla extract with 1 tablespoon liqueur or spirit of choice (e.g., Kahlua, Grand Marnier, Irish Cream, whiskey, dark rum).

# CABERNET-CHOCOLATE

## *Fudge Sauce*

*So easy, so delicious—use this decadent sauce to dress up light versions of ice cream, pound cake, brownies, and just about anything else you can think of. You can also serve it as a fondue with an assortment of fresh fruit and angel food cake cubes.*

1   14-OUNCE CAN FAT-FREE SWEETENED
    CONDENSED MILK
¾   CUP CABERNET OR OTHER DRY RED WINE
7   TABLESPOONS UNSWEETENED COCOA POW-
    DER (NOT DUTCH PROCESS)
1   TEASPOON VANILLA EXTRACT

In a small saucepan whisk the sweetened condensed milk, wine, and cocoa powder until blended. Cook 10 minutes over low heat. Remove from heat and whisk in vanilla; cool. **Makes 18 servings.**

**Cook's Note:** The sauce will keep, tightly covered in the refrigerator, for up to 2 weeks.

NUTRITION PER SERVING (1½ TABLESPOONS):
CALORIES 73; FAT .27G (POLY .01G, MONO .09G, SAT .16G);
PROTEIN 1.5G; CHOLESTEROL .56MG; CARBOHYDRATE 1G.

# Chocolate Syrup

*This syrup is perfectly delicious over light ice cream, fruit, and sorbet or as a base for an intense chocolate milk and hot cocoa (use 1 cup milk with ⅓ cup syrup).*

1  CUP WATER

½  CUP SUGAR

⅔  CUP UNSWEETENED COCOA POWDER (NOT DUTCH PROCESS)

¼  TEASPOON SALT

1  TEASPOON VANILLA

Bring water and sugar to a boil, whisking until sugar is dissolved. Whisk in the cocoa powder and salt and simmer, whisking, until slightly thickened, about 3 minutes.

Remove syrup from heat and add vanilla, then cool (syrup will continue to thicken as it cools). **Makes 16 servings.**

**Cook's Note:** Syrup will keep, tightly covered in the refrigerator, for up to 2 weeks.

NUTRITION PER SERVING (1½ TABLESPOONS):
CALORIES 32; FAT .49G (POLY .02G, MONO .17G, SAT .29G);
PROTEIN 1G; CHOLESTEROL 0MG; CARBOHYDRATE 8G.

# Chocolate-Raspberry Sauce

*A dream-come-true dessert sauce: so easy to make, yet so very impressive (and delicious, too). Drizzle it over raspberry or chocolate sorbet, low-fat vanilla ice-cream, or reduced-fat pound cake for dessert on demand.*

---

⅔ CUP SUGAR

¼ CUP UNSWEETENED COCOA POWDER (NOT
   DUTCH PROCESS)

1 TABLESPOON CORNSTARCH

½ CUP WATER

6 TABLESPOONS SEEDLESS RASPBERRY JAM

OPTIONAL: 4 TEASPOONS RASPBERRY LIQUEUR
   (E.G., CHAMBORD)

---

Whisk together sugar, cocoa, and cornstarch in a small saucepan. Gradually whisk in water and jam. Bring to a simmer over medium heat, whisking constantly.

Remove from the heat and stir in liqueur, if using. Let cool slightly. **Makes 14 servings.**

⟡ **Cook's Note:** Sauce will keep, tightly covered in the refrigerator, for up to 2 weeks.

NUTRITION PER SERVING (1½ TABLESPOONS):
CALORIES 72; FAT .22G (POLY .01G, MONO .07G, SAT .13G);
PROTEIN .5G; CHOLESTEROL 0MG; CARBOHYDRATE 18G.

# Chocolate-Coconut Sauce

*I am a sucker for desserts that taste and look exceptional, but are in fact a breeze to prepare. Case in point: this tropical chocolate sauce. It is exceptional partnered with fresh tropical fruit and mango sorbet.*

½ CUP CANNED FAT-FREE SWEETENED CON-
DENSED MILK

½ CUP CANNED LITE UNSWEETENED COCONUT
MILK

2 TABLESPOONS UNSWEETENED COCOA POW-
DER (NOT DUTCH PROCESS)

2 OUNCES BITTERSWEET CHOCOLATE,
CHOPPED

¾ TEASPOON COCONUT EXTRACT (OR TO
TASTE)

⅛ TEASPOON SALT

1 TABLESPOON DARK RUM

In a heavy saucepan whisk together the sweetened condensed milk and coconut milk. Bring the mixture to a simmer over medium heat. Whisk in the cocoa powder and chocolate, whisking until chocolate is melted and the sauce is smooth.

Whisk in the coconut extract, salt, and rum. Serve the sauce warm or at room temperature over ice cream. **Makes 16 servings.**

**Cook's Note:** Sauce will keep, tightly covered in the refrigerator, for up to 2 weeks.

NUTRITION PER SERVING (1½ TABLESPOONS):
CALORIES 52; FAT 1.7G (POLY .05G, MONO .48G, SAT 1.1G);
PROTEIN 1G; CHOLESTEROL .25MG; CARBOHYDRATE 2.5G.

# Chocolate-Orange Sauce

*Embellished with orange marmalade and orange liqueur, this velvety sauce is a supremely sophisticated topping for ice cream and for fruits such as fresh strawberries and bananas. There's also something to be said for sampling it by the spoonful, straight from the fridge.*

1 CUP CANNED FAT-FREE EVAPORATED MILK

6 TABLESPOONS ORANGE MARMALADE

3 OUNCES BITTERSWEET CHOCOLATE, FINELY CHOPPED

2 TABLESPOONS UNSWEETENED COCOA POWDER (NOT DUTCH PROCESS)

PINCH OF SALT

1 TABLESPOON ORANGE LIQUEUR (E.G., GRAND MARNIER OR TRIPLE SEC)

In a heavy-bottomed saucepan bring the evaporated milk and marmalade to a simmer, whisking. Remove pan from heat and add the chocolate, cocoa powder, and a pinch of salt. Let the mixture stand for 3 minutes, then whisk it until it is smooth; whisk in the liqueur. Serve warm or at room temperature. **Makes 16 servings**.

NUTRITION PER SERVING (1½ TABLESPOONS):
CALORIES 62; FAT 1.7G (POLY .06G, MONO .57G, SAT 1G);
PROTEIN 2G; CHOLESTEROL .64MG; CARBOHYDRATE 11G.

# 5. SAVORY

*Chocolate*

LIME TORTILLA SOUP WITH SHRIMP & CHIPOTLE CHILES, MOROCCAN CHICKPEA SOUP, ULTIMATE BLACK BEAN SOUP, EXOTIC, SPICED PUMPKIN SOUP, CHICKEN, STRAWBERRY, & MESCLUN SALAD WITH **COCOA** VINAIGRETTE, NORTH INDIAN-SPICED CHICKEN, MANGO & RICE SALAD, SPICY HOISIN-**COCOA** BBQ CHICKEN, PAN-ASIAN CHICKEN LETTUCE WRAPS, RASPBERRY-GLAZED CHICKEN, **COCOA**-RUBBED CHICKEN WITH BARBECUE TABLE MOP, PORK CHOPS MOLE, GRILLED PORK KEBABS WITH CUBAN **COCOA**-RUM GLAZE, PORK MEDALLIONS WITH PORT-**CHOCOLATE** PAN SAUCE, MALAYSIAN PORK TENDERLOIN WITH MANGO SAMBAL, SLOW-COOKED CHAR SIU PORK ROAST, PORK TOURNEDOS WITH **CHOCOLATE** GASTRIQUE AND FRESH CHERRY SALSA, GRILLED LAMB CHOPS WITH HONEYED-RED WINE GLAZE, PUNJABI-SPICED SALMON WITH CUCUMBER-MINT RAITA, PASTA, SHRIMP & MANGO SALAD WITH CITRUS-**COCOA** VINAIGRETTE, BRAISED MAHOGANY TOFU, SPANISH BLACK BEAN BURGERS WITH OLIVE-ORANGE RELISH, SMOKY-LIME PICADILLO WRAP, BEEF & BEER CHILI WITH LIME CREMA, GINGER & DARK BEER-BRAISED BEEF, ADOBO FLANK STEAK WITH ORANGE & AVOCADO SALSA, TEJAS MEATLOAF, CABERNET-GLAZED BEEF STEW, CARIBBEAN BLACK BEANS WITH **COCOA** & RUM, ROASTED AUTUMN VEGETABLES, SPICY CHICKPEAS WITH SPINACH & BASMATI RICE, FIRE-ROASTED RED PEPPER-**COCOA** KETCHUP, BRAISED CAULI-FLOWER & POTATOES WITH NORTH INDIAN SPICES, AND MORE . . .

# Lime Tortilla Soup

## WITH SHRIMP & CHIPOTLE CHILES

*Long on flavor and short on time, this classic Mexican soup makes a great weeknight supper. Bright with lime, the broth gets a deeper flavor from a touch of cocoa powder.*

| | | | |
|---|---|---|---|
| 1 | TABLESPOON OLIVE OIL | 2 | 15-OUNCE CANS GOLDEN HOMINY, DRAINED |
| 1 | CUP FINELY CHOPPED ONION | 1 | CUP FROZEN CORN |
| 1 | CUP FINELY CHOPPED CARROT | ¾ | CUP CANNED CRUSHED TOMATOES |
| 1 | MEDIUM RED BELL PEPPER, SEEDED AND CHOPPED | 2 | TEASPOONS CHOPPED CANNED CHIPOTLE CHILES |
| 6 | GARLIC CLOVES, MINCED | 1 | POUND FROZEN UNCOOKED, PEELED & DEVEINED SMALL SHRIMP (THAWED) |
| 2 | TEASPOONS GROUND CUMIN | | |
| 1 | TEASPOON DRIED OREGANO | ½ | CUP CHOPPED FRESH CILANTRO |
| 2 | TABLESPOONS UNSWEETENED COCOA POWDER (NOT DUTCH PROCESS) | 3 | TABLESPOONS FRESH LIME JUICE |
| | | 3 | CUPS REDUCED-FAT TORTILLA CHIPS, COARSELY CRUSHED |
| 2 | TABLESPOONS HONEY | | |
| 7 | CUPS CANNED LOW-SALT CHICKEN BROTH | | |

Heat olive oil in large, heavy pot over medium heat. Add onion, carrot, bell pepper, garlic, cumin, and oregano. Sauté until vegetables are crisp-tender, about 10 minutes.

Add the cocoa powder, honey, chicken broth, hominy, corn, crushed tomatoes, and chipotle chiles; bring to simmer. Reduce heat, cover, and simmer 30 minutes. Season to taste with salt and pepper.

Bring soup to simmer over medium heat. Add shrimp and cook until opaque in center, stirring occasionally, about 3 minutes. Stir in chopped fresh cilantro and lime juice. Divide soup among 10 soup bowls. Top soup with crushed tortilla chips, dividing equally. **Makes 10 servings.**

NUTRITION PER SERVING (ABOUT 1¼ CUPS SOUP AND ¼ CUP CRUSHED CHIPS):
CALORIES 223; FAT 4.1G (POLY .73G, MONO 1.3G, SAT .51G);
PROTEIN 16G; CHOLESTEROL 73.5MG; CARBOHYDRATE 33G.

# MOROCCAN
## *Chickpea Soup*

*Adding cocoa powder to the broth of this hearty vegetarian soup enriches and enhances the flavors of the herbs and spices, making it taste like it has been simmering on the stove all day.*

1½ CUPS FINELY CHOPPED ONION

¾ CUP FINELY CHOPPED CELERY

2½ TABLESPOONS OLIVE OIL

3 CLOVES GARLIC, MINCED

2 TABLESPOONS UNSWEETENED COCOA POWDER (NOT DUTCH PROCESS)

2½ TEASPOONS GROUND CUMIN

1½ TEASPOONS GROUND TURMERIC

1 TEASPOON BLACK PEPPER

1 TEASPOON GROUND CINNAMON

½ TEASPOON GROUND CORIANDER

1 28-OUNCE CAN PURÉED TOMATOES

1 CUP CHOPPED FRESH CILANTRO, DIVIDED USE

1 15-OUNCE CAN CHICKPEAS, DRAINED

7 CUPS VEGETABLE BROTH OR CHICKEN BROTH

2 CUPS FINE EGG NOODLES

½ CUP CHOPPED FRESH PARSLEY

1½ TABLESPOONS FRESH LEMON JUICE

ACCOMPANIMENT: LEMON WEDGES

Cook the onion and celery in olive oil in a 4-quart heavy pot over moderately low heat, stirring occasionally, until softened. Add garlic, cocoa powder, cumin, turmeric, pepper, cinnamon, and coriander; cook and stir 3 minutes.

Stir in tomato purée, ½ cup cilantro, chickpeas, and vegetable broth. Bring to a boil, then reduce heat and simmer, uncovered, about 15 minutes.

Stir in noodles and cook, stirring, until tender, about 3 minutes. Stir in parsley, remaining ½ cup cilantro, lemon juice, and salt and pepper to taste. Ladle into bowls and serve with lemon wedges. **Makes 8 servings.**

NUTRITION PER SERVING (ABOUT 1⅔ CUPS SOUP):
CALORIES 257; FAT 6.1G (POLY .99G, MONO 3.6G, SAT .96G);
PROTEIN 11G; CHOLESTEROL 24.8MG; CARBOHYDRATE 40G.

# ULTIMATE
## *Black Bean Soup*

*A soup from your pantry and refrigerator: canned pumpkin and cocoa powder are the secrets behind the deep flavor of this black bean soup that make it worthy of its "ultimate" eponym.*

3   15-OUNCE CANS BLACK BEANS (ABOUT
     4½ CUPS), RINSED AND DRAINED

1   CUP DRAINED CANNED DICED TOMATOES

1   TABLESPOON UNSALTED BUTTER

1½ CUPS CHOPPED ONION

4   CLOVES GARLIC, MINCED

1½ TABLESPOONS GROUND CUMIN

1   TEASPOON SALT

½   TEASPOON FRESHLY GROUND BLACK
     PEPPER

3   TABLESPOONS UNSWEETENED COCOA
     POWDER (NOT DUTCH PROCESS)

4   CUPS CANNED BEEF BROTH

1   16-OUNCE CAN SOLID PACK PUMPKIN

½   CUP DRY SHERRY

1½ CUPS FINELY DICED LEAN COOKED HAM

3   TABLESPOONS SHERRY VINEGAR

½   CUP REDUCED-FAT SOUR CREAM

In a food processor coarsely purée the beans and tomatoes.

Melt the butter in a large pot and cook the onion, garlic, cumin, salt, and pepper over moderate heat, stirring, until onion is softened and beginning to brown. Stir in bean mixture and cocoa powder. Stir in beef broth, pumpkin, and Sherry until blended.

Simmer soup, uncovered, stirring occasionally, 25 minutes.

Just before serving, add ham and vinegar and simmer soup, stirring, until heated through. Season soup with salt and pepper. Serve with dollops of sour cream. **Makes 10 servings.**

NUTRITION PER SERVING (ABOUT 1¼ CUPS):
CALORIES 193; FAT 5.3G (POLY .49G, MONO 2.1G, SAT 2.5G);
PROTEIN 13G; CHOLESTEROL 20.1MG; CARBOHYDRATE 25G.

# Pumpkin Soup

*Serenity in a spoon, this soup is so good, and so good for you. Pumpkin is rich in carotenoids, which have been linked to a host of health-promoting activities, including maintenance of heart, lung, and eye health. But all you need to know is that this soup is delicious and is so easy and inexpensive to prepare that it will become part of your standard repertoire.*

| | |
|---|---|
| 1 TABLESPOON BUTTER | 1⅓ CUPS CANNED LITE UNSWEETENED COCONUT MILK |
| ¾ CUP CHOPPED CARROT | |
| ¾ CUP CHOPPED CELERY | 2 TABLESPOONS UNSWEETENED COCOA POWDER (NOT DUTCH PROCESS) |
| 1 LARGE RIPE BANANA, CHOPPED | |
| 1 CUP CHOPPED ONION | 1½ TEASPOONS MILD CURRY POWDER |
| 2 GARLIC CLOVES, MINCED | ½ TEASPOON NUTMEG |
| 2 BAY LEAVES | ½ TEASPOON CINNAMON |
| 4½ CUPS CANNED LOW-SODIUM CHICKEN BROTH | ½ TEASPOON CORIANDER |
| | ¼ TEASPOON ALLSPICE |
| 2 CUPS CANNED SOLID PACK PUMPKIN | ⅛ TEASPOON CLOVES |
| | ¼ CUP CHOPPED FRESH CHIVES |

Melt butter in heavy large pot over medium-high heat. Add the carrot, celery, banana, onion, garlic, and bay leaves. Sauté until vegetables are soft, about 10 minutes. Discard bay leaves.

Transfer mixture to a blender or food processor and blend until smooth. Return mixture to pot. Add the chicken broth, pumpkin, coconut milk, cocoa powder, curry powder, nutmeg, cinnamon, coriander, allspice, and cloves. Simmer soup over medium-high heat 15 minutes to blend flavors. Cool slightly.

Season soup to taste with salt and pepper. Divide among 8 bowls. Sprinkle with chives and serve. **Makes 8 servings.**

NUTRITION PER SERVING (ABOUT 1 CUP):
CALORIES 99; FAT 4.2G (POLY .11G, MONO .97G, SAT 3.0G);
PROTEIN 4G; CHOLESTEROL 4.0MG; CARBOHYDRATE 13.8G.

# Chicken, Strawberry, and Mesclun Salad

## WITH COCOA VINAIGRETTE

*This recipe proves that salad isn't just a bag of lettuce and bottled dressing. It can be a mix of many flavors that satisfies on every level. Using precooked chicken makes this dish a snap to throw together for lunch. Serve with slices of hearty whole-grain peasant bread to complement the fruit and tart-sweet vinaigrette.*

| | |
|---|---|
| 2 CUPS SHREDDED OR CHOPPED COOKED CHICKEN BREAST | 1½ TABLESPOONS BALSAMIC VINEGAR |
| 2 CUPS QUARTERED STRAWBERRIES | 2 TEASPOONS UNSWEETENED COCOA POWDER (NOT DUTCH PROCESS) |
| ½ CUP PEELED, FINELY CHOPPED JICAMA | 2 TEASPOONS WATER |
| ⅓ CUP FINELY CHOPPED RED ONION | 1½ TEASPOONS SUGAR |
| 2 TABLESPOONS GOLDEN RAISINS | ½ TEASPOON PAPRIKA |
| 1 TABLESPOON SESAME SEEDS, TOASTED | ⅛ TEASPOON SALT |
| 1 TEASPOON DRIED TARRAGON | ⅛ TEASPOON BLACK PEPPER |
| 1½ TABLESPOONS EXTRA-VIRGIN OLIVE OIL | 4 CUPS MESCLUN SALAD GREENS |

In a large bowl combine the chicken, strawberries, jicama, red onion, and raisins.

In a small bowl combine the sesame seeds, tarragon, olive oil, vinegar, cocoa powder, water, sugar, paprika, salt, and black pepper, stirring well with a whisk. Pour over chicken mixture, tossing well to coat. Cover and chill 1 hour. Serve over mesclun greens. **Makes 4 servings.**

NUTRITION PER SERVING (¼ OF SALAD):
CALORIES 277; FAT 13.1G (POLY 2.7G, MONO 6.5G, SAT 2.7G);
PROTEIN 27G; CHOLESTEROL 75.7MG; CARBOHYDRATE 14G.

# Chicken, Mango, & Rice Salad

*When you want to go all out without the fat, try this colorful main-dish salad. The cocoa-spice rub makes for a deeply flavorful contrast to the bright, fresh flavors of mango, bell pepper and cucumber.*

| | |
|---|---|
| 2 TABLESPOONS MILD CURRY POWDER | 1 CUP BOTTLED REDUCED-FAT SESAME-GINGER VINAIGRETTE (E.G., NEWMAN'S OWN BRAND) |
| 2 TABLESPOONS GROUND CUMIN | |
| 1 TEASPOON GROUND GINGER | 2 CUPS COOKED, COOLED BASMATI RICE |
| 1 TEASPOON SALT | 8 CUPS MESCLUN SALAD GREENS |
| ¼ TEASPOON CAYENNE PEPPER | 2 LARGE RED BELL PEPPERS, SEEDED AND CUT INTO THIN STRIPS |
| 2 TABLESPOONS UNSWEETENED COCOA POWDER (NOT DUTCH PROCESS) | 2 LARGE FIRM-RIPE MANGOES, PEELED, PITTED, AND DICED |
| 4 4-OUNCE SKINLESS, BONELESS CHICKEN BREAST HALVES | 1 MEDIUM CUCUMBER, PEELED, SEEDED, AND SLICED |

Preheat oven to 350°F. Spray a baking sheet with nonstick cooking spray.

In a small bowl mix the curry powder, cumin, ginger, salt, pepper, and cocoa. Lightly spray each chicken breast with nonstick cooking spray. Sprinkle 1 heaping teaspoon cocoa-curry mixture over each chicken breast (reserve remaining spice mix for dressing). Rub spice mixture all over each breast. Place coated chicken on prepared baking sheet.

Bake the chicken 20–25 minutes or until juices are clear. Cool. Cut into strips.

In a large bowl whisk the remaining cocoa-curry mixture and vinaigrette until blended. Set aside ¼ cup of the dressing. Add the chicken and rice to the bowl, tossing to coat. Cover and refrigerate until chilled.

To serve, toss the mesclun, bell peppers, mango, and cucumbers with the reserved ¼ cup dressing to coat. Divide between 6 plates and top with the chicken-rice mixture. **Makes 6 servings.**

NUTRITION PER SERVING (⅙ OF SALAD):
CALORIES 305; FAT 7.4G (POLY .79G, MONO 1.0G, SAT 1.6G);
PROTEIN 25G; CHOLESTEROL 60.2MG; CARBOHYDRATE 36G.

# SPICY HOISIN-COCOA BBQ

# *Chicken*

*Hoisin sauce is a powerhouse pantry item. Thick and reddish-brown, it is a sweet-spicy Chinese sauce made from soybeans, garlic, chile peppers, and various spices. Inexpensive and readily available in supermarkets where soy sauce is shelved, it packs a tremendous punch of flavor with minimal calories. Here it coalesces with a touch of cocoa powder, sherry, and soy sauce to make a delectable chicken dish that can be assembled in minutes. I like to serve the chicken with brown rice and a crisp Asian-style slaw.*

---

6   TABLESPOONS HOISIN SAUCE

2   TABLESPOONS RICE WINE OR DRY SHERRY

1½ TABLESPOONS LOW-SODIUM SOY SAUCE

1½ TABLESPOONS KETCHUP

1½ TABLESPOONS UNSWEETENED COCOA POW-
    DER (NOT DUTCH PROCESS)

1   TABLESPOON PACKED LIGHT BROWN SUGAR

1   TABLESPOON FINELY GRATED PEELED
    FRESH GINGER

3   GARLIC CLOVES, MINCED

½   TEASPOON CRUSHED RED PEPPER FLAKES

4   CHICKEN DRUMSTICKS, SKINNED AND
    TRIMMED (ABOUT 2 POUNDS)

4   CHICKEN THIGHS, SKINNED AND TRIMMED
    (ABOUT 2 POUNDS)

Preheat oven to 500°F. Line a large shallow baking pan (1 inch deep) with foil.

In a large bowl whisk together all ingredients except chicken. Add chicken and toss to coat. Transfer chicken mixture (scrape out all of the sauce) to the prepared pan.

Roast chicken in upper third of oven until chicken is cooked through and glaze is brown, 20–30 minutes. Serve, spooning sauce over chicken. **Makes 4 servings.**

NUTRITION PER SERVING (1 THIGH AND 1 DRUMSTICK):
CALORIES 367; FAT 13.2G (POLY 3.3G, MONO 5.2G, SAT 4.2G);
PROTEIN 43G; CHOLESTEROL .25MG; CARBOHYDRATE 16G.

# Chicken Lettuce Wraps

*These fresh and pretty wraps are favorites with kids and adults alike. Cocoa powder coaxes out the subtle layers of spice in the hoisin sauce, making an irresistible sauce for the chicken-vegetable filling. If someone at the dinner table has a peanut allergy, simply substitute roasted cashews for the peanuts.*

| | |
|---|---|
| 3 TABLESPOONS HOISIN SAUCE | 3 TABLESPOONS SALTED, DRY-ROASTED PEANUTS |
| 2½ TABLESPOONS FRESH LIME JUICE | |
| 1 TABLESPOON UNSWEETENED COCOA POWDER (NOT DUTCH PROCESS) | 2 CUPS PACKAGED CABBAGE-AND-CARROT COLESLAW MIX |
| 2 TEASPOONS LOW-SODIUM SOY SAUCE | 1 CUP CANNED SLICED WATER CHESTNUTS, DRAINED |
| 1 TEASPOON GROUND GINGER | |
| 1 TEASPOON DARK SESAME OIL | 2 CUPS DICED COOKED CHICKEN BREAST |
| ⅛ TEASPOON CAYENNE PEPPER | 12 BIBB LETTUCE LEAVES |
| 1 GARLIC CLOVE, MINCED | |

Whisk the hoisin sauce, lime juice, cocoa powder, soy sauce, ginger, sesame oil, pepper, and garlic in a small bowl until blended.

In a medium bowl combine the peanuts, coleslaw mix, water chestnuts, and chicken, tossing well to combine.

Spoon about ⅓ cup chicken salad in the center of each lettuce leaf. Top each with 2 teaspoons sauce. Roll up; secure with a wooden pick. **Makes 4 servings.**

NUTRITION PER SERVING (3 WRAPS):
CALORIES 239; FAT 8.2G (POLY 2.0G, MONO 2.9G, SAT 1.7G);
PROTEIN 30G; CHOLESTEROL 72.6MG; CARBOHYDRATE 15G.

# RASPBERRY-GLAZED

*Chicken*

*Workaday chicken breasts are transformed into a luxurious dish accented with cocoa powder and balsamic vinegar. Couscous makes an easy accompaniment.*

½ TEASPOON DRIED THYME

½ TEASPOON SALT, DIVIDED USE

4 4-OUNCE SKINLESS, BONELESS CHICKEN
   BREAST HALVES

2 TEASPOONS CANOLA OIL

½ CUP MINCED SHALLOT

⅓ CUP SEEDLESS RASPBERRY JAM

2 TABLESPOONS BALSAMIC VINEGAR

2½ TEASPOONS UNSWEETENED COCOA POW-
   DER (NOT DUTCH PROCESS)

¼ TEASPOON PEPPER

OPTIONAL: 1 TABLESPOON SNIPPED CHIVES

Combine the thyme and ¼ teaspoon salt in a small cup. Sprinkle over chicken; set aside.

Heat oil in a large nonstick skillet coated over medium-high heat until hot. Add the shallots and sauté 5 minutes.

Add chicken to skillet and sauté 6 minutes on each side or until done. Remove chicken from skillet to a plate. Tent with foil to keep warm.

Reduce heat to medium-low. Add jam, vinegar, cocoa powder, pepper, and remaining ¼ teaspoon salt, stirring constantly until the jam melts. Spoon raspberry-cocoa sauce over chicken. If desired, sprinkle with chives. **Makes 4 servings.**

NUTRITION PER SERVING (1 BREAST AND 1½ TABLESPOONS SAUCE):
CALORIES 281; FAT 6.1G (POLY 1.5G, MONO 2.7G, SAT 1.3G);
PROTEIN 33G; CHOLESTEROL 90.3MG; CARBOHYDRATE 21G.

# Cocoa-Rubbed Chicken

## WITH BARBECUE TABLE MOP

*In this recipe, a "dry rub" of chili powder, cocoa powder, brown sugar, and cayenne flavors the chicken before it is cooked, and a spicy-sweet "mop" is served alongside.*

| | |
|---|---|
| ½ CUP CHILI POWDER | 2 TEASPOONS GRATED ORANGE ZEST |
| ¼ CUP UNSWEETENED COCOA POWDER (NOT DUTCH PROCESS) | 1 TABLESPOON SOY SAUCE |
| | 1 TEASPOON HOT PEPPER SAUCE (SUCH AS TABASCO) |
| 3 TABLESPOONS BROWN SUGAR | |
| 2 TEASPOONS CAYENNE PEPPER | 2 3½-POUND CHICKENS, QUARTERED, BACK-BONES DISCARDED |
| 1 CUP MESQUITE BARBECUE SAUCE | |
| ¾ CUP KETCHUP | OPTIONAL: 3 CUPS MESQUITE WOOD CHIPS, SOAKED IN COLD WATER 1 HOUR |
| ⅓ CUP FRESHLY SQUEEZED ORANGE JUICE | |

To make the cocoa rub, mix the chili powder, cocoa powder, brown sugar, and cayenne pepper in a small bowl until blended; set aside.

To make the mop, mix the barbecue sauce, ketchup, orange juice, orange zest, soy sauce, and hot pepper sauce in a medium bowl until blended; set aside.

Arrange the chicken in single layer on large baking sheet. Season with salt and pepper. Sprinkle cocoa rub generously on both sides of chicken, pressing to adhere. Let stand at room temperature 1 hour.

Prepare grill to medium-high heat. When coals are white, place chicken, skin side down, on grill rack away from direct heat. Cover grill and cook chicken until cooked through, turning every 5 minutes and covering grill, about 35–40 minutes (cocoa rub may look slightly burned). Serve chicken hot or warm, skin removed, passing mop separately. **Makes 8 servings.**

NUTRITION PER SERVING (1 CHICKEN QUARTER AND ¼ CUP MOP):
CALORIES 276; FAT 8.0G (POLY 2.2G, MONO 2.7G, SAT 2.1G);
PROTEIN 32G; CHOLESTEROL 88.1MG; CARBOHYDRATE 22G.

# Pork Chops Mole

*This rendition of mole, made into a simple weeknight supper of pork chops, doesn't hit you over the head with the flavor of chocolate. Quite the opposite: the chocolate is indiscernible as a separate taste, and instead works by imparting richness and a slow-cooked flavor to this otherwise very quick weeknight supper.*

| | |
|---|---|
| 4 4-OUNCE BONELESS PORK LOIN CHOPS (ABOUT ½ INCH THICK) | ½ OUNCE BITTERSWEET CHOCOLATE, FINELY CHOPPED |
| ½ CUP DARK BEER | 1 TEASPOON ANCHO CHILE POWDER |
| 2 TEASPOONS UNSWEETENED COCOA POWDER (NOT DUTCH PROCESS) | 1 TEASPOON DRIED OREGANO |
| 1 CUP CHOPPED ONION | 1 TEASPOON GROUND CUMIN |
| 1 MEDIUM RED BELL PEPPER, SEEDED AND CUT INTO STRIPS | ½ TEASPOON SALT |
| 1 14.5-OUNCE CAN DICED TOMATOES WITH GARLIC AND ONION, UNDRAINED | ⅛ TEASPOON CINNAMON |
| | PINCH OF GROUND CLOVES |
| | ½ CUP MINCED FRESH CILANTRO |

Heat a large nonstick skillet coated with cooking spray over medium-high heat. Cook chops 4 minutes on each side or until browned. Remove from pan to a shallow dish. Add beer and cocoa powder to pan, scraping to loosen browned bits. Cook 3-4 minutes until liquid is reduced by half. Pour mixture over chops. Cover and set aside.

Reheat skillet coated with cooking spray over medium-high heat. Add the onion and bell pepper and cook 4–5 minutes or until tender. Stir in tomatoes; cook 1 minute. Add the chocolate, chile powder, oregano, cumin, salt, cinnamon, and cloves. Add the pork chops and beer mixture; bring to a boil. Cover, reduce heat to medium-low, and cook 5 minutes, stirring occasionally. Serve, sprinkling with cilantro. **Makes 4 servings.**

NUTRITION PER SERVING (1 PORK CHOP PLUS ¼ OF MOLE SAUCE):
CALORIES 276; FAT 10.8G (POLY 1.7G, MONO 4.4G, SAT 3.7G);
PROTEIN 27G; CHOLESTEROL 71MG; CARBOHYDRATE 14G.

# Grilled Pork Kebabs

## WITH CUBAN COCOA-RUM GLAZE

*Treat your friends to a summer party in the backyard with these tender kebabs, enhanced with dark rum and a trio of favorite flavors: cocoa, cinnamon, and coffee. Spicy black beans, purchased rolls, and fresh fruit or sorbet seal the meal.*

| | |
|---|---|
| 1 TABLESPOON OLIVE OIL | 4 CUPS HOT BREWED COFFEE |
| ½ CUP CHOPPED ONION | 3 TABLESPOONS UNSWEETENED COCOA |
| 1 TABLESPOON GRATED PEELED FRESH GINGER | POWDER (NOT DUTCH PROCESS) |
| 2 GARLIC CLOVES, CHOPPED | 1 TEASPOON GROUND CINNAMON |
| ¼ TEASPOON CAYENNE PEPPER | 1 TABLESPOON BUTTER, SOFTENED |
| 1½ TABLESPOONS DARK MOLASSES (NOT BLACKSTRAP) | ½ TEASPOON SALT |
| ½ CUP DARK RUM | 2 POUNDS PORK TENDERLOIN, TRIMMED |

Heat olive oil in a large skillet over medium-high heat. Add onion; sauté 5 minutes. Add ginger and garlic and sauté 2 minutes. Stir in cayenne pepper and molasses. Remove from heat and carefully stir in rum. Return to heat and cook mixture 2 minutes.

Stir the coffee, cocoa powder, and cinnamon into onion mixture. Bring to a boil and cook until reduced to 1½ cups, about 20 minutes. Remove from heat and cool 15 minutes. Place mixture in a blender or food processor and process until smooth. Stir in butter and salt.

Cut pork lengthwise into 8½-inch-wide strips. Thread pork strips onto 8 (10-inch) skewers.

Prepare grill to medium-high heat.

Place kebabs on grill rack coated with nonstick cooking spray. Grill 4 minutes on each side or until desired degree of doneness, turning and basting frequently with cocoa-rum mixture. Serve any remaining sauce on the side. **Makes 8 servings.**

NUTRITION PER SERVING (1 SKEWER): CALORIES 199; FAT 7.6G (POLY 1.5G, MONO 2.9G, SAT 2.7G); PROTEIN 26G; CHOLESTEROL 87MG; CARBOHYDRATE 5G.

# *Pork Medallions*

## WITH PORT-CHOCOLATE PAN SAUCE

*Rich enough to qualify as comfort food, these pork medallions—pork tenderloin cut into 16 medallions—also appeal to those with a more refined palate. The velvety sauce is made by whisking unsweetened chocolate into the sweet cranberry-port wine mixture at the end.*

| | |
|---|---|
| 1   CUP RUBY PORT | ¼   TEASPOON FRESHLY GROUND BLACK |
| ⅓   CUP DRIED CRANBERRIES |    PEPPER |
| 1   TEASPOON DIJON MUSTARD | ½   OUNCE UNSWEETENED CHOCOLATE, FINELY |
| 1   TABLESPOON CANOLA OIL |    CHOPPED |
| 1½ POUNDS PORK TENDERLOIN, TRIMMED | OPTIONAL: FRESH PARSLEY SPRIGS |
| ½   TEASPOON SALT | |

Combine the port, cranberries, and mustard in a small bowl; set aside.

Heat the oil in a large nonstick skillet over low heat for 2 minutes. Cut the pork crosswise into 16 pieces. Sprinkle evenly with salt and pepper.

Place the pork in the pan and cook 4 minutes on each side or until golden brown. Remove pork from pan. Stir in wine mixture, scraping to loosen browned bits. Increase heat to high and bring mixture to a boil. Cook until reduced to ½ cup, about 2–3 minutes. Remove sauce from heat. Stir in chocolate with a whisk until melted and smooth.

Serve sauce over pork. Garnish with parsley, if desired. **Makes 4 servings.**

NUTRITION PER SERVING (4 MEDALLIONS AND 2 TABLESPOONS SAUCE):
CALORIES 308; FAT 11.7G (POLY 1.7G, MONO 5.5G, SAT 3.5G);
PROTEIN 25G; CHOLESTEROL 73.1MG; CARBOHYDRATE 16G.

# Malaysian Pork Tenderloin

## WITH MANGO SAMBAL

*For the best tasting sambal—a generic name for any paste-like condiment made with chiles— begin with a ripe mango (or ripen in a paper bag). First peel the skin off the mango. Slice it lengthwise on either side of the pit into 4 slices. Chop with a kitchen knife.*

1   LARGE FIRM-RIPE MANGO, PEELED, PITTED, AND CHOPPED

1½ TEASPOONS SUGAR

2   TEASPOONS FRESH LIME JUICE

1¼ TEASPOONS FISH SAUCE (NAAM PLA)

1   TEASPOON MINCED, SEEDED JALAPEÑO

1   TABLESPOON UNSWEETENED COCOA POW-DER (NOT DUTCH PROCESS)

1   TABLESPOON PACKED LIGHT BROWN SUGAR

1¼ TEASPOONS CHILI POWDER

1   TEASPOON PAPRIKA

¾   TEASPOON SALT

¾   TEASPOON GROUND CUMIN

½   TEASPOON GROUND GINGER

¼   TEASPOON GARLIC POWDER

¼   TEASPOON DRIED THYME

1   1-POUND PORK TENDERLOIN, TRIMMED

To prepare the sambal, combine the mango, sugar, lime juice, fish sauce and jalapeño in a small bowl. Set aside while preparing pork.

For the pork, combine the cocoa powder, brown sugar, chili powder, paprika, salt, cumin, ginger, garlic powder, and dried thyme in a small bowl. Rub pork tenderloin with spice mixture. Loosely cover pork with plastic wrap and refrigerate for 20 minutes.

Preheat oven to 425°F. Spray a broiler pan with nonstick cooking spray. Place pork on the prepared broiler pan.

Roast the pork 18–20 minutes or until meat thermometer registers 160°F. Let stand 5 minutes; cut into ¼-inch-thick slices. Serve the sambal with the pork. **Makes 4 servings.**

NUTRITION PER SERVING (¼ OF THE PORK PLUS ABOUT ¼ CUP SAMBAL):
CALORIES 217; FAT 6.7G (POLY .72G, MONO 3.0G, SAT 2.4G);
PROTEIN 25G; CHOLESTEROL 66.9MG; CARBOHYDRATE 14G.

# Char Siu Pork Roast

*You may never order take-out again once you try this char siu shredded pork (a Chinese version of barbecue), made simple in a slow cooker. To round out the meal, try sticky rice and steamed snow peas drizzled with toasted sesame oil and toasted sesame seeds.*

| | |
|---|---|
| ⅓ CUP HOISIN SAUCE | 3 CLOVES GARLIC, MINCED |
| ⅓ CUP LOW-SODIUM SOY SAUCE | 2 TEASPOONS DARK SESAME OIL |
| 3 TABLESPOONS LIGHT MOLASSES | ¼ TEASPOON FIVE-SPICE POWDER |
| 3 TABLESPOONS KETCHUP | 2 POUNDS BONELESS BOSTON BUTT PORK |
| 2 TABLESPOONS UNSWEETENED COCOA | ROAST, TRIMMED |
| POWDER (NOT DUTCH PROCESS) | ½ CUP CANNED REDUCED-SODIUM CHICKEN |
| 1 TABLESPOON MINCED PEELED FRESH | BROTH |
| GINGER | |

In a small bowl whisk the hoisin sauce, soy sauce, molasses, ketchup, cocoa powder, ginger, garlic, sesame oil, and five-spice powder, stirring well with a whisk. Place in a large ziplock plastic bag. Add pork to bag and seal. Marinate in refrigerator at least 2 hours, turning occasionally.

Place pork and marinade in an electric slow cooker. Cover and cook on low for 8 hours.

Remove pork from slow cooker using a slotted spoon. Place on a cutting board or work surface. Cover with aluminum foil to keep warm.

Add chicken broth to sauce in slow cooker. Cover and cook on low for 30 minutes or until sauce thickens. Shred pork with fingers or 2 forks. Serve pork with sauce. **Makes 8 servings.**

NUTRITION PER SERVING (⅛ OF THE PORK AND 2 TABLESPOONS SAUCE):
CALORIES 234; FAT 8.1G (POLY 1.4G, MONO 3.5G, SAT 2.6G);
PROTEIN 27G; CHOLESTEROL 67.2MG; CARBOHYDRATE 13G.

# Pork Tournedos

## WITH CHOCOLATE GASTRIQUE AND FRESH CHERRY SALSA

*Gastrique is essentially the French version of sweet & sour sauce, made by reducing vinegar or wine with sugar and, sometimes, fruit. A tournedo is a fancy name for a center-cut boneless pork loin chop. Coupled with a fresh cherry salsa, this pork-gastrique combination flirts with extravagance.*

| | |
|---|---|
| 1 CUP FRESH, PITTED CHERRIES CUT INTO ¼-INCH DICE | 1 TABLESPOON UNSWEETENED COCOA POWDER (NOT DUTCH PROCESS) |
| 2 TABLESPOONS FINELY CHOPPED RED ONION | ¼ TEASPOON SALT |
| ¼ TEASPOON FRESHLY GRATED LEMON ZEST | 6 1½-INCH-THICK CENTER-CUT BONELESS PORK LOIN CHOPS |
| 1 TABLESPOON FRESH LEMON JUICE | FRESHLY GROUND BLACK PEPPER |
| 2 TABLESPOONS MINCED FRESH MINT LEAVES | 1 TABLESPOON UNSALTED BUTTER |
| 1 CUP RED-WINE VINEGAR | |
| 3 TABLESPOONS RED CURRANT JELLY | |

In a bowl combine the cherries, red onion, lemon zest, lemon juice, mint, and salt to taste and let stand, covered, at room temperature. Salsa may be made 2 hours ahead and kept at room temperature, covered.

In a small saucepan simmer vinegar until reduced to about 3 tablespoons. Whisk in jelly, cocoa powder, and salt, whisking until smooth. Keep warm, covered.

Season pork with pepper and salt. In a 12-inch heavy skillet melt butter over moderately high heat until foam subsides and sauté pork until golden, about 3 minutes on each side.

Continue cooking pork, covered, over moderate heat until just cooked through, about 5 minutes more.

Divide chocolate gastrique among 6 plates and top with pork and salsa. **Makes 6 servings.**

NUTRITION PER SERVING (1 TOURNEDO, 1½ TABLESPOONS GASTRIQUE, AND ¼ CUP SALSA):
CALORIES 202; FAT 5.3G (POLY .47G, MONO 1.8G, SAT 2.5G);
PROTEIN 26G; CHOLESTEROL 67.6MG; CARBOHYDRATE 13G.

# Grilled Lamb Chops

## WITH HONEYED-RED WINE GLAZE

*The glaze for these elegant chops combines simplicity with deep, distinct flavors.*

| | |
|---|---|
| 1 CUP DRY RED WINE | 2 TEASPOONS RED WINE VINEGAR |
| 1 TABLESPOON OLIVE OIL | ½ TEASPOON SALT |
| 3 TABLESPOONS CHOPPED FRESH OREGANO | ½ TEASPOON GROUND BLACK PEPPER |
| 2 TABLESPOONS MINCED GARLIC | 8 1- TO 1¼-INCH-THICK LOIN LAMB CHOPS, |
| 1½ TABLESPOONS UNSWEETENED COCOA | TRIMMED |
| POWDER (NOT DUTCH PROCESS) | 2 TABLESPOONS HONEY |

In a large glass baking dish mix the red wine, olive oil, oregano, garlic, cocoa powder, vinegar, salt, and pepper. Arrange lamb chops in single layer in dish; turn to coat. Cover and refrigerate at least 2 hours, turning and basting often. (Can be prepared 1 day ahead. Keep chilled.)

Remove chops from marinade. Boil marinade in a small saucepan over high heat until reduced by half. Stir in the honey. Cool.

Prepare barbecue to medium-high heat. Transfer lamb to plate. Grill lamb to desired doneness, turning and basting with marinade often, about 10 minutes for medium-rare. **Makes 4 servings.**

NUTRITION PER SERVING (2 CHOPS):
CALORIES 402; FAT 15.8G (POLY .96G, MONO 7.5G, SAT 5.5G);
PROTEIN 44G; CHOLESTEROL 82.1MG; CARBOHYDRATE 11G.

# Punjabi-Spiced Salmon

## WITH CUCUMBER-MINT RAITA

*Cooking the salmon fillets with the skin on protects the delicate flesh and removing the skin at the end is easier than taking it off while it's raw. If you do not have an ovenproof skillet, wrap the handle of a skillet with foil to "ovenproof" it.*

| | |
|---|---|
| 1 CUP NONFAT YOGURT | ½ TEASPOON GROUND TURMERIC |
| ¼ CUP PEELED, SEEDED, AND DICED CUCUMBER | ½ TEASPOON FENNEL SEEDS, CRUSHED |
| ¼ CUP THINLY SLICED GREEN ONIONS | ½ TEASPOON BLACK PEPPER |
| ¼ CUP MINT LEAVES, MINCED | ¼ TEASPOON GROUND CINNAMON |
| 2 TEASPOONS GRATED LEMON ZEST | ¼ TEASPOON GROUND CARDAMOM |
| 2 TEASPOONS UNSWEETENED COCOA POWDER (NOT DUTCH PROCESS) | 4 (6-OUNCE) SALMON FILLETS (ABOUT 1¼ INCHES THICK) |
| 1 TEASPOON GROUND CUMIN | ½ TEASPOON SALT |
| 1 TEASPOON GROUND CORIANDER | 1 TEASPOON OLIVE OIL |

Preheat oven to 400°F.

In a small bowl combine the yogurt, cucumber, green onions, mint, and lemon zest. Season with salt and pepper to taste and set aside.

In a shallow dish combine the cocoa powder, cumin, coriander, turmeric, fennel, pepper, cinnamon and cardamom. Sprinkle fillets with the salt, then dredge in spice mixture.

Heat the oil in a large ovenproof skillet over medium-high heat. Add the fillets, skin sides up, and cook 5 minutes or until bottoms are golden. Turn fillets over. Transfer skillet to oven and roast 10 minutes or until fish flakes easily when tested with a fork. Remove skin from fillets, discarding skin. Serve with the raita. **Makes 4 servings.**

NUTRITION PER SERVING ( 1 FILLET AND ⅓ CUP RAITA):
CALORIES 301; FAT 15.4G (POLY 3.2G, MONO 7.7G, SAT 2.7G);
PROTEIN 36G; CHOLESTEROL 111MG; CARBOHYDRATE 3G.

# *Pasta, Shrimp, and Mango Salad*

## WITH CITRUS-COCOA VINAIGRETTE

*The dressing on this salad is so good—you'll want to make it for many other occasions. Use it as a dressing for soft lettuce (i.e., Bibb or butter lettuce), potato salad, or fresh fruit salad, or use it as an accompaniment to grilled shrimp, chicken, or pork.*

¼ CUP BOTTLED MANGO CHUTNEY

¼ CUP FRESH ORANGE JUICE

1½ TABLESPOONS FRESH LIME JUICE

2 TABLESPOONS WATER

2 TEASPOONS UNSWEETENED COCOA POW-
DER (NOT DUTCH PROCESS)

1 TEASPOON MINCED CANNED CHIPOTLE
CHILE IN ADOBO SAUCE

1 TEASPOON GROUND CUMIN

1 GARLIC CLOVE, MINCED

1 POUND MEDIUM SHRIMP, COOKED AND
PEELED

4 CUPS COOKED MEDIUM SEASHELL PASTA
(ABOUT 2 CUPS UNCOOKED PASTA)

2 LARGE, FIRM-RIPE MANGOES, PEELED,
PITTED, AND DICED

1 MEDIUM RED BELL PEPPER, SEEDED AND
CUT INTO VERY THIN STRIPS

⅓ CUP CHOPPED FRESH CILANTRO

1 5-OUNCE BAG BABY SPINACH

Place the chutney, orange juice, lime juice, water, cocoa powder, chile, cumin, and garlic in a blender and purée until smooth. Season with salt and pepper to taste.

In a large bowl combine the shrimp, cooked pasta, mango, and red bell pepper. Add the cilantro and citrus-cocoa dressing, tossing to coat. Cover and refrigerate at least 8 hours. Divide spinach among 8 dinner plates; top with equal portions of the salad. **Makes 8 main-dish servings.**

NUTRITION PER SERVING (⅛ OF SALAD AND SPINACH):
CALORIES 348; FAT 3.7G (POLY 1.4G, MONO .57G, SAT .72G);
PROTEIN 38G; CHOLESTEROL 258.4MG; CARBOHYDRATE 38G.

# Braised Mahogany Tofu

*Salty, sweet, and tangy, braised tofu takes on a meaty texture in this wholly satisfying entrée. Fresh ginger, sesame oil, orange zest, and five-spice powder add a satisfying fragrance to the sauce, perfect for spooning over nutty brown rice.*

| | | | |
|---|---|---|---|
| 1 | CUP CANNED TOMATO SAUCE | 3 | GARLIC CLOVES, MINCED |
| ½ | CUP BOTTLED HOISIN SAUCE | 1 | TABLESPOON TOASTED SESAME OIL |
| ¼ | CUP WATER | 1 | POUND FIRM OR EXTRA-FIRM TOFU, DRAINED AND CUT INTO 1-INCH CUBES |
| ¼ | CUP LOW-SODIUM SOY SAUCE | | |
| 2 | TABLESPOONS UNSWEETENED COCOA POWDER (NOT DUTCH PROCESS) | 2 | CUPS (1-INCH) SLICED GREEN ONIONS |
| 1 | TABLESPOON GRATED ORANGE ZEST | 1 | CUP CHOPPED ONION |
| 1 | TABLESPOON GRATED PEELED FRESH GINGER | 1 | CUP PEELED, DIAGONALLY SLICED CARROT |
| 2 | TABLESPOONS MOLASSES (NOT BLACKSTRAP) | 1 | MEDIUM RED BELL PEPPER, SEEDED AND DICED |
| 1 | TABLESPOON RICE VINEGAR | 2 | ROMA TOMATOES, SEEDED AND DICED |
| 2 | TEASPOONS CHINESE FIVE-SPICE POWDER | | OPTIONAL: HOT COOKED BROWN OR WHITE RICE |
| ½ | TEASPOON CAYENNE PEPPER | | |

In a medium bowl whisk the tomato sauce, hoisin sauce, water, soy sauce, cocoa powder, orange zest, ginger, molasses, rice vinegar, five-spice powder, cayenne, and garlic until well blended.

Heat sesame oil in a large nonstick skillet over medium heat. Add tofu and cook 6 minutes or until browned, turning occasionally.

Add tomato sauce mixture, green onions, onion, carrot, bell pepper, and tomatoes. Bring to a boil. Cover, reduce heat, and simmer 15 minutes or until vegetables are crisp-tender. Serve over rice, if desired. **Makes 4 servings.**

NUTRITION PER SERVING (¼ OF TOFU MIXTURE):
CALORIES 250; FAT 8.2G (POLY 3.6G, MONO 3.0G, SAT 1.2G);
PROTEIN 10G; CHOLESTEROL .96MG; CARBOHYDRATE 38G.

# Spanish Black Bean Burgers

## WITH OLIVE-ORANGE RELISH

*You have never had a vegetarian burger like this one: aromatic without being overly spicy, this dish has a touch of the exotic but will please traditionalists, too. The two-ingredient relish hits on sweet, salty, and sour, complementing the smoky, herbed black bean patties and tangy Manchego.*

½ CUP PIMENTO-STUFFED OLIVES, COARSELY CHOPPED

3 TABLESPOONS ORANGE MARMALADE

1 15-OUNCE CAN BLACK BEANS, RINSED AND DRAINED

½ CUP DRY BREADCRUMBS

¼ CUP MINCED RED ONION

1 TABLESPOON UNSWEETENED COCOA POWDER (NOT DUTCH PROCESS)

1 TEASPOON SWEET (NOT HOT) SMOKED PAPRIKA (PIMENTON)

1 TEASPOON DRIED OREGANO

1 CLOVE GARLIC, MINCED

1 LARGE EGG

1 CUP COARSELY GRATED, LOOSELY PACKED MANCHEGO CHEESE

4 WHOLE WHEAT HAMBURGER BUNS

2 CUPS FRESH PRECLEANED BABY SPINACH LEAVES

To prepare relish, combine the olives and marmalade in a small bowl; set aside.

To prepare burgers, place black beans in a large bowl and coarsely mash with a fork. Stir in the breadcrumbs, red onion, cocoa powder, paprika, oregano, garlic, and egg. Divide bean mixture into 4 equal portions, shaping each into a ½-inch-thick patty.

Prepare grill to medium-high heat. Spray grill rack with nonstick cooking spray.

Place patties on prepared grill rack. Grill 5 minutes. Turn patties with a spatula. Sprinkle with equal amounts of Manchego and grill 5 minutes longer.

To serve, place one patty on the bottom half of each bun. Top with equal amounts of relish and spinach leaves, then the top half of bun. **Makes 4 servings.**

NUTRITION PER SERVING (1 ASSEMBLED BURGER):
CALORIES 389; FAT 11.3G (POLY 1.5G, MONO 5.4G, SAT 3.5G);
PROTEIN 17G; CHOLESTEROL 60.1MG; CARBOHYDRATE 57G.

## SMOKY-LIME

# *Picadillo Wrap*

*This is a quick and easy version of picadillo, which is a sweet-and-sour meat stew popular in many Spanish-speaking countries. Here it gets a touch of smokiness from chipotle chile powder (smoked jalapeños) and citrus from fresh lime juice and zest. Serve with light sweet potato chips and fresh fruit for dessert.*

| | |
|---|---|
| 2 POUNDS EXTRA-LEAN GROUND BEEF | 2 TABLESPOONS UNSWEETENED COCOA POW-DER (NOT DUTCH PROCESS) |
| 1 TABLESPOON DRIED OREGANO | |
| 2 TEASPOONS CHIPOTLE CHILE POWDER | ¼ CUP CHOPPED PIMENTO-STUFFED OLIVES |
| ¼ TEASPOON SALT | 3 TABLESPOONS MINCED FRESH CILANTRO LEAVES |
| 3 GARLIC CLOVES, MINCED | |
| 1 6-OUNCE CAN TOMATO PASTE | 2 TABLESPOONS FRESH LIME JUICE |
| 2 CUPS WATER | 2 TEASPOONS GRATED LIME ZEST |
| ½ CUP GOLDEN RAISINS | 8 6-INCH FLOUR TORTILLAS |

Place a skillet over medium-high heat until hot. Add ground beef and cook, breaking up meat with the back of a spoon, until browned. Add oregano, chile powder, salt, and garlic, and sauté 1 minute. Stir in tomato paste and sauté 2 minutes.

Stir in water, raisins, and cocoa powder. Bring mixture to a boil. Reduce heat and simmer 20 minutes. Stir in olives, cilantro, lime juice, and lime zest.

Warm tortillas according to package directions. Spoon about ½ cup beef mixture down center of each tortilla. Roll up and serve. **Makes 8 servings.**

NUTRITION PER SERVING (1 WRAP):
CALORIES 324; FAT 9.4G (POLY .76G, MONO 4.5G, SAT 3.4G);
PROTEIN 29G; CHOLESTEROL 70.3MG; CARBOHYDRATE 31G.

# Beef and Beer Chili

## WITH LIME CREMA

*A Texas-inspired version of a hearty classic, this recipe is just right for a family meal or casual party. The dark beer and cocoa powder make the beef taste beefier.*

1½ POUNDS EXTRA-LEAN GROUND BEEF

1½ CUPS CHOPPED ONIONS

4   GARLIC CLOVES, FINELY CHOPPED

¼   CUP CHILI POWDER

2½ TABLESPOONS UNSWEETENED COCOA POW-
    DER (NOT DUTCH PROCESS)

1   14.5-OUNCE CAN BEEF BROTH

½   CUP CANNED PURÉED TOMATOES

½   CUP DARK BEER

2   TEASPOONS CHIPOTLE CHILE POWDER

2   TABLESPOONS YELLOW CORNMEAL

1   15.5-OUNCE CAN SMALL RED BEANS,
    RINSED AND DRAINED

¾   REDUCED-FAT SOUR CREAM

1   TABLESPOON FRESH LIME JUICE

1½ TEASPOONS GRATED LIME ZEST

OPTIONAL: REDUCED-FAT TORTILLA CHIPS

Heat heavy large pot over high heat. Add the ground beef and sauté until cooked through, breaking up meat with the back of a spoon, about 8 minutes. Transfer to a large bowl.

Add onions and garlic to same pot. Sauté until onions are tender, 8 minutes. Add chili powder and cocoa powder. Sauté until fragrant, 3 minutes. Add cooked beef, beef broth, tomatoes, beer, and chipotle powder. Cover partially; simmer until chili is thick, stirring often, about 1 hour 10 minutes.

Gradually stir cornmeal into chili. Stir in beans. Simmer until heated through. Season generously with salt and pepper. (Can be made 1 day ahead. Cover and chill. Rewarm over medium heat.)

In a small bowl whisk sour cream, lime juice, and lime zest. Season with salt.

Spoon chili into bowls. Spoon lime crema atop chili. Serve with chips, if desired. **Makes 8 servings.**

NUTRITION PER SERVING (⅛ OF CHILI AND 2 TABLESPOONS CREMA):
CALORIES 338; FAT 11.2G (POLY .6G, MONO 4.4G, SAT 5.3G);
PROTEIN 41G; CHOLESTEROL 112.7MG; CARBOHYDRATE 16G.

# Ginger and Dark Beer-Braised Beef

*Although often called "gingerroot," ginger is actually a rhizome. The forms found at the market are pieces of the rhizome, called a "hand." Purchase fresh ginger with a smooth, unblemished skin; if you break off a piece of the hand, the texture should be firm and crisp and the fragrance fresh and spicy. Note that it isn't added to the braise until the final 30 minutes of cooking; this is to get more gingery oomph, since the flavor fades the longer it cooks.*

| | | | |
|---|---|---|---|
| 1 | POUND BEEF STEW MEAT, TRIMMED | 1 | 3-INCH CINNAMON STICK |
| ¼ | TEASPOON PEPPER | 1 | 2-INCH PIECE PEELED FRESH GINGER, CUT |
| 1 | TEASPOON CANOLA OIL | | INTO SLICES |
| 3 | TABLESPOONS LOW-SODIUM SOY SAUCE | 2 | CUPS PEELED, THINLY SLICED CARROT |
| 1 | 12-OUNCE BOTTLE DARK BEER | 2 | CUPS WELL-CLEANED SLICED LEEKS, WHITE |
| 2 | TABLESPOONS UNSWEETENED COCOA | | PARTS ONLY (ABOUT 2 MEDIUM) |
| | POWDER (NOT DUTCH PROCESS) | 6 | CUPS HOT COOKED COUSCOUS |
| 2 | WHOLE GREEN ONIONS | | |

Cut meat into ¾-inch cubes, and sprinkle with pepper.

Heat oil in a Dutch oven over medium-high heat. Add beef, and cook 3 minutes or until browned, stirring frequently. Add the soy sauce, beer, cocoa powder, green onions, and cinnamon stick. Bring to a boil. Cover meat mixture, reduce heat, and simmer 1 hour.

Add the ginger, carrot, and leeks. Cook, uncovered, an additional 30 minutes or until vegetables are tender. Discard gingerroot, green onions, and cinnamon stick. Serve over couscous. **Makes 6 servings.**

NUTRITION PER SERVING (ABOUT 1 CUP STEW AND 1 CUP COUSCOUS): CALORIES 458; FAT 6.4G (POLY 1.8G, MONO 1.8G, SAT 1.6G); PROTEIN 31G; CHOLESTEROL 44MG; CARBOHYDRATE 71G.

# Adobo Flank Steak

## WITH ORANGE & AVOCADO SALSA

*No need to wait until the summer grilling season to make this steak. Simply fire up the broiler and place the flank steak on a nonstick broiler pan, then broil, 6 minutes per side. Talk about a delicious cold-weather escape!*

¼ CUP SHERRY VINEGAR

2 TABLESPOONS FRESH THYME LEAVES

2 TABLESPOONS UNSWEETENED COCOA POWDER (NOT DUTCH PROCESS)

2 TABLESPOONS PACKED DARK BROWN SUGAR

2 TEASPOONS GROUND CUMIN

1½ TEASPOONS KOSHER SALT

½ TEASPOON GROUND CLOVES

3 GARLIC CLOVES, PEELED

1 CANNED CHIPOTLE CHILE (PACKED IN ADOBO SAUCE), SEEDS REMOVED

1 1½-POUND FLANK STEAK, TRIMMED

1 TABLESPOON FRESH LIME JUICE

1 TABLESPOON HONEY

1½ CUPS CANNED, WELL-DRAINED MANDARIN ORANGES

1 MEDIUM AVOCADO, PEELED, PITTED, AND DICED

⅔ CUP FINELY CHOPPED RED ONION

⅓ CUP CHOPPED FRESH CILANTRO

In a blender place the vinegar, thyme, cocoa powder, brown sugar, cumin, salt, cloves, garlic, and chipotle chile. Process until smooth, scraping sides occasionally.

Combine vinegar mixture and steak in a large ziplock plastic bag. Seal and marinate in refrigerator 24 hours. Remove steak from bag and discard marinade.

Prepare grill to medium high heat. Spray grill rack with nonstick cooking spray.

Place steak on prepared grill rack and cook 6 minutes on each side or until desired degree of doneness. Remove steak to cutting board and let rest 5 minutes.

While the steak rests, whisk the lime juice and honey in a medium bowl until blended. Add the oranges, avocado, red onion, and cilantro to the bowl. Season to taste with salt and pepper.

Cut steak diagonally across the grain into thin slices. Serve steak with the salsa. **Makes 6 servings.**

NUTRITION PER SERVING (⅙ OF STEAK AND ½ CUP SALSA):
CALORIES 285; FAT 13.2G (POLY .93G, MONO 6.3G, SAT 4.4G);
PROTEIN 25G; CHOLESTEROL 56.7MG; CARBOHYDRATE 19G.

# Tejas Meatloaf

*With the additions of cumin, chili powder, and cilantro, this meatloaf has a southwestern accent, so round out the menu with corn muffins and coleslaw.*

| | |
|---|---|
| 1 CUP KETCHUP | ½ CUP FRESHLY GRATED PARMESAN CHEESE |
| 1 TABLESPOON WORCESTERSHIRE SAUCE | ½ CUP SHREDDED CARROT |
| 2 TEASPOONS CHILI POWDER | ¼ CUP MINCED FRESH CILANTRO |
| 1 TABLESPOON BALSAMIC VINEGAR | 1 TEASPOON GROUND CUMIN |
| 2 TABLESPOONS UNSWEETENED COCOA POWDER (NOT DUTCH PROCESS), DIVIDED USE | ½ TEASPOON BLACK PEPPER |
| | 2 LARGE GARLIC CLOVES, MINCED |
| ¼ CUP BREADCRUMBS | 1½ POUNDS EXTRA-LEAN GROUND BEEF |
| ½ CUP 1% LOW-FAT MILK | ½ POUND LEAN GROUND PORK |
| 1 CUP FINELY CHOPPED ONION | 1 LARGE EGG, LIGHTLY BEATEN |

Preheat oven to 350°F. Spray an 8½-inch loaf pan with nonstick cooking spray.

In a small bowl combine the ketchup, Worcestershire sauce, chili powder, vinegar, and 1 tablespoon cocoa powder.

In a large bowl combine the breadcrumbs and milk. Add the onion, Parmesan cheese, carrot, cilantro, cumin, pepper, garlic, ground beef, ground pork, egg, ½ cup ketchup mixture and remaining 1 tablespoon cocoa powder. Gently mix with hands until well blended. Shape beef mixture into a loaf in the prepared pan.

Bake meatloaf 55 minutes. Brush remaining ketchup mixture over top. Bake an additional 15 minutes. Let stand 10 minutes. Remove meatloaf from pan. Cut into 8 slices. **Makes 8 servings.**

NUTRITION PER SERVING (1 SLICE):
CALORIES 262; FAT 9.6G (POLY .7G, MONO 3.7G, SAT 3.9G); PROTEIN 29G; CHOLESTEROL 102MG; CARBOHYDRATE 14G.

# Beef Stew

*Homey and old-fashioned goes sophisticated in this trim stew thanks to the additions of dry red wine, hoisin sauce, and cocoa powder. It can be on the stove in a flash, where it simmers undisturbed for an hour—leaving you free to relax, unwind, and enjoy a few sips of the leftover Cabernet Sauvignon you'll have from this recipe.*

| | | | |
|---|---|---|---|
| 1 | TEASPOON CANOLA OIL | 1½ | TABLESPOONS UNSWEETENED COCOA POWDER (NOT DUTCH PROCESS) |
| 1½ | POUNDS BONED RUMP ROAST, CUT INTO 1-INCH CUBES | 2 | BAY LEAVES |
| 3 | GARLIC CLOVES, MINCED | 4 | CUPS (⅓-INCH-THICK) SLICED ONION, SEPARATED INTO RINGS |
| 1 | CUP CABERNET SAUVIGNON OR OTHER DRY RED WINE | 12 | OUNCES MUSHROOMS, TRIMMED AND HALVED |
| ½ | TEASPOON SALT | 1 | TABLESPOON CORNSTARCH |
| 1 | 14.5-OUNCE CAN NO-SALT-ADDED DICED TOMATOES, UNDRAINED | 1 | TABLESPOON WATER |
| 1¼ | CUPS CANNED FAT-FREE BEEF BROTH | 2 | TABLESPOONS CHOPPED FRESH FLAT-LEAF PARSLEY |
| ¼ | CUP HOISIN SAUCE | | |

Heat oil in a Dutch oven over medium-high heat. Add half of the beef, and cook for 5 minutes or until browned, turning occasionally. Remove from pan, and keep warm. Repeat procedure with remaining beef.

Return beef to pot. Add garlic and cook 1 minute. Stir in the wine, salt, tomatoes, beef broth, hoisin sauce, cocoa powder, and bay leaves; bring to a boil. Cover, reduce heat, and simmer 1 hour. Add the onions and mushrooms and bring to a boil. Partially cover, reduce heat, and simmer for 1 hour or until the beef is tender.

In a small cup mix the cornstarch and water. Reduce heat to medium, add cornstarch mixture and simmer until sauce thickens, stirring occasionally, about 8 minutes. Discard bay leaves. Season stew with salt and pepper. Serve, sprinkled with parsley. **Makes 6 servings.**

NUTRITION PER SERVING (ABOUT 1⅓ CUPS STEW):
CALORIES 250; FAT 5.8G (POLY .8G, MONO 2.2G, SAT 1.9G);
PROTEIN 28G; CHOLESTEROL 65MG; CARBOHYDRATE 19G.

# Caribbean Black Beans

## WITH COCOA & RUM

*Perfect for a backyard barbecue, these spicy-sweet beans have a distinct Caribbean flair thanks to a generous splash of dark rum, a sprinkling of spices, and a kick of heat.*

| | |
|---|---|
| 5 OUNCES FRESH CHORIZO | 2 TABLESPOONS PACKED LIGHT BROWN SUGAR |
| 1⅓ CUPS CHOPPED ONION | 2 TABLESPOONS WORCESTERSHIRE SAUCE |
| 4 GARLIC CLOVES, MINCED | 2 TABLESPOONS HOT SAUCE (OR TO TASTE) |
| ½ CUP MOLASSES | 2 TEASPOONS GROUND GINGER |
| ½ CUP KETCHUP | ¼ TEASPOON ALLSPICE |
| ½ CUP DARK RUM | 3 15-OUNCE CANS BLACK BEANS, RINSED AND |
| ¼ CUP DIJON MUSTARD | DRAINED |
| 2 TABLESPOONS UNSWEETENED COCOA POWDER (NOT DUTCH PROCESS) | |

Cook chorizo in a large saucepan over medium heat until browned, stirring to crumble. Remove sausage with slotted spoon and wipe out all but 1 teaspoon fat with a paper towel.

Add onion and garlic to pan. Cook 5 minutes or until onion is tender. Stir in molasses, ketchup, rum, mustard, cocoa powder, brown sugar, Worcestershire sauce, hot sauce, ginger, and allspice. Bring mixture to a boil. Reduce heat, and simmer 5 minutes, stirring occasionally.

Stir in the chorizo and beans. Simmer for 1 hour over low heat, stirring occasionally. **Makes 10 servings.**

NUTRITION PER SERVING (¾ CUP BEANS):
CALORIES 247; FAT 5.3G (POLY .45G, MONO 2.6G, SAT 2.0G);
PROTEIN 10G; CHOLESTEROL 12.5MG; CARBOHYDRATE 39G.

# Vegetables

*Toss and roast: orange marmalade and shallots bring color and sweetness to a fall harvest of root vegetables. The touch of cocoa powder can't be skipped: it adds a nuance of flavor to the caramelized vegetables that will keep guests guessing.*

| | |
|---|---|
| 4 CUPS OF 1-INCH CUBED PEELED SWEET POTATO | 2½ TABLESPOONS ORANGE MARMALADE |
| 3 CUPS OF 1-INCH CUBED PEELED RUTABAGA | 2 TABLESPOONS LEMON JUICE |
| 2 CUPS OF 1-INCH CUBED SLICED PARSNIP | 1 TABLESPOON DIJON MUSTARD |
| 1 TABLESPOON OLIVE OIL | 1 TABLESPOON UNSWEETENED COCOA POWDER (NOT DUTCH PROCESS) |
| 6 LARGE SHALLOTS, ENDS TRIMMED, QUARTERED | ¼ TEASPOON SALT |
| ¼ CUP PACKED DARK BROWN SUGAR | ⅛ TEASPOON NUTMEG |
| | ⅛ TEASPOON CAYENNE PEPPER |

Preheat oven to 400°F. Spray a large shallow roasting pan with nonstick cooking spray.

In a large bowl combine the sweet potato, rutabaga, and parsnip. Arrange the vegetables in a single layer in the prepared pan.

Roast vegetables 45 minutes, stirring twice.

In a small saucepan set over medium-high heat combine the brown sugar, marmalade, lemon juice, mustard, cocoa powder, salt, nutmeg, and cayenne. Bring to a boil. Reduce heat and simmer 1 minute. Pour mixture over vegetables and toss gently to coat.

Roast an additional 15 minutes or until vegetables are tender. **Makes 8 servings.**

NUTRITION PER SERVING (⅛ OF ROASTED VEGETABLES):
CALORIES 202; FAT 2.5G (POLY 1.0G, MONO .7G, SAT .6G);
PROTEIN 3G; CHOLESTEROL 0MG; CARBOHYDRATE 45G.

# Spicy Chickpeas

## WITH SPINACH & BASMATI RICE

*Basmati rice makes a fragrant base for this vegetarian entree—but it's the coalescence of aromatic spices and citrus, flavoring the chickpeas and spinach, that are the real focus of the dish.*

| | |
|---|---|
| 2 TEASPOONS OLIVE OIL | 1 10-OUNCE PACKAGE FRESH SPINACH, ROUGHLY CHOPPED |
| 3 CUPS CHOPPED ONION | 2 TEASPOONS CHILI POWDER |
| 2 TEASPOONS GROUND GINGER | 2 15.5-OUNCE CANS CHICKPEAS (GARBANZO BEANS), RINSED AND DRAINED |
| 4 GARLIC CLOVES, MINCED | |
| ½ CUP WATER | 2 TEASPOONS FRESH LEMON JUICE |
| ⅓ CUP CANNED TOMATO PASTE | 2 TEASPOONS GRATED LEMON ZEST |
| 2 TEASPOONS UNSWEETENED COCOA POWDER (NOT DUTCH PROCESS) | 2 CUPS HOT COOKED BASMATI RICE |
| 1 TEASPOON MILD CURRY POWDER | OPTIONAL ACCOMPANIMENTS: PLAIN FAT-FREE YOGURT AND LEMON WEDGES |
| 1 TEASPOON GROUND CUMIN | |
| ½ TEASPOON SALT | |

Heat the oil in a large nonstick skillet over medium-high heat. Add the onion, ginger, and garlic; sauté 4 minutes or until mixture begins to brown. Add the water, tomato paste, cocoa powder, curry powder, cumin, and salt; cook 1 minute, stirring constantly.

Stir in the spinach, chili powder, and chickpeas; cover. Reduce heat; cook 5 minutes or until spinach wilts and mixture is heated. Stir in lemon juice and zest. Serve over rice. Garnish with yogurt and lemon wedges, if desired. **Makes 4 servings.**

NUTRITION PER SERVING (1¼ CUPS CHICKPEAS AND ½ CUP RICE):
CALORIES 406; FAT 5G (POLY 1.4G, MONO 2.4G, SAT .8G);
PROTEIN 14G; CHOLESTEROL 0MG; CARBOHYDRATE 77G.

# Butternut Squash Purée

## WITH WINTER SPICES

*A new kind of aromatherapy: cinnamon, cumin, pepper, ginger, and cardamom in a sensational squash purée. Other orange-fleshed squash—such as kabocha or acorn—will also work in this warming side dish.*

| | | | |
|---|---|---|---|
| 2 | TABLESPOONS OLIVE OIL | ¼ | TEASPOON GROUND GINGER |
| 1 | TABLESPOON UNSWEETENED COCOA POWDER (NOT DUTCH PROCESS) | ¼ | TEASPOON GROUND CARDAMOM |
| ¾ | TEASPOON SALT | 10 | CUPS OF 1-INCH CUBED PEELED BUTTERNUT SQUASH (ABOUT 3¾ POUNDS) |
| ¼ | TEASPOON GROUND CINNAMON | 1 | LARGE RED ONION, CUT INTO 1-INCH PIECES |
| ¼ | TEASPOON GROUND CUMIN | ¼ | CUP WATER |
| ¼ | TEASPOON FRESHLY GROUND BLACK PEPPER | 1 | TABLESPOON PACKED LIGHT BROWN SUGAR |

Preheat oven to 375°F. Line a large, rimmed baking sheet with foil.

In a large bowl whisk the olive oil, cocoa powder, salt, cinnamon, cumin, pepper, ginger, and cardamom. Add the squash and red onion and toss well to coat. Transfer the squash mixture to the prepared baking sheet.

Bake 50–55 minutes or until squash is tender. Place squash mixture, ¼ cup water, and brown sugar in a large food processor and process until smooth. Serve immediately. **Makes 6 servings.**

NUTRITION PER SERVING (ABOUT 1 CUP PURÉE):
CALORIES 208; FAT 5.1G (POLY .7G, MONO 3.5G, SAT .9G);
PROTEIN 4G; CHOLESTEROL 0MG; CARBOHYDRATE 42G.

# Braised Cauliflower

## & POTATOES WITH NORTH INDIAN SPICES

*Sure, brightly colored vegetables are packed with nutrition, but so too cauliflower: it's low in calories (25 calories per cup) and high in dietary fiber, vitamin C, vitamin K, vitamin B6, folate, thiamin, and more. It even has 2 grams of protein per cup. Here it gets the high-flavor treatment, in combination with potatoes, thanks to a host of North Indian herbs and spices.*

| | |
|---|---|
| 2 TABLESPOONS CANOLA OIL, DIVIDED USE | 2 TEASPOONS UNSWEETENED COCOA POWDER (NOT DUTCH PROCESS) |
| 2 BAKING POTATOES, PEELED, HALVED LENGTHWISE, AND SLICED (ABOUT 1¾ POUNDS) | 1½ TEASPOONS GROUND CUMIN |
| 4 GARLIC CLOVES, MINCED | 1 TEASPOON GROUND TURMERIC |
| 3 TABLESPOONS CHOPPED PEELED FRESH GINGER | ½ TEASPOON CAYENNE PEPPER |
| ½ CUP CANNED CRUSHED TOMATOES | 5 CUPS FRESH OR FROZEN, THAWED CAULIFLOWER FLORETS |
| ⅓ CUP WATER | ⅓ CUP CHOPPED FRESH CILANTRO |
| 1½ TEASPOONS SALT | 1 TEASPOON GARAM MASALA |

Heat 1½ tablespoons oil in a large heavy pot or Dutch oven set over medium-high heat. Add potatoes, garlic, and ginger and stir-fry for 6–7 minutes or until potatoes are crisp-tender.

Stir the tomatoes, water, salt, cocoa powder, cumin, turmeric, and cayenne into the pot. Stir in the cauliflower. Cover, then reduce heat and simmer 20–25 minutes or until vegetables are tender. Uncover and drizzle with the remaining canola oil, cilantro, and garam masala, tossing well. **Makes 6 servings.**

NUTRITION PER SERVING (ABOUT ¾ CUP):
CALORIES 203; FAT 5.3G (POLY 2.8G, MONO 1.3G, SAT .9G);
PROTEIN 5G; CHOLESTEROL 0MG; CARBOHYDRATE 36G.

# Summertime Salsa

*Why summertime? Because this salsa is loaded with peak summer vegetables, a true round-up from the garden or farmer's market.*

½ CUP SEEDED, FINELY CHOPPED RED BELL PEPPER

¼ CUP FINELY CHOPPED RED ONION

¼ CUP PEELED, DICED CUCUMBER

¼ CUP SEEDED, DICED PLUM TOMATO

3 TABLESPOONS CHOPPED FRESH BASIL

2 TABLESPOONS CHOPPED CELERY

2 TABLESPOONS SEEDED, CHOPPED JALAPEÑO PEPPER

2 TABLESPOONS UNSWEETENED COCOA POWDER (NOT DUTCH PROCESS)

2 TABLESPOONS OLIVE OIL

2 TABLESPOONS BALSAMIC VINEGAR

1 TABLESPOON FRESH LIME JUICE

1 TEASPOON DRIED THYME

½ TEASPOON SALT

½ TEASPOON GROUND CUMIN

½ TEASPOON CHILI POWDER

¼ TEASPOON BLACK PEPPER

3 GARLIC CLOVES, MINCED

2 15-OUNCE CANS BLACK BEANS, RINSED AND DRAINED

Combine all ingredients in a medium bowl, stirring well to combine. Cover and chill at least 2 hours or up to overnight. **Makes 16 servings.**

NUTRITION PER SERVING (ABOUT ⅓ CUP):
CALORIES 93; FAT 2.3G (POLY .3G, MONO 1.3G, SAT .7G);
PROTEIN 5G; CHOLESTEROL 0MG; CARBOHYDRATE 14G.

# Roasted Onions

*The sweet-acidic pungency of balsamic is mellowed by the smoothness of cocoa powder, making this simple side dish come alive. Serve it alongside chicken, beef, turkey, or pork.*

| | |
|---|---|
| 3 LARGE SWEET ONIONS (ABOUT 1¾ POUNDS) | 1 TABLESPOON OLIVE OIL |
| ⅓ CUP BALSAMIC VINEGAR | 1 TEASPOON DRIED THYME |
| 2 TEASPOONS UNSWEETENED COCOA POWDER (NOT DUTCH PROCESS) | ½ TEASPOON DRIED BASIL |
| | ¼ TEASPOON SALT |
| | ⅛ TEASPOON PEPPER |

Preheat oven to 450°F. Spray an 11 x 7-inch baking dish with nonstick cooking spray

Peel onions, leaving roots intact. Cut each onion into 6 wedges.

Place onion wedges in prepared dish. In a small bowl combine the vinegar, cocoa, olive oil, thyme, basil, salt, and pepper. Pour vinegar mixture over onion wedges, tossing gently to coat.

Cover and bake onions for 25 minutes. Uncover and bake an additional 45 minutes or until tender. **Makes 6 servings.**

NUTRITION PER SERVING (½ AN ONION):
CALORIES 74; FAT 2.8G (POLY .3G, MONO 1.7G, SAT .8G);
PROTEIN 1.6G; CHOLESTEROL 0MG; CARBOHYDRATE 12G.

## SASSY, SPICY

# Baked Beans

*Baked beans are one of my comfort foods—I remember eating them with toast as a child (one of mother's "I am too exhausted to make dinner tonight" meals). But these sassy beans aren't nursery food: they have a grown-up kick thanks to the addition of chipotle chile powder. Serve them with grilled meats in the summer or pan-roasted light sausages or rotisserie chicken in the winter.*

| | |
|---|---|
| 1 TEASPOON CANOLA OIL | 2 TABLESPOONS DIJON MUSTARD |
| 4 OUNCES (¼ PACKAGE) LITE SMOKED SAUSAGE, DICED SMALL | 2 TEASPOONS CHIPOTLE CHILE POWDER |
| 2½ CUPS CHOPPED ONION | ¼ TEASPOON SALT |
| 1 CUP FAT-FREE, LOW-SODIUM CHICKEN BROTH | ¼ TEASPOON GROUND CLOVES |
| ⅓ CUP CIDER VINEGAR | ¼ TEASPOON GROUND ALLSPICE |
| ⅓ CUP BOTTLED MESQUITE BARBECUE SAUCE | 1 15-OUNCE CAN BLACK BEANS, RINSED AND DRAINED |
| ⅓ CUP DARK MOLASSES (NOT BLACKSTRAP) | 1 15-OUNCE CAN KIDNEY BEANS, RINSED AND DRAINED |
| ¼ CUP PACKED BROWN SUGAR | 1 15-OUNCE CAN PINTO BEANS, RINSED AND DRAINED |
| 2 TABLESPOONS UNSWEETENED COCOA POWDER (NOT DUTCH PROCESS) | |

Preheat oven to 325°F.

Heat the oil in a Dutch oven over medium-high heat. Add the smoked sausage and sauté 2 minutes. Add the onion and sauté 5 minutes, stirring occasionally. Stir in the chicken broth and remaining ingredients.

Transfer the Dutch oven to the oven and bake, uncovered, for 1 hour. **Makes 10 servings.**

NUTRITION PER SERVING (ABOUT ¾ CUP):
CALORIES 178; FAT 1.1G (POLY .20, MONO .46G, SAT .32G);
PROTEIN 8G; CHOLESTEROL 5MG; CARBOHYDRATE 39G.

# *4-Bean Salad*

*Super-easy to make and loaded with flavor, this protein-packed salad makes a great lunch on its own or a cooling side dish for summertime grilled meats. It keeps well, covered, in the refrigerator for up to three days.*

½ CUP BALSAMIC VINEGAR

¼ CUP WATER

2 TABLESPOONS UNSWEETENED COCOA POW-
DER (NOT DUTCH PROCESS)

2 TABLESPOONS DIJON MUSTARD

1 TABLESPOON DRIED BASIL

1 TABLESPOON OLIVE OIL

2 GARLIC CLOVES, MINCED

1 TEASPOON PACKED LIGHT BROWN SUGAR

1 TEASPOON DRIED THYME

¼ TEASPOON SALT

¼ TEASPOON PEPPER

1 16-OUNCE CAN KIDNEY BEANS, RINSED
AND DRAINED

1 15-OUNCE CAN BLACK BEANS, RINSED AND
DRAINED

1 15-OUNCE CAN CHICKPEAS (GARBANZO
BEANS), RINSED AND DRAINED

1 CUP FROZEN WHOLE-KERNEL CORN, THAWED

1 CUP FROZEN SHELLED EDAMAME, THAWED

1 CUP CHOPPED RED ONION

In a large bowl whisk the vinegar, water, cocoa powder, mustard, basil, olive oil, garlic, brown sugar, thyme, salt, and pepper until well blended. Add the kidney beans, black beans, chickpeas, corn, edamame, and onion, tossing gently to combine.

Cover and let marinate in refrigerator at least 4 hours, stirring occasionally. Serve, chilled, with a slotted spoon. **Makes 8 servings.**

NUTRITION PER SERVING (ABOUT 1¼ CUPS):
CALORIES 217; FAT 4.0G (POLY .9G, MONO 1.8G, SAT .8G);
PROTEIN 11G; CHOLESTEROL 0MG; CARBOHYDRATE 37G.

# Grilled Fruit

## WITH SAVORY COCOA-GINGER GLAZE

*This is a delicious side dish alongside summertime grilled meats, especially pork and chicken.*

| | |
|---|---|
| 3 TABLESPOONS PACKED BROWN SUGAR | 4 FIRM-RIPE PLUMS, EACH CUT INTO 8 WEDGES |
| 2 TABLESPOONS UNSWEETENED COCOA POWDER (NOT DUTCH PROCESS) | 4 FIRM-RIPE PEACHES, PEELED AND EACH CUT INTO 8 WEDGES |
| 2 TABLESPOONS HOISIN SAUCE | ½ RIPE PINEAPPLE (1 AND ½ POUNDS), PEELED, CORED, AND CUT INTO 1-INCH PIECES |
| 2 TABLESPOONS LOW-SODIUM SOY SAUCE | |
| 1 TABLESPOON MINCED PEELED FRESH GINGER | |
| 1 TEASPOON GRATED ORANGE ZEST | 8 (8-INCH) WOODEN SKEWERS SOAKED IN WATER 1 HOUR |
| 2 TABLESPOONS FRESH ORANGE JUICE | |

Prepare grill to medium-high heat.

To make the glaze, in a small bowl whisk the brown sugar, cocoa powder, hoisin sauce, soy sauce, ginger, orange zest, and orange juice until blended.

Thread about 4 pieces of fruit onto each skewer. Brush the fruit with the glaze.

When fire is medium-hot (you can hold your hand 5 inches above rack 3 to 4 seconds), grill fruit in batches on grill rack sprayed with nonstick cooking spray, turning and basting once with glaze, until browned and slightly softened, about 5 minutes total. Serve fruit on skewers with remaining glaze on the side. **Makes 8 servings.**

NUTRITION PER SERVING (1 SKEWER):
CALORIES 88; FAT .62G (POLY .08G, MONO .14G, SAT .15G);
PROTEIN 2G; CHOLESTEROL .04MG; CARBOHYDRATE 22G.

# *Popcorn*

*I tend to prefer sweet to savory—except in the case of popcorn. I find it difficult to watch a movie—any movie—without at least a few handfuls of the stuff. This cocoa and spice version is particularly addictive. Serve it with glasses of homemade limeade for an unforgettable combination.*

| | |
|---|---|
| ¾ CUP POPCORN KERNELS | 1½ TEASPOONS GROUND CUMIN |
| 1 TABLESPOON CANOLA OIL | ½ TEASPOON CHIPOTLE CHILE POWDER |
| 1 TABLESPOON UNSWEETENED COCOA POW-DER (NOT DUTCH PROCESS) | 1 TEASPOON SALT |
| | 1 TABLESPOON BUTTER, MELTED |

In a Dutch oven combine the popcorn kernels, oil, cocoa powder, cumin, chile powder, and salt.

Cover and shake vigorously for 7 minutes over medium-high heat or until all kernels are popped. Drizzle with melted butter. **Makes 8 servings.**

> **Cook's Note:** Store the popcorn in an airtight container for up to 3 days.

NUTRITION PER SERVING (2 CUPS):
CALORIES 91; FAT 4.0G (POLY .86G, MONO 1.8G, SAT 1.0G);
PROTEIN 2G; CHOLESTEROL 4MG; CARBOHYDRATE 13G.

# *Snack Mix*

*Pack this delectable mix into small ziplock bags and stash in the car or desk drawer at work for a satisfying snack fix. You can vary the proportions of cereal to pretzels and crackers.*

| | |
|---|---|
| 2   CUPS CRISSCROSS CORN CEREAL (E.G., CHEX) | 1½ TABLESPOONS BUTTER, MELTED |
| 1   CUP TINY PRETZEL TWISTS | 1   TABLESPOON BOTTLED BBQ SAUCE |
| ½   CUP REDUCED-FAT WHEAT CRACKERS (E.G., WHEAT THINS) | 2   TEASPOONS UNSWEETENED COCOA POWDER (NOT DUTCH PROCESS) |
| ½   CUP REDUCED-FAT CHEDDAR CRACKERS (E.G., CHEEZ-IT) | 1   TEASPOON CHILI POWDER |
| | 1   TEASPOON GROUND CUMIN |
| | ¼   TEASPOON SALT |

Preheat oven to 250°F. Spray a baking sheet with nonstick cooking spray.

Combine the cereal, pretzels, and crackers in a medium bowl.

In a small bowl or cup combine the melted butter, BBQ sauce, cocoa powder, chili powder, cumin, and salt. Drizzle over cereal mixture, tossing to coat. Spread mixture evenly onto prepared baking sheet.

Bake 25–30 minutes or until crisp, stirring twice. Store in an airtight container for up to 1 week. **Makes 8 servings.**

NUTRITION PER SERVING (½ CUP):
CALORIES 106; FAT 3.7G (POLY .15G, MONO 1.2G, SAT 1.4G);
PROTEIN 2G; CHOLESTEROL 6.1MG; CARBOHYDRATE 17G.

# CARAMELIZED ONION AND

## *Black Bean Spread*

*Delicious on crusty bread, whole grain crackers, or as a dip with vegetables, this rich-tasting spread also makes a great foundation for a vegetarian sandwich. It will keep in the refrigerator for up to one week—perfect for when the munchies strike.*

| | |
|---|---|
| 1 TABLESPOON OLIVE OIL | 2½ TEASPOONS UNSWEETENED COCOA POWDER (NOT DUTCH PROCESS) |
| 2 CUPS CHOPPED ONION | 1 TEASPOON PAPRIKA |
| 1 15-OUNCE CAN BLACK BEANS, RINSED AND DRAINED | ½ TEASPOON SALT |
| 2 TEASPOONS BALSAMIC VINEGAR | 3 TABLESPOONS CHOPPED FRESH CILANTRO, DIVIDED USE |
| 2 TEASPOONS GROUND CUMIN | |

Heat oil in a large nonstick skillet over medium-high heat. Add onion and sauté 10 minutes or until golden.

Place the cooked onion, beans, vinegar, cumin, cocoa powder, paprika, salt, and 2 tablespoons cilantro in a food processor; process until smooth. Place bean mixture in a bowl. Sprinkle with remaining 1 tablespoon cilantro. **Makes 16 servings.**

NUTRITION PER SERVING (1½ TABLESPOONS):
CALORIES 39; FAT 1.1G (POLY .20G, MONO .64G, SAT .14G);
PROTEIN 2G; CHOLESTEROL 0MG; CARBOHYDRATE 6G.

# Ancho Mole Poblano

*Chile power: dried ancho chiles pack heat in this traditional (but much lower fat) mole, mellowed by the earthy flavors of cocoa and chocolate. Serve it with chicken, tofu, or shrimp, or use it to add flavor to quick black bean burrito wraps or enchiladas. Freeze the extra sauce in 1-cup or 2-cup increments for speedy weeknight dinners.*

| | |
|---|---|
| 4 DRIED ANCHO CHILES, STEMMED, SEEDED, TORN INTO LARGE PIECES | 2 TABLESPOONS UNSWEETENED COCOA POWDER (NOT DUTCH PROCESS) |
| 2 6-INCH CORN TORTILLAS | ¼ TEASPOON GROUND CUMIN |
| 4 WHOLE CANNED PLUM TOMATOES (FROM 14.5-OUNCE CAN), DRAINED | ¼ TEASPOON GROUND CINNAMON |
| | ⅛ TEASPOON GROUND CLOVES |
| 1 14-OUNCE CAN REDUCED-SODIUM CHICKEN BROTH | ½ CUP SEEDLESS RAISINS |
| | 1¼ CUPS WATER, DIVIDED USE |
| ¾ CUP CHOPPED ONION | 1 OUNCE BITTERSWEET CHOCOLATE, CHOPPED |
| ¼ CUP SLICED ALMONDS | 1 TABLESPOON FRESH LIME JUICE |
| 4 GARLIC CLOVES, MINCED | ¾ TEASPOON SALT |

Heat a large nonstick skillet over medium-high heat. Add chiles; cook 1 minute on each side. Place chiles in a medium bowl and cover with hot water. Let stand at room temperature 30 minutes, then drain.

Place 1 tortilla in a large nonstick pan set over medium-high heat. Cook 1½ minutes on each side or until browned. Repeat with second tortilla. Place drained chiles, tomatoes, tortillas, and chicken broth in a blender. Process until smooth.

Coat the same large nonstick pan with nonstick cooking spray. Set over medium-high heat and add the chopped onion; sauté for 3 minutes. Add almonds and garlic; sauté for 1 minute. Stir in cocoa powder, cumin, cinnamon, and cloves; sauté for 15 seconds.

Place onion mixture, raisins, and ¼ cup water in blender with chile mixture. Process until smooth.

Place chile mixture, remaining 1 cup water, and chocolate in a large saucepan. Cook over medium heat, partially covered, 18–20 minutes, stirring occasionally. Remove from heat. Stir in lime juice and salt. **Makes about 4 cups, 16 servings.**

NUTRITION PER SERVING (¼ CUP): CALORIES 55; FAT 2.1G (POLY .32G, MONO 1.0G, SAT .81G); PROTEIN 2G; CHOLESTEROL 0MG; CARBOHYDRATE 9G.

# Creamy Pumpkin Mole

*This is what luxury tastes like. Pair the sauce with grilled chicken, pork, and shrimp for a show-off dinner for yourself and a favorite circle of friends. It freezes quite well, so use what you need and freeze the rest for a quick weeknight meal at a future date.*

| | | | |
|---|---|---|---|
| 2 | DRIED ANCHO CHILES, STEMMED, SEEDED, TORN INTO LARGE PIECES | 3 | CUPS CANNED LOW-SODIUM CHICKEN BROTH, DIVIDED USE |
| 5 | TEASPOONS CANOLA OIL, DIVIDED USE | 2 | CANNED CHIPOTLE CHILES, SEEDED |
| 1 | 3-INCH-DIAMETER SLICED WHITE ONION (½ INCH THICK), SEPARATED INTO RINGS | 1 | CUP CANNED SOLID PACK PUMPKIN |
| 2 | GARLIC CLOVES, PEELED | 1 | CUP CANNED LITE COCONUT MILK |
| 2 | 6-INCH CORN TORTILLAS | 1½ | TABLESPOONS FRESH LIME JUICE |
| ¾ | CUP DRAINED CANNED DICED TOMATOES | 1 | TABLESPOON PACKED DARK BROWN SUGAR |
| 2 | TABLESPOONS UNSWEETENED COCOA POWDER (NOT DUTCH PROCESS) | ¼ | CUP CHOPPED FRESH CILANTRO |

Heat a large pot over medium-high heat. Add chiles and cook 1 minute on each side. Place chiles in a medium bowl and cover with hot water. Let stand at room temperature 30 minutes, then drain.

In same large pot, heat 3 teaspoons oil over medium-high heat. Add the onion rings and garlic. Sauté until brown, about 4 minutes. Transfer to a food processor. Add tortillas to pot, stirring with wooden spoon 2 minutes. Add the tortillas, tomatoes, and cocoa powder in the food processor. Purée until smooth. Transfer tomato purée to small bowl (do not clean processor).

Place ancho chiles in processor. Add ½ cup chicken broth and 2 chipotle chiles. Purée until smooth.

Add remaining 2 teaspoons oil to the same large pot. Heat over medium-high heat. Add ancho chile purée. Cook and stir 1–2 minutes until purée thickens and darkens. Add tomato purée. Simmer until thick, stirring often, about 4 minutes. Whisk in pumpkin and remaining 2½ cups chicken broth. Bring to boil. Reduce heat to medium-low. Simmer 30 minutes. Whisk in coconut milk, lime juice, brown sugar, and cilantro. Season to taste with salt. **Makes about 4 cups, 16 servings.**

NUTRITION PER SERVING (¼ CUP): CALORIES 48; FAT 2.4G (POLY .45G, MONO .96G, SAT .93G); PROTEIN 2G; CHOLESTEROL 0MG; CARBOHYDRATE 6G.

# Cabernet-Chocolate BBQ Sauce

*This luscious sauce is basted on the meat—think beef, pork, and chicken—as it grills. It is also great on top of burgers or served alongside purchased rotisserie chicken.*

| | |
|---|---|
| 1 TABLESPOON OLIVE OIL | 1 OUNCE BITTERSWEET CHOCOLATE, CHOPPED |
| 1 LARGE GARLIC CLOVE, MINCED | 1 TABLESPOON BALSAMIC VINEGAR |
| ¼ TEASPOON GROUND CUMIN | 1 TABLESPOON SOY SAUCE |
| ¼ TEASPOON GROUND CHIPOTLE CHILE POWDER | 2 TEASPOONS UNSWEETENED COCOA POWDER (NOT DUTCH PROCESS) |
| ⅓ CUP CABERNET OR OTHER DRY RED WINE | ⅛ TEASPOON LIQUID SMOKE |
| ½ CUP BOTTLED KETCHUP | |

Heat olive oil in medium, heavy-bottomed saucepan over medium heat. Add the garlic, cumin, and chipotle chile powder; stir 1 minute. Add the wine and simmer 2 minutes. Stir in the ketchup, chocolate, vinegar, soy sauce, cocoa powder, and liquid smoke; simmer 2 minutes longer. Remove from heat and cool completely. **Makes about 16 servings.**

**Cook's Note:** Sauce will keep, tightly covered in the refrigerator, for up to 2 weeks.

NUTRITION PER SERVING (1 TABLESPOON):
CALORIES 28; FAT 1.5G (POLY .13G, MONO .85G, SAT .51G);
PROTEIN .5G; CHOLESTEROL 0MG; CARBOHYDRATE 3G.

# *Barbecue Sauce*

*Fresh ginger and crushed red pepper flakes spike this fantastic sauce. Serve it with shrimp, salmon, pork, or chicken.*

---

| | |
|---|---|
| ½ CUP HOISIN SAUCE | 1 TABLESPOON HONEY |
| 2 TABLESPOONS RICE VINEGAR (NOT SEASONED) | ⅓ CUP MINCED SHALLOT |
| 1 OUNCE UNSWEETENED CHOCOLATE, CHOPPED | 2 GARLIC CLOVES, MINCED |
| 2 TEASPOONS UNSWEETENED COCOA POWDER (NOT DUTCH PROCESS) | 1 TABLESPOON MINCED PEELED FRESH GINGER |
| 1 TABLESPOON ASIAN FISH SAUCE | ⅛ TEASPOON CHINESE FIVE-SPICE POWDER |
| 1 TABLESPOON SOY SAUCE | ⅛ TEASPOON CRUSHED RED PEPPER FLAKES |
| | ⅓ CUP SUGAR |

Stir together all ingredients except sugar in a medium bowl.

Cook sugar in a dry heavy saucepan over moderate heat, undisturbed, until it begins to melt. Continue to cook, stirring occasionally with a fork, until sugar is melted into a deep golden caramel. Tilt pan and carefully pour in hoisin mixture (caramel will harden and steam vigorously).

Cook over moderately low heat, stirring, until caramel is dissolved and sauce is smooth and thickened, about 6–8 minutes. Remove from heat and cool to room temperature. **Makes about 24 servings.**

»  **Cook's Note:** Sauce will keep, tightly covered in the refrigerator, for up to 2 weeks.

NUTRITION PER SERVING (2 TABLESPOONS):
CALORIES 41; FAT .99G (POLY .03 G, MONO .22G, SAT .45G);
PROTEIN .5G; CHOLESTEROL .08MG; CARBOHYDRATE 9G.

# FIRE-ROASTED RED PEPPER–COCOA

## Ketchup

*Transform everything from burgers to shrimp to roasted potatoes with this homemade take on ketchup. The fire-roasted tomatoes are worth seeking—they add a smoky depth of flavor that really makes the recipe. Look for them where all of the other varieties of canned tomatoes are shelved in the supermarket.*

| | |
|---|---|
| 1 14.5-OUNCE CAN FIRE-ROASTED DICED TOMATOES (E.G., MUIR GLEN), UNDRAINED | 2 TABLESPOONS RED WINE VINEGAR |
| 1 7.25-OUNCE JAR ROASTED RED PEPPERS, DRAINED | 2 TABLESPOONS UNSWEETENED COCOA POWDER (NOT DUTCH PROCESS) |
| 1 CUP CHOPPED ONION | 1 TABLESPOON FENNEL SEEDS |
| ½ CUP DRY RED WINE | 2 TEASPOONS CHOPPED GARLIC |
| 6 TABLESPOONS PACKED LIGHT BROWN SUGAR | 1½ TEASPOONS ANCHO CHILE POWDER |
| | 1½ TEASPOONS GROUND CUMIN |
| 2 TABLESPOONS TOMATO PASTE | 1 BAY LEAF |

Combine all ingredients in large, heavy saucepan over high heat. Bring to boil. Reduce heat to medium and simmer until reduced to about 3 cups, about 30 minutes. Discard bay leaf.

Working in batches, purée ketchup in blender until smooth. Season with salt and pepper. Cool slightly, then chill until cold. **Makes about 24 servings.**

**Cook's Note:** Ketchup can be prepared 1 week ahead. Cover and keep refrigerated for up to 3 weeks. The ketchup also freezes extremely well.

NUTRITION PER SERVING (2 TABLESPOONS):
CALORIES 24; FAT .07G (POLY .01G, MONO .02G, SAT .04G);
PROTEIN .5G; CHOLESTEROL .03MG; CARBOHYDRATE 5G.

# Rustic Rub

*You'll have more spice rub than you need for one night of grilling. Use it to season everything from meats to seafood to vegetables.*

½  CUP PAPRIKA

½  TEASPOON CAYENNE PEPPER

5  TABLESPOONS BLACK PEPPER

6  TABLESPOONS ONION POWDER

3  TABLESPOONS SALT

2½ TABLESPOONS DRIED OREGANO

2½ TABLESPOONS DRIED THYME

3  TABLESPOONS PACKED DARK BROWN
   SUGAR

¼  CUP UNSWEETENED COCOA POWDER (NOT
   DUTCH PROCESS)

Combine all ingredients in medium bowl until blended. Store in airtight container in cool, dry place. Apply as a dry rub or seasoning on poultry, pork, beef, seafood, salads, soups, or vegetables. **Makes about 1¾ cups.**

 **Cook's Note:** Store in cool dry place for up to 4 months.

NUTRITION PER SERVING (2 TABLESPOONS):
CALORIES 24; FAT .20G (POLY .01G, MONO .07G, SAT .12G);
PROTEIN .5G; CHOLESTEROL 0MG; CARBOHYDRATE 6G.

# Tex-Mex Spice Rub

*Homemade rubs are a quick way to transform roasted meat, poultry, and vegetables into something out of the ordinary. This one is particularly good on steak and potatoes. And if you do not have all of the spices in your pantry, you can improvise with what's on hand to create your own unique blend.*

| | |
|---|---|
| ½ CUP PACKED DARK BROWN SUGAR | 2 TEASPOONS SALT (PREFERABLY SEA SALT) |
| ½ CUP CHILI POWDER | 2 TEASPOONS DRIED OREGANO LEAVES |
| ¼ CUP PAPRIKA | ½ CUP UNSWEETENED COCOA POWDER (NOT DUTCH PROCESS) |
| 1 TABLESPOON GROUND CUMIN | |
| 1 TEASPOON GARLIC POWDER | 1 TABLESPOON INSTANT ESPRESSO POWDER |
| 1 TEASPOON CAYENNE PEPPER | |

Combine all ingredients in medium bowl until blended. Store in airtight container in cool, dry place. Apply as a dry rub or seasoning on poultry, pork, beef, seafood, or vegetables. **Makes about 2 cups.**

**Cook's Note:** Store in cool dry place for up to 4 months.

NUTRITION PER SERVING (2 TABLESPOONS):
CALORIES 24; FAT .34G (POLY .01G, MONO .11G, SAT .20G);
PROTEIN .5G; CHOLESTEROL 0MG; CARBOHYDRATE 6G.

# APPENDIX A
## ON-LINE CHOCOLATE AND COCOA POWDER RESOURCES

It would be impossible to list all of the great sources available for purchasing chocolate and cocoa powder online, but these are a few of my favorites.

**www.amazon.com**
Find virtually every chocolate and cocoa product you need in their gourmet foods section, from Green & Black's to Guittard to Ghirardelli.

**www.chocolatesource.com**
An excellent online gourmet chocolate and cocoa source, which includes premium brands such as Callebaut, El Rey, Schokinag, Green & Black's, Lindt, Scharffen Berger, Valrhona, and Belcolade.

**www.chocosphere.com**
A virtual chocolate paradise, this site will amaze you with their diversity of offerings. All the premiere chocolates and cocoas are here, as well as many, many regional and international brands that would otherwise be very hard to locate.

**www.dagobachocolate.com**
Superior chocolate and cocoa powder in every sense of the word. This Ashland, Oregon-based company produces organic chocolate and cocoa that will make you weak in the knees—it is just that good. Order their products directly from their website (and be sure to sign up for their Tao of Cacao newsletter, too).

**www.greenandblacks.com**
Simply incredible chocolate and cocoa powder—and it's organic, too.

**www.kingarthurflour.com**

One of the most trusted websites for cooks and bakers, this is the online companion to the ever-popular baker's catalog. In addition to Schokinag, Scharffen Berger, Guittard, Callebaut, Valrhona chocolates, and cocoa powder, they also have just about everything else you need to cook and bake, save for fresh groceries.

**www.penzeys.com**

An excellent source for an extensive assortment of herbs, spices, and seasonings at excellent prices, Penzeys also sells cocoa powder in bulk. It is a good source for extracts, vanilla beans, and crystallized ginger, too.

**www.scharffenberger.com**

Ok, I am prejudiced—this is my favorite chocolate and cocoa source, and not just because their factory is located minutes from my childhood home. You can order this superior chocolate directly from their website, as well as sign up for their free newsletter (it's great) and take a virtual factory tour.

**www.worldwidechocolate.com**

Much like chocosphere.com, World Wide Chocolate has an extensive variety of premiere and harder-to-find chocolates. In addition, they offer warm weather shipping boxes: for about $6.00 extra you can be assured that your chocolate won't arrive as a box of fondue.

# APPENDIX B:
## ESPECIALLY LOW-CALORIE RECIPES
### (150 CALORIES OR LESS PER SERVING)

# APPENDIX C
## ESPECIALLY LOW-FAT RECIPES
### (3 GRAMS TOTAL FAT OR LESS PER SERVING)

# BIBLIOGRAPHY

Adamson, G. E., G. Cao, J. F. Hammerstone, P. H. Jacobs, B. C. Kremers, S. A. Lazarus, A. E. Mitchell et al. "HPLC Method for the Quantification of Procyanidins in Cocoa and Chocolate Samples and Correlation to Total Antioxidant Capacity." *Journal of Agricultural and Food Chemistry* 47 (1999): 4184–88.

Arai, Y., W. Watanabe, M. Kimira, K. Shimol, R. Mochizuki, and N. Kinae. "Dietary Intakes of Flavonoids, Flavones and Isoflavones by Japanese Women and the Inverse Correlation between Quercetin Intake and Plasma LDL Cholesterol Concentration." *Journal of Nutrition* 130 (2000): 2243–50.

Arts, I. C. W., P. C. H. Hollman, and D. Kromhout. "Chocolate as a Source of Tea Flavonoids." *Lancet* 354 (1999): 488.

Bazzano, L. A., J. He, and L. G. Ogden. "Fruit and Vegetable Intake and Risk of Cardiovascular Disease in U.S. Adults: The First National Health and Nutrition Examination Survey Epidemiologic Follow-up Study." *American Journal of Clinical Nutrition* 76 (2002): 93–99.

Brownlee, Christen. "Cocoa Compound Increases Brain's Blood Flow." *Science News* 171, no. 9 (2007): 142.

Buijsse, Brian, Edith J. M. Feskens, Frans J. Kok, and Daan Kromhout. "Cocoa Intake, Blood Pressure, and Cardiovascular Mortality." *Archives of Internal Medicine* 166, no. 4 (2006): 411–17.

Coe, M., and S. Coe. *The True History of Chocolate.* London: Thames & Hudson, 1996.

Corriher, S. *Cookwise: The Secrets of Cooking Revealed.* New York: Morrow, 1997.

Dillinger, T. L., P. Barriga, S. Escarcega, M. Jiminez, D. Salazar Lowe, and L. E. Grivette. "Food of the Gods: Cure for Humanity? A Cultural History of the Medicinal and Ritual Use of Chocolate." *Journal of Nutrition* 130, no. suppl 8S (2000): 2057S–72S.

Engler, M. B., M. M. Engler, and C. Y. Chen. "Flavonoid-rich Dark Chocolate Improves Endothelial Function and Increases Plasma Epicatechin Concentrations in Healthy Adults." *Journal of the American College of Nutrition* 23 (2004): 197–204.

Engler, Mary B., and Marguerite M. Engler. "The Emerging Role of Flavonoid-Rich Cocoa and Chocolate in Cardiovascular Health and Disease." *Nutrition Reviews* 64, no. 3 (2006): 109–118.

Fraga, Cesar G., Actis-Goretta, Lucas, Ottaviani, I. Javier, Carrasquedo, Fernando, Lotito, B. Silvina, Lazarus, Sheryl, Schmitz, H. Harold, and Carl L. Keen. "Regular Consumption of a Flavanol-rich Chocolate Can Improve Oxidant Stress in Young Soccer Players." *Clinical and Developmental Immunology* 12, no. 1 (2005): 11–17.

Grassi, D., C. Lippi, S. Necozione, G. Desideri, and C. Ferri. "Short-term Administration of Dark Chocolate Is Followed by a Significant Increase in Insulin Sensitivity and a Decrease in Blood Pressure in Healthy Persons." *American Journal of Clinical Nutrition* 81 (2005): 611–14.

Hammerstone, J., S. Lazarus, A. Mitchell, R. Rucker, and H. H. Schmitz. "Identification of Procyanidins in Cocoa (Theobroma Cacao) and Chocolate using High-performance Liquid Chromatography/mass Spectrometry." *Journal of Agricultural and Food Chemistry* 47 (1999): 490–96.

Hannum, Sandra M., Harold H. Schmitz, and Carl L. Keen. "Chocolate: A Heart-healthy Food? Show Me the Science!" *Nutrition Today* 37, no. 3 (2002): 103.

Harborne, J. B., and C. A. Williams. "Advances in Flavonoid Research since 1992." *Phytochemistry* 55 (2000): 481–504.

Heiss, C., A. Dejam, P. Kleinbongard, T. Schewe, H. Sies, and M. Kelm. "Vascular Effects of Cocoa Rich in Flavan-3-ols." *Journal of the American Medical Association* 290 (2003): 1030–31.

Hu, F. B., M. J. Stampfer, and J. E. Manson. "Dietary Saturated Fats and Their Food Sources in Relation to the Risk of Coronary Heart Disease in Women." *American Journal of Clinical Nutrition* 70: (1999) 1001–8.

Huxley, R. R., and H. A. Neil. "The Relation between Dietary Flavonol Intake and Coronary Heart Disease Mortality: A Meta-analysis of Prospective Cohort Studies." *European Journal of Clinical Nutrition* 57 (2003): 904–8.

Innes, A. J., G. Kennedy, M. McLaren, A. J. Bancroft, and J. J. Belch. "Dark Chocolate Inhibits Platelet Aggregation in Healthy Volunteers." *Platelets* 14 (2003): 325–27.

Jacobsen, R. *Chocolate Unwrapped: The Surprising Health Benefits of America's Favorite Passion.* Montpelier, VT: Invisible Cities Press LLC, 2003.

Knekt, P., J. Kumpulainen, R. Jarvinen, H. Rissanen, M. Heliovaara, A. Reunanen, T. Hakulinen, and A. Aromaa. "Flavonoid Intake and Risk of Chronic Diseases." *American Journal of Clinical Nutrition* 76 (2002): 560–68.

Kris-Etherton, P. M., and C. L. Keen. "Evidence that the Antioxidant Flavonoids in Tea and Cocoa are Beneficial for Cardiovascular Health." *Current Opinion in Lipidology* 13 (2002): 41–49.

Lecumberri, Elena, Luis Goya, Raquel Mateos, Mario Alía, Sonia Ramos, María Izquierdo-Pulido, and Laura Bravo. "A Diet Rich in Dietary Fiber from Cocoa Improves Lipid

Profile and Reduces Malondialdehyde in Hypercholesterolemic Rats." *Nutrition* 23, no. 4 (2007): 332–41.

Mathur, S., S. Devaraj, S. M. Grundy, and I. Jialal. "Cocoa Products Decrease Low Density Lipoprotein Oxidative Susceptibility But Do Not Affect Biomarkers of Inflammation in Humans." *Journal of Nutrition* 132 (2002): 3663–67.

Matsui, Naoko, Ryoichi Ito, Eisaku Nishimura, Mariko Yoshikawa, Masatoshi Kato, Masanori Kamei, Haruki Shibata et al. "Ingested Cocoa Can Prevent High-fat Diet-Induced Obesity by Regulating the Expression of Genes for Fatty Acid Metabolism." *Nutrition* 21, no. 5 (2005): 594–601.

McGee, H. *On Food and Cooking: The Science and Lore of the Kitchen.* New York: Scribner, 2004.

Mennen, L. I., D. Sapinho, and A. de Bree. "Consumption of Foods Rich in Flavonoids Is Related to a Decreased Cardiovascular Risk in Apparently Healthy French Women." *Journal of Nutrition* 134 (2004): 923–26. EBSCO Publishing Citations, EBSCOhost (accessed April 27, 2007).

Middleton, E. Jr, C. Kandaswami, and T. C. Theoharides. "The Effects of Plant Flavonoids on Mammalian Cells: Implications for Inflammation, Heart Disease, and Cancer." *Pharmacological Reviews* 52 (2000): 673–751.

Murphy, K. J., A. K. Chronopoulos, I. Singh et al. "Dietary Flavanols and Procyanidins Oligomers from Cocoa (Theobroma cacao) Inhibit Platelet Function." *American Journal of Clinical Nutrition* 77 (2003): 1466–73.

Mursu, J., S. Voutilainen, and T. Nurmi. "Dark Chocolate Consumption Increases HDL Cholesterol Concentration and Chocolate Fatty Acids May Inhibit Lipid Peroxidation in Healthy Humans." *Free Radical Biology and Medicine* 37 (2004): 1351–59.

Nijveldt, T. J., E. van Nood, D. E. C. van Hoorn, R. G. Boelens, K. van Norren, and P. A. M. van Leeuwen. "Flavonoids: A Review of Probable Mechanisms of Action and Potential Applications." *American Journal of Clinical Nutrition* 74 (2001): 418–25.

Othman, Azizah, Amin Ismail, Nawalyah Abdul Ghani, and Ilham Adenan. "Antioxidant Capacity and Phenolic Content of Cocoa Beans." *Food Chemistry* 100, no. 4 (2007): 1523–30.

Pearson, Debra A., Roberta R. Holt, Dietrich Rein, Teresa Paglieroni, Harold H. Schmitz, and Carl L. Keen. "Flavanols and Platelet Reactivity." *Clinical and Developmental Immunology* 12, no. 1 (2005): 1–9.

Polagruto, John A., Janice F. Wang-Polagruto, Marlia M. Braun, Luke Lee, Catherine Kwik-Uribe, and Carl L. Keen. "Cocoa Flavanol-Enriched Snack Bars Containing Phytosterols Effectively Lower Total and Low-Density Lipoprotein Cholesterol Levels." *Journal of the American Dietetic Association* 106, no. 11 (2006): 1804–13.

Presilla, M. *The New Taste of Chocolate: A Cultural and Natural History of Cacao with Recipes.* Berkeley: Ten Speed Press, 2001.

Rein, D., T. G. Paglieroni, T. Wun, D. A. Pearson, H. H. Schmitz, R. Gosselin, and C. L. Keen. "Cocoa Inhibits Platelet Activation and Function." *American Journal of Clinical Nutrition* 72 (2000): 30–35.

Rosenblum, M. *Chocolate: A Bittersweet Saga of Dark and Light.* New York: North Point Press, 2006.

Schewe, T., C. Sadik, L. O. Klotz, T. Yoshimoto, H. Kuhn, and H. Sies. "Polyphenols of Cocoa: Inhibition of Mammalian 15-Lipoxygenase." *Biological Chemistry* 382 (2001): 1687–96. EBSCO Publishing Citations, EBSCOhost (accessed April 27, 2007).

Schramm, D. D., J. F. Wang, R. R. Holt et al. "Chocolate Procyanidins Decrease the Leukotriene-Prostacyclin Ratio in Humans and Human Aortic Endothelial Cells." *American Journal of Clinical Nutrition* 73 (2001): 36–40. EBSCO Publishing Citations, EBSCOhost (accessed April 27, 2007).

Schroeter, H, R. R. Holt, T. J. Orozco, H. H. Schmitz, and C. L. Keen. "Milk and Absorption of Dietary Flavanols." *Nature* 426 (2003): 787–88.

Schroeter, Hagen, Christian Heiss, Jan Balzer, Petra Kleinbongard, Carl L. Keen, Norman K. Hollenberg, Helmut Sies, Catherine Kwik-Uribe, Harold H. Schmitz, and Malte Kelm. "(-)-Epicatechin Mediates Beneficial Effects of Flavanol-rich Cocoa on Vascular Function in Humans." *Proceedings of the National Academy of Sciences of the United States of America* 103, no. 4 (2006): 1024–29.

Vinson, J. A., J. Proch, and L. Zubik. "Phenol Antioxidant Quantity and Quality in Foods: Cocoa, Dark Chocolate, and Milk Chocolate." *Journal of Agricultural Food Chemistry* 47 (1999): 4821–24.

Wan, Y., J. A. Vinson, T. D. Etherton, J. Proch, S. A. Lazarus, and P. M. Kris-Etherton. "Effects of Cocoa Powder and Dark Chocolate on LDL Oxidative Susceptibility and Prostaglandin Concentrations in Humans." *American Journal of Clinical Nutrition* 74 (2001): 596–602.

Wiswedel, Ingrid, Daniela Hirsch, Siegfried Kropf, Martin Gruening, Eberhard Pfister, Tankred Schewe, and Helmut Sies. "Flavanol-rich Cocoa Drink Lowers Plasma F2-Isoprostane Concentrations in Humans." *Free Radical Biology and Medicine* 37, no. 3 (2004): 411–21.

# INDEX